George Alfred Henty, William Heysham Overend

On the Irrawaddy

A Story of the first Burmese War

George Alfred Henty, William Heysham Overend

On the Irrawaddy
A Story of the first Burmese War

ISBN/EAN: 9783744749688

Printed in Europe, USA, Canada, Australia, Japan

Cover: Foto ©ninafisch / pixelio.de

More available books at **www.hansebooks.com**

ON THE IRRAWADDY

MR. HENTY'S HISTORICAL TALES.

Crown 8vo, Cloth elegant, Olivine edges. Illustrated.

THE CAT OF BUBASTES: A Story of Ancient Egypt. 5s.
THE YOUNG CARTHAGINIAN: A Story of the Times of Hannibal. 6s.
FOR THE TEMPLE: A Tale of the Fall of Jerusalem. 6s.
BERIC THE BRITON: A Story of the Roman Invasion. 6s.
THE DRAGON AND THE RAVEN: Or, The Days of King Alfred. 5s.
WULF THE SAXON: A Story of the Norman Conquest. 6s.
A KNIGHT OF THE WHITE CROSS: The Siege of Rhodes. 6s.
THE LION OF ST. MARK: A Story of Venice in the 14th Century. 6s.
THE LION OF THE NORTH: A Tale of Gustavus Adolphus. 6s.
ST. BARTHOLOMEW'S EVE: A Tale of the Huguenot Wars. 6s.
IN FREEDOM'S CAUSE: A Story of Wallace and Bruce. 6s.
ST. GEORGE FOR ENGLAND: A Tale of Cressy and Poitiers. 5s.
BY RIGHT OF CONQUEST: Or, With Cortez in Mexico. 6s.
BY PIKE AND DYKE: A Tale of the Rise of the Dutch Republic. 6s.
BY ENGLAND'S AID: Or, The Freeing of the Netherlands. 6s.
UNDER DRAKE'S FLAG: A Tale of the Spanish Main. 6s.
ORANGE AND GREEN: A Tale of the Boyne and Limerick. 5s.
A JACOBITE EXILE: In the Service of Charles XII. 5s.
BONNIE PRINCE CHARLIE: A Tale of Fontenoy and Culloden. 6s.
WHEN LONDON BURNED: A Story of the Great Fire. 6s.
THE BRAVEST OF THE BRAVE: Or, With Peterborough in Spain. 5s.
WITH WOLFE IN CANADA: Or, The Winning of a Continent. 6s.
WITH CLIVE IN INDIA: Or, The Beginnings of an Empire. 6s.
THROUGH THE SIKH WAR: A Tale of the Punjaub. 6s.
TRUE TO THE OLD FLAG. The American War of Independence. 6s.
IN THE REIGN OF TERROR. The French Revolution. 5s.
HELD FAST FOR ENGLAND: A Tale of the Siege of Gibraltar. 5s.
THROUGH RUSSIAN SNOWS: A Story of Napoleon's Retreat from Moscow. 5s.
ONE OF THE 28TH: A Story of Waterloo. 5s.
IN GREEK WATERS: A Story of the Grecian War (1821). 6s.
THE TIGER OF MYSORE: The War with Tippoo Saib. 6s.
THROUGH THE FRAY: A Story of the Luddite Riots. 6s.
MAORI AND SETTLER: A Story of the New Zealand War. 5s.
BY SHEER PLUCK: A Tale of the Ashanti War. 5s.
FOR NAME AND FAME: Or, Through Afghan Passes. 5s.
WITH LEE IN VIRGINIA: A Story of the American Civil War. 6s.
THE DASH FOR KHARTOUM: A Tale of the Nile Expedition. 6s.
CONDEMNED AS A NIHILIST: A Story of Escape from Siberia. 5s.

LONDON: BLACKIE & SON, LIMITED; GLASGOW AND DUBLIN.

"STANLEY GAVE A SUDDEN SPRING AND BURIED HIS KNIFE IN THE LEOPARD."

ON THE IRRAWADDY

A STORY OF

THE FIRST BURMESE WAR

BY

G. A. HENTY

Author of "With Clive in India", "In the Heart of the Rockies", "Through Russian Snows"
"When London Burned", "The Dash for Khartoum", "Through the Sikh War", &c.

WITH EIGHT ILLUSTRATIONS BY W. H. OVEREND

LONDON
BLACKIE & SON, Limited, 50 OLD BAILEY, E.C.
GLASGOW AND DUBLIN
1897

PREFACE.

With the exception of the terrible retreat from Afghanistan, none of England's many little wars have been so fatal in proportion to the number of those engaged as our first expedition to Burma. It was undertaken without any due comprehension of the difficulties to be encountered from the effects of climate and the deficiency of transport; the power and still more the obstinacy and arrogance of the Court of Ava were altogether underrated; and it was considered that our possession of her ports would assuredly bring the enemy, who had wantonly forced the struggle upon us, to submission. Events, however, proved the completeness of the error. The Burman policy of carrying off every boat on the river, laying waste the whole country and driving away the inhabitants and the herds, maintained our army as prisoners in Rangoon through the first wet season, and caused the loss of half the white officers and men first sent there. The subsequent campaign was no less fatal, and although large reinforcements had been sent, fifty per cent of the whole died, so that less than two thousand fighting men remained in the ranks when the expedition arrived within a short distance of Ava. Not until the last Burmese army had been scattered did the Court of Ava submit to the by no means onerous terms we imposed. Great, indeed, was the contrast presented by this first invasion of the country with the last war in 1885, which brought about the final annexation of Burma. Then a fleet of steamers conveyed the troops up the noble river, while in 1824 a solitary steamer was all that India could furnish to aid the flotilla of row-boats. No worse government has ever existed than that of Burma when, with the boast that she intended to drive the British out of India, she began the war; no people were ever kept down by a more grinding tyranny, and the occupation of the country by the British has been an even greater blessing to the population than has that of India. Several works, some by eye-witnesses, others compiled from official documents, appeared after the war. They differ remarkably in the relation of details, and still more in the spelling of the names both of persons and places. I have chiefly followed those given in the narratives of Mr. H. H. Wilson, and of Major Snodgrass, the military secretary to the commander of the expedition.

CONTENTS.

Chap.		Page
I.	A New Career,	11
II.	The Outbreak of War,	28
III.	A Prisoner,	45
IV.	A Ruined Temple,	64
V.	With Brigands,	82
VI.	Among Friends,	101
VII.	On the Staff,	119
VIII.	The Pagoda,	137
IX.	Victories,	157
X.	The Advance,	176
XI.	Donabew,	196
XII.	Harry Carried Off,	215
XIII.	Preparing a Rescue,	236
XIV.	In the Temple,	256
XV.	The Attack,	276
XVI.	Rejoining,	296
XVII.	The Pride of Burma Humbled,	316
XVIII.	In Business Again,	336

ILLUSTRATIONS.

	Page
"Stanley gave a sudden spring and buried his knife in the leopard", ... *Frontispiece*.	82
Stanley is brought before Bandoola the Burmese General, ...	47
"They forced the canoe behind bushes so as to be entirely concealed", ...	99
The Burmese make a Great Effort to Capture Pagoda Hill, ...	152
"Stanley cut down the man who was about to fire the hut", ...	204
"The great snake moved his head higher and higher, hissing angrily", ...	252
"In vain the Burmese tried to force their way into the chamber", ...	278
"The old Burmese general was carried from point to point in a litter", ...	314

ON THE IRRAWADDY.

CHAPTER I.

A NEW CAREER.

 PARTY was assembled in a room of an hotel in Calcutta at the end of the year 1822. It consisted of a gentleman, a lady in deep mourning, a boy of between fourteen and fifteen, and two girls of thirteen and twelve.

"I think you had better accept my offer, Nellie," the gentleman was saying. "You will find it hard work enough to make both ends meet with these two girls, and Stanley would be a heavy drain on you. The girls cost nothing but their clothes, but he must go to a decent school, and then there would be the trouble of thinking what to do with him afterwards. If I could have allowed you a couple of hundred a year it would have been altogether different, but you see I am fighting an uphill fight myself, and need every penny that I can scrape together. I am getting on, and I can see well enough that, unless something occurs to upset the whole thing, I shall be doing a big trade one of these days, but every halfpenny of profit has to go into the business. So, as you know, I cannot help you at present, though by the time the girls grow up I hope I shall be able to do so, and that to a good extent. I feel sure that it would not be a bad thing for Stanley; he will soon get to be useful to me, and in three or four years will be a valuable assistant. Speaking Hindustani as well as he does, he won't be very long in picking up enough of the various dialects in Kathee and Chittagong for our purpose, and by twenty he will have a share of the business, and be on the highway towards making his fortune. It will be infinitely better than anything he is likely to find in England, and he will be doing a man's work at the age when he would still be a schoolboy in England. I have spoken to him about it. Of course he does not like leaving you, but he says that he should like it a thousand times better than perhaps having to go into some humdrum office in England.'

"Thank you, Tom," Mrs. Brooke said with a sigh. "It will be very hard to part with him,—terribly hard,—but I see that it is by far the best thing for him, and, as you say. in a monetary way it will be a relief to me. I think I can manage very comfortably on the pension, in some quiet place at home with the two girls, but Stanley's schooling would be a heavy drain. I might even manage that, for I might earn a little money by painting, but there would be the question of what to do with him when he left school, and without friends or influence it will be hopeless to get him into any good situation. You see, Herbert's parents have both died since he came out here, and though he was distantly related to the Earl of Netherley, he was only a second cousin or something of that kind, and knew nothing about the family, and of course I could not apply to them."

"Certainly not, Nellie," her brother agreed. "There is nothing so hateful as posing as a poor relation—and that is a connection rather than a relationship. Then you will leave the boy in my hands?"

"I am sure that it will be best," she said with a tremor

in her voice, "and at any rate I shall have the comfort of knowing that he will be well looked after."

Mrs. Brooke was the widow of a captain in one of the native regiments of the East India Company. He had, six weeks before this, been carried off suddenly by an outbreak of cholera, and she had been waiting at Calcutta in order to see her brother before sailing for England. She was the daughter of an English clergyman, who had died some seventeen years before. Nellie, who was then eighteen, being motherless as well as fatherless, had determined to sail for India. A great friend of hers had married and gone out a year before. Nellie's father was at that time in bad health, and her friend had said to her at parting: "Now mind, Nellie, I have your promise that if you should find yourself alone here, you will come out to me in India. I shall be very glad to have you with me, and I don't suppose you will be on my hands very long; pretty girls don't remain single many months in India." So, seeing nothing better to do, Nellie had, shortly after her father's death, sailed for Calcutta.

Lieutenant Brooke was also a passenger on board the *Ava*, and during the long voyage he and Nellie Pearson became engaged, and were married from her friend's house a fortnight after their arrival. Nellie was told that she was a foolish girl, for that she ought to have done better, but she was perfectly happy. The pay and allowances of her husband were sufficient for them to live upon in comfort, and though, when the children came, there was little to spare, the addition of pay when he gained the rank of captain was ample for their wants. They had been in fact a perfectly happy couple—both had bright and sunny dispositions and made the best of everything, and she had never had a serious care until he was suddenly taken away from her.

Stanley had inherited his parents' disposition, and as his sisters, coming so soon after him, occupied the greater portion of his mother's care, he was left a good deal to his own devices, and became a general pet in the regiment, and was equally at home in the men's lines and in the officers' bungalows. The native language came as readily to him as English, and by the time he was ten he could talk in their own tongue with the men from the three or four different districts from which the regiment had been recruited. His father devoted a couple of hours a day to his studies; he did not attempt to teach him Latin, which would, he thought, be altogether useless to him, but gave him a thorough grounding in English and Indian history and arithmetic, and insisted upon his spending a certain time each day in reading standard English authors.

Tom Pearson, who was five years younger than his sister, had come out to India four years after her. He was a lad full of life and energy. As soon as he left school, finding himself the master of a hundred pounds, the last remains of the small sum that his father had left behind him, he took a second-class passage to Calcutta. As soon as he had landed he went round to the various merchants and offices, and finding that he could not, owing to a want of references, obtain a clerkship, he took a place in the store of a Parsee merchant who dealt in English goods.

Here he remained for five years, by which time he had mastered two or three native languages, and had obtained a good knowledge of business. He now determined to start on his own account; he had lived hardly, saving up every rupee not needed for actual necessaries, and at the end of the five years he had in all a hundred and fifty pounds. He had long before this determined that the best opening for trade was among the tribes on the eastern borders of the British territory, and had specially devoted himself to the study of the languages of Kathee and Chittagong. Investing the greater portion of his money in goods suitable for the trade, he embarked at Calcutta in a vessel bound for Chittagong. There he took passage in a native craft going up the great river to Sylhet, where he established his head-quarters, and thence, leaving the greater portion of his goods in the care of a native merchant with whom his late employer had had dealings, started with a native, and four donkeys on which his goods were packed, to trade among the wild tribes.

His success fully equalled his anticipations, and gradually he extended his operations, going as far east as Manipur and south almost as far as Chittagong. The firm in Calcutta, from whom he had in the first place purchased his goods, sent him up fresh stores as he required them, and soon, seeing the energy with which he was pushing his business, gave him considerable credit, and he was able to carry on his operations on an increasingly larger scale. Sylhet remained his head-quarters, but he had a branch at Chittagong whither goods could be sent direct from Calcutta, and from this he drew his supplies for his trade in that province. Much of his business was carried on by means of the waterways and the very numerous streams that covered the whole country, and enabled him to carry his goods at a far cheaper rate than he could transport them by land, and for this purpose he had a boat specially fitted up with a comfortable cabin. He determined from the first to sell none but the best goods in the market, and thus he speedily gained the confidence of the natives, and the arrival of his boats was eagerly hailed by the villagers on the banks of the rivers.

He soon found that money was scarce, and that to do a

good business he must take native products in barter for his goods, and that in this way he not only did a much larger trade, but obtained a very much better price for his wares than if he had sold only for money; and he soon consigned considerable quantities to the firm in Calcutta, and by so doing obtained a profit both ways. He himself paid a visit to Calcutta every six months or so, to choose fresh fashions of goods and to visit the firm, with whom his dealings every year became more extensive. But though laying the foundations for an extensive business, he was not, as he told his sister, at present in a position to help her, for his increasing trade continually demanded more and more capital, and the whole of his profits were swallowed up by the larger stocks that had to be held at his depots at Sylhet, Chittagong, and at the mouths of the larger rivers. Twice since he had been out he had met his sister at Calcutta, and when she came down after her husband's death and heard from Tom's agents that he would probably arrive there in the course of a fortnight, she decided to wait there and meet him. He was greatly grieved at her loss, and especially so as he was unable to offer her a home; for as his whole time was spent in travelling, it was impossible for him to do so; nor indeed would she have accepted it. Now that her husband was gone, she yearned to be back in England again; it was, too, far better for the girls that she should take them home. But when he now offered to take the boy, she felt that, hard as it would be to leave Stanley behind, the offer was a most advantageous one for him.

The boy's knowledge of Indian languages, which would be of immense advantage to him in such a life, would be absolutely useless in England, and, from what Tom told her of his business, there could be little doubt that the prospects were excellent. Stanley himself, who now saw his uncle for the first time, was attracted to him by the energy and cheeriness of manner that had rendered him so successful in business, and he was stirred by the enterprise and adventure of the life he proposed for him. More than once in the little-frequented rivers that stretched into Kathee his boats had been attacked by wild tribesmen, and he had to fight hard to keep them off; petty chiefs had at times endeavoured to obstruct his trading, and when at Manipur, he had twice been witness of desperate fights between rival claimants for the throne. All this was to a boy brought up among soldiers irresistibly fascinating, especially as the alternative seemed to be a seat in a dull counting-house in England. He was then delighted when his mother gave her consent to his remaining with his uncle, grieved as he was at being parted from her and his sisters. The thought that he should in time be able to be of assistance to her was a pleasant one, and aided him to support the pain of parting, when, a week later, she sailed with the girls for England.

"I suppose you have not done any shooting, Stanley?" his uncle asked.

"Not with a gun, but I have practised sometimes with pistols. Father thought that it would be useful."

"Very useful; and you must learn to shoot well with them and with fowling-piece and rifle. What with river thieves, and dacoits, and wild tribes, to say nothing of wild beasts, a man who travels about as I do, wants to be able to shoot straight. The straighter you shoot, the less likely you are to have to do so. I have come to be a good shot myself, and whenever we row up a river I constantly practise either at floating objects in the water, or at birds or other marks in the trees. I have the best weapons that money can buy. It is my one extravagance, and the result is that to my boatmen and the men about me my shooting seems to be marvellous; they tell others of it, and the result is that I am regarded with great respect. I have no doubt whatever that it has saved me from much trouble, for the natives have almost got to believe that I only have to point my gun, and the man I wish to kill falls dead, however far distant."

Two days after the departure of Mrs. Brooke her brother and Stanley started down the Hoogly in a native trader.

"She is a curious-looking craft, uncle."

"Yes; she would not be called handsome in home waters, but she is uncommonly fast, and I find her much more convenient in many ways than a British merchantman."

"Is she yours, uncle?"

"No, she is not mine, and I do not exactly charter her, but she works principally for me. You see the wages are so low that they can work a craft like this for next to nothing. Why, the captain and his eight men together don't get higher pay than the boatswain of an English trader. The captain owns the vessel; he is quite content if he gets a few rupees a month in addition to what he considers his own rate of pay; his wife and his two children live on board. If the craft can earn twenty rupees a week, he considers that he is doing splendidly. At the outside he would not pay his men more than four rupees a month each, and I suppose that he would put down his services at eight, so that would leave him forty rupees a month as the profit earned by the ship. In point of fact I keep him going pretty steadily. He makes trips backwards and forwards between the different depots; carries me up the rivers for a considerable distance; does a little trade on his own account,—not in goods such as I sell, you know, but purely native stores; takes a little freight when he can get it, and generally a few native passengers.

"I pay him fifteen rupees a week, and I suppose he earns from five to ten in addition, so that the arrangement suits us both admirably. I keep the stern cabin for myself. As you see, she has four little brass guns which I picked up for a song at Calcutta, and there are twenty-four muskets aft. It is an arrangement that the crew are to practise shooting once a week, so they have all come to be pretty fair shots, and the captain himself can send a two-pound shot from those little guns uncommonly straight. You will be amused when you see us practising for action. The captain's wife and the two boys load the guns, and do it very quickly too; he runs round from gun to gun, takes aim, and fires; the crew shout and yell and bang away with their muskets; I take the command, and give a few pice among them if the firing has been accurate. We have been attacked once or twice in the upper waters, but have always managed to beat the robbers off without much difficulty. The captain fires away till they get pretty close, and I pepper them with my rifles; I have three of them. When they get within fifty yards, the crew open fire, and as they have three muskets each, they can make it very hot for the pirates. I have a store of hand grenades, and if they push on, I throw two or three on board when they get within ten yards, and that has always finished the matter. They don't understand the things bursting in the middle of them. I don't mean to say that my armament would be of much use if we were trading along the coast of the Malay Peninsula or among the Islands, but it is quite enough to deal with the petty robbers of these rivers."

"But I thought that you had a boat that you went up the rivers in, uncle?"

"Yes; we tow a row-boat and a store-boat up behind this craft as far as she can go, that is, as long as she has wind enough to make against the sluggish stream. When she can go no further, I take to the row-boat; it has eight rowers, carries a gun—it is a twelve-pounder howitzer that I have had cut short so that it is only about a foot long. Of course it won't carry far, but that is not necessary. Its charge is a pound of powder and a ten-pound bag of bullets, and at a couple of hundred yards the balls scatter enough to sweep two or three canoes coming abreast, and as we can charge and fire the little thing three times in a minute, it is all that we require for practical purposes; it is only on a few of the rivers we go up that there is any fear of trouble. On the river from Sylhet to the east and its branches in Kathee, or, as it is sometimes called, Kasi, the country is comparatively settled. The Goomtee beyond Oudypore is well enough until it gets into Kaayn, which is what they call independent. That is to say, it owns no authority, and some villages are peaceable and well-disposed, while others are savage. The same may be said of the Munnoo and Fenny rivers. For the last two years I have done a good deal of trade in Assam up the Brahmaputra river. As far as Rungpoor there are a great many villages on the banks, and the people are quiet and peaceable."

"Then you don't go further south than Chittagong, uncle?"

"No. The Burmese hold Aracan on the south, and indeed for some distance north of it there is no very clearly defined border. You see the great river runs from Rangoon very nearly due north, though with a little east in it, and extends along at the back of the districts I trade with; so that the Burmese are not very far from Manipur, which indeed stands on a branch of the Irrawaddy, of which another branch runs nearly up to Rungpoor. We shall have big trouble with them one of these days; indeed we have had troubles already. You see the Burmese are a great and increasing power, and have so easily conquered all their neighbours that they regard themselves as invincible. Until the beginning of the eighteenth century the Burmese were masters of Pegu; then the people of that country, with the help of the Dutch and Portuguese, threw off their yoke. But the Burmese were not long kept down, for in 1753 Alompra, a hunter, gathered a force round him, and, after keeping up an irregular warfare for some time, was joined by so many of his countrymen that he attacked and captured Ava, conquered the whole of Pegu, and in 1759 the English trading colony at Negrais were massacred.

"This, however, was not the act of Alompra, but of the treachery of a Frenchman named Levine, and of an Armenian, who incited the Burmese of the district to exterminate the English, hoping, no doubt, thus to retrieve in a new quarter the fortunes of France, which in India were being extinguished by the genius of Clive. The English were at the time far too occupied with the desperate struggle they were having in India to attempt to revenge the massacre of their countrymen at Negrais. Very rapidly the Burman power spread. They captured the valuable Tenasserim coast from Siam, repulsed a formidable invasion from China, annexed Aracan and dominated Manipur, and thus became masters of the whole tract of country lying between China and Hindustan. As they now bordered upon our territory, a mission was sent in 1794 to them from India, with a proposal for the settlement of boundaries, and for the arrangement of trade between the two countries. Nothing came of it, for the Burmese had already proposed to themselves the conquest of India, and considered the mission as a proof of the terror that their advance had inspired among us.

"After the conquest by them of Aracan in 1784, there had been a constant irritation felt against us by the Burmese, owing to the fact that a great number of fugitives from that country had taken refuge in the swamps and islands of Chittagong, from which they from time to time issued and made raids against the Burmese. In 1811 these fugitives, in alliance with some predatory chiefs, invaded Aracan in force, and being joined by the subject population there, expelled the Burmese. These, however, soon reconquered the province. The affair was, nevertheless, unfortunate, since the Burmese naturally considered that as the insurrection had begun with an invasion by the fugitives in Chittagong, it had been fomented by us. This was in no way the fact: we had no force there capable of keeping the masses of fugitives in order, but we did our best, and arrested many of the leaders when they returned after their defeat. This, however, was far from satisfying the Burmese. A mission was sent to Ava to assure them of our friendly intentions, and that we had had nothing whatever to do with the invasion, and would do all we could to prevent its recurrence. The Burmese government declined to receive the mission.

"We ourselves had much trouble with the insurgents, for, fearful of re-entering Burma after their defeat, they now carried on a series of raids in our territory, and it was not until 1816 that these were finally suppressed. Nevertheless the court of Ava remained dissatisfied, and a fresh demand was raised for the surrender of the chiefs who had been captured, and of the whole of the fugitives living in the government of Chittagong. The Marquis of Hastings replied that the British government could not, without a violation of the principles of justice, deliver up those who had sought its protection; that tranquillity now existed; and there was no probability of a renewal of the disturbances, but that the greatest vigilance should be used to prevent and punish the authors of any raid that might be attempted against Aracan. A year later a second letter was received, demanding on the part of the king the cession of Ramoo, Chittagong, Moorshedabad, and Dacca, that is to say, of the whole British possessions east of the Ganges. Lord Hastings simply replied that if it was possible to suppose that the demand had been dictated by the king of Ava, the British government would be justified in regarding it as a declaration of war.

"To this the Burmese made no reply; doubtless they had heard of the successes we had gained in Central India, and had learned that our whole force was disposable against them. Three years ago the old king died, and a more warlike monarch succeeded him. Since 1810 they have been mixed up in the troubles that have been going on in Assam, where a civil war had been raging. One party or other has sought their assistance, and fighting has been going on there nearly incessantly, and two months ago the Burmese settled the question by themselves taking possession of the whole country. This has, of course, been a serious blow to me. Although disorder has reigned, it has not interfered with my trading along the banks of the river; but now that the Burmese have set up their authority, I shall, for a time anyhow, be obliged to give up my operations there, for they have evinced considerable hostility to us—have made raids near Rungpoor on our side of the river, and have pulled down a British flag on an island in the Brahmaputra. We have taken, in consequence, the principality of Cachar under our protection—indeed its two princes, seeing that the Burmese were beginning to invade their country, invited us to take this step—and we thus occupy the passes from Manipur into the low country of Sylhet."

"I wonder that you have been able to trade in Manipur, uncle, as the Burmese have been masters there."

"I am not trading with the capital itself, and the Burmese have been too occupied with their affairs in Assam to exercise much authority in the country. Besides, you see there has not been war between the two countries. Our merchants at Rangoon still carry on their trade up the Irrawaddy, and in Assam this spring the only trouble I had, was, that I had to pay somewhat higher tolls than I had done before. However, now that Cachar is under our protection, I hope that I shall make up for my loss of trade in Assam by doing better than before in that province."

"I thought you called it Kathee, uncle?"

"So it is generally named; but as it is spoken of as Cachar in the proclamation assuming the protectorate, I suppose it will be called so in future; but all these names out here are spelt pretty much according to fancy."

While this conversation had been going on the boat had been running fast down the river, passing several European vessels almost as if they had been standing still.

"I should not have thought that a boat like this would pass these large ships," Stanley said.

"We have a good deal to learn in the art of sailing yet," his uncle replied. "A great many of these Indian dhows can run away from a square-rigged ship in light weather. I don't know whether it is the lines of their hulls or the cut of the sails, but there is no doubt about their speed. They seem to skim over the water while our bluff-bowed craft shove their way through it. I suppose some day we shall adopt these long sharp bows; when we do it will make a wonderful difference in our rate of sailing. Then, too, these craft have a very light draft of water; but, on the other hand, they have a deep keel which helps them to lie close to the wind, and that long overhanging bow renders them capital craft in heavy weather, for as they meet the sea they rise over it gradually, instead of its hitting them full on the bow as it does our ships. We have much to learn yet in the way of shipbuilding."

The trader had his own servant with him, and the man now came up and said that a meal was ready, and they at once entered the cabin. It was roomy and comfortable, and was, like the rest of the boat, of varnished teak. There were large windows in the stern; it had a table with two fixed benches, and there were broad, low sofas on each side. Above these the muskets were disposed in racks, while at the end by the door were Tom Pearson's own rifles, four brace of pistols, and a couple of swords. Ten long spears were suspended from the roof of the cabin in leather slings. The floor, like the rest of the cabin, was varnished.

"It looks very comfortable, uncle."

"Yes; you see I live quite half my time on board, the rest being spent in the boat. My man is a capital cook. He comes from Chittagong, and is a Mug."

"What are Mugs, uncle?"

"They are the original inhabitants of Aracan. He was one of those who remained there after the Burmese had conquered it, and speaks their language as well as his own. I recommend you to begin it with him at once. If things settle down in Assam, it will be very useful for you in arranging with the Burmese officials. You won't find it very easy, though of course your knowledge of three or four Indian tongues will help you. It is said to be a mixture of the old Tali, Sanscrit, Tartar, and Chinese. The Tartar and Chinese words will of course be quite new to you—the other two elements will resemble those that you are familiar with. I talk to the man in Hindustani; he picked up a little of it at Chittagong, and has learned a good deal more during the two years that he has been with me, and through that you will be able to learn Burmese."

A week later the dhow entered the harbour. Stanley had passed most of his time in conversation with Khyen, Tom's servant. The facility his tongue had acquired in the Indian languages was of great benefit to him, and he speedily picked up a good many Burmese sentences.

For the next six months he continued, with his uncle, the work the latter had carried on, and enjoyed it much. They sailed up the sluggish rivers, with their low, flat shores, in the dhow, towing the row-boat and the store-boat behind them. The crews of these boats lived on board the dhow until their services were required, helping in its navigation and aiding the crew when the wind dropped and sweeps were got out. The villages along the banks were for the most part small, but were very numerous. At each of these the dhow brought up. There was in almost all cases sufficient water to allow of her being moored alongside the banks, and as soon as she did so the natives came on board to make their purchases and dispose of their produce. In addition to the European and Indian goods carried, the dhow was laden with rice, for which there was a considerable demand at most of the villages. As soon as he had learned the price of the various goods and their equivalent in the products of the country, Stanley did much of the bartering, while his uncle went ashore and talked with the head men of the village, with all of whom he made a point of keeping on good terms, and so securing a great portion of the trade that might otherwise have been carried by native craft.

Three times during the six months the dhow had gone

back to Calcutta to fetch fresh supplies of goods, and to take in another cargo of rice, while the trader proceeded higher up the river in his own boats. While on the voyage Stanley always had the rifle and fowling-piece, that his uncle had handed over for his special use, leaning against the bulwark, close at hand, and frequently shot water-fowl, which were so abundant that he was able to keep not only their own table supplied, but to furnish the crew and boatmen with a considerable quantity of food. They had had no trouble with river pirates, for these had suffered so heavily in previous attacks upon the dhow that they shunned any repetition of their loss. At the same time every precaution was taken, for owing to the intestine troubles in Cachar and Assam, fugitives belonging to the party that happened for the time to be worsted were driven to take refuge in the jungles near the rivers, and to subsist largely on plunder, the local authorities being too feeble to root them out. The boats, therefore, were always anchored in the middle of the stream at night and two men were kept on watch. To the south as well as in the north the trading operations were more restricted, for the Burmese became more and more aggressive. Elephant hunters in the hills that formed the boundary of the British territory to the east were seized and carried off, twenty-three in one place being captured and six in another—all being ill-treated and imprisoned, and the remonstrances of the Indian government treated with contempt by the Rajah of Aracan.

It was evident that the object of the Burmese was to possess themselves of this hill country in order that they might, if they chose, pour down at any time into the cultivated country round the town of Ramoo.

"There is no doubt, Stanley," said his uncle one day, "we shall very shortly have a big war with the Burmese.

The fact that these constant acts of aggression are met only by remonstrances on our part increases their arrogance, and they are convinced that we are in mortal terror of them. They say that in Assam their leaders are openly boasting that ere long they will drive us completely from India, and one of their generals has confidently declared that after taking India they intend to conquer England. With such ignorant people there is but one argument understood, namely, force; and sooner or later we shall have to give them such a hearty thrashing that they will be quiet for some time. Still, I grant that the difficulties are great. Their country is a tremendous size, the beggars are brave, and the climate, at any rate near the sea-coast, is horribly unhealthy. Altogether it will be a big job, but it will have to be done, or in a very short time we shall see them marching against Calcutta."

CHAPTER II.

THE OUTBREAK OF WAR.

ON the last day of September, 1823, just a year after Stanley had joined his uncle, the dhow sailed into Chittagong, which had now taken the place of Sylhet, as the traders' chief depôt, the latter place being too near the Burmese in Assam for him to care about keeping a large stock of his goods there. He went ashore as soon as the dhow cast anchor, Stanley remaining on board.

"The fat is all in the fire, Stanley," Tom Pearson said when he returned. "The Burmese have attacked and killed some of our troops, and it is certain that the government cannot put up with that."

"Where was it, uncle?"

"Down at the mouth of the Naaf. As you know that is the southern boundary of the province, and there was a row there in January. One of our native boats laden with rice was coming up the river, on our side of the channel, when an armed Burmese boat came across and demanded duty. Of course, our fellows said they were in their own waters, whereupon the Burmese fired upon them and killed the steersman. There were reports then that bodies of Burmese troops were moving about on their side of the river, and that it was feared they would cross over and burn some of our villages. Accordingly our guard at the mouth of the river was increased to fifty men, and a few of these were posted on the island of Shapuree. This island lies close to our shore, and indeed the channel between can be forded at low water. It has always formed part of the province of Chittagong, and there has never been any question raised by the Burmese as to this. However, the viceroy of Aracan called upon our resident here to withdraw the guard, asserting the right of the king of Ava to the island.

"Since then letters have passed to and fro, but I hear that the Burmese have settled the question by landing on Shapuree. One night last week they attacked our post there, killed and wounded four of the sepoys, and drove the rest off the island. The Indian government have put up with a great deal rather than engage in so costly and difficult an operation as a war with Burma, but it is impossible that we can stand this."

The Indian government, however, used every endeavour to avert the necessity for war, although the Rajah of Aracan lost no time in writing a letter to the government of Calcutta, stating that he had occupied the island of Shapuree, and that unless they submitted quietly to this act of justice, the cities of Dacca and Moorshedabad would be forcibly seized. In order, however, to postpone, at any rate, the outbreak of war, the government of Bengal resolved to give the court of Ava an opportunity to withdraw from the position taken up. They therefore acted as if the attack on the guard at Shapuree had been the action of the viceroy of Aracan alone, and addressed a declaration to the Burmese government recapitulating the facts of the case, pointing out that Shapuree had always been acknowledged by Burma as forming part of the province of Chittagong, and calling upon the government to disavow the action of the local authorities.

The Burmese considered this, as it was in fact, a proof that the government of India was reluctant to enter upon a contest with them, and confirmed Burma in its confident expectation of annexing the eastern portions of Bengal, if not of expelling the English altogether. In the meantime Shapuree had been reoccupied by us. The Burmese, after driving out the little garrison, had retired, and two months after the attack two companies of the 20th Native Infantry arrived by sea from Calcutta and landed there. A stockade was built, and two six-pounders placed in position. Another company was stationed on the mainland, and the *Planet* and three gunboats, each carrying a twelve-pounder, were stationed in the river. The Burmese at once collected large bodies of troops, both in Aracan and Assam. The government of Bengal made preparations to defend our frontier, and especially the position in the north, as an advance of the Burmese in this direction would not only threaten the important towns of Dacca and Moorshedabad, but would place the invaders in dangerous proximity to Calcutta. Accordingly a portion of the 10th and 23rd Native Infantry, and four companies of the Rungpoor local force, were marched to Sylhet, and outposts thrown forward to the frontier.

Seeing that the Burmese operations would probably commence in the north, Tom Pearson had, after completing his arrangements at Chittagong, sailed north to remove his depots from Sylhet and other places that would be exposed to an attack from that direction. They reached Sylhet the first week in January. By this time Stanley, from his constant conversation with his uncle's servant, had come to speak Burmese as fluently as the Indian languages. He was now nearly sixteen, tall for his age and active; but owing to the hot climate and the absence of vigorous exercise, he was less broad and muscular than most English lads of his age.

They found on landing that news had arrived two days before that a powerful army of Burmese had entered Cachar from Manipur and had defeated the troops of Jambhir Sing, that 4000 Burmese and Assamese had advanced from Assam into Cachar, and had begun to stockade themselves at Bickrampore at the foot of the Bhortoka Pass, and that the third division was crossing into the district of Jyntea immediately to the north of Sylhet. There was a complete panic in the town, and the ryots were flocking in from all the surrounding country with their families and belongings, and were making their way down the country in boats to Dacca.

"I am afraid, Stanley, there is an end of trade for the present. What we see here is doubtless taking place all over Cachar, and it would be just as bad down at Chittagong. It is a heavy blow, for I have done remarkably well this year, and was building up the foundations for a good business. No doubt when this trouble is over I shall be able to take it up again, and it may be if we thrash the

Burmese heartily, which we are sure to do in the long run, it may even prove a benefit; still there is no doubt that it is a very bad business for me. However, as just at present there is nothing whatever to be done, I propose, as soon as the goods are all on board, to take a holiday and go out and have a look at the fighting."

"You will take me with you, uncle?" Stanley asked eagerly.

"Certainly, lad, we don't mean to do any fighting ourselves, but only to look on; and it may be that after it is over you may be able to make yourself useful if they want to ask questions of any Burmese prisoners."

"You think that there is no chance of their beating us?"

"I should think not, though of course there is no saying; still, I don't think these fellows will be able to stand against our troops. Of course, they have no idea whatever of our style of fighting, and have never met any really formidable foes, so that I imagine we shall make pretty short work of them. However, as we shall be mounted—for I will hire a couple of horses, there have been plenty of them driven into the town—we shall be able to make a bolt of it if necessary. Of course we will take our rifles and pistols with us."

The goods were not placed on board the dhow, but in what was called the store-boat, as the trader had determined to take up his abode in his row-boat, which could move about much faster than the dhow, and to allow the captain of that craft to make a good thing of it by taking down to Dacca as many of the fugitives as she would hold.

Finding that the Burmese division that had entered Jyntea was intrenching itself at a few miles' distance, Major Newton, the officer commanding on the Sylhet frontier, concentrated his force at Jatrapur, a village five miles beyond the Sylhet boundary. Tom Pearson had introduced himself to Major Newton and asked permission to accompany his force, saying that his nephew would be able, if necessary, to communicate with the Burmese either before or after the action, and that both would willingly act as aides-de-camp. The offer was accepted with thanks, and they rode out with him on the evening of the 16th of January, 1824, to Jatrapur.

At one o'clock in the morning the troops were roused, and marched an hour later. At daybreak they came in sight of the stockade, and a few shots were at once fired upon the advanced guard by the Burmese. A portion of their force was lying in a village hard by.

Major Newton at once divided his command into two bodies; one of these was led by Captain Johnston against the front of the stockade, the other under Captain Rowe attacked the village adjoining. The Burmese stationed there gave way after a very faint resistance. They were accustomed to rely always on stockades, and this attack upon them when not so protected, shook them at once. Those in the stockade, however, made a resolute resistance. Captain Rowe, after gaining possession of the village, and seeing the occupants in full flight, moved his force to aid the other division; and the Burmese, dispirited by the defeat of their countrymen, and finding themselves attacked on two sides, gave way and fled, leaving a hundred dead behind them, while on the British side but six sepoys were killed.

The Burmese fled to the hills at a speed that rendered pursuit hopeless by the more heavily-armed troops, and the fugitives soon rallied and effected their junction with the division advancing from Manipur. After the action Major Newton returned to Sylhet, and a few days later Mr. Scott, who had been appointed commissioner, arrived there, and, advancing to Bhadrapur, opened communications with the Burmese. As, however, it became evident that the latter were only negotiating in order to gain time to intrench themselves near Jatrapur, to which they had returned, he again placed the matter in the hands of the military commanders.

The Burmese force amounted to about six thousand men. They had erected strong stockades on each bank of the river Surma, and had thrown a bridge across to connect them. Captain Johnston advanced with a wing of the 10th Native Infantry, a company of the 23rd Native Infantry, and a small party of men of a local corps. Small as was this force, he divided it into two parties; one of these under Captain Rowe crossed the river, and then both moved against the enemy. The Burmese opened fire as they advanced, but the sepoys marched gallantly forward, and drove the enemy out of their unfinished intrenchments at the point of the bayonet. The Assam division retreated hastily to the Bhortoka Pass, while the Manipur force stockaded itself at Doodpatnee.

The Assam division was first attacked, and the stockade carried at the point of the bayonet. Lieutenant-colonel Bowen, who now commanded, then moved against the position at Doodpatnee. This was very strong; steep hills covered the rear, while the other faces of the intrenchments were defended by a deep ditch fourteen feet wide, with a *chevaux de frise* of pointed bamboos on its outer edge. Although the position was attacked with great gallantry, it was too strong to be captured by so small a force, and they were obliged to withdraw to Jatrapur with the loss of one officer killed and four wounded, and about one hundred and fifty sepoys killed and wounded. However, their bravery had not been without effect, for the Burmese evacuated their stockade and retreated to Manipur, leaving Cachar free from its invaders. Thus in less than three weeks the Burmese invasion of the northern provinces had been hurled back by a British force of less than a tenth of that of the invaders.

Stanley and his uncle had been present at all these engagements, and in the absence of any cavalry had done good service in conveying messages and despatches, and the lad had several times acted as interpreter between the officers and Burmese prisoners. Both received letters from the commissioner thanking them for the assistance that they had rendered.

"That last affair was unfortunate, Stanley, and it is evident that these stockades of theirs are nasty places to attack, and that they ought to be breached by guns before the men are sent forward to storm them. However, as the Burmese have gone, our repulse does not matter much. Well, I felt sure that we should thrash them, but I certainly gave them credit for having a great deal more pluck than they have shown. As it is, if there is nothing fresh takes place here, the natives and little traders will soon be coming back from Dacca, and business will be better than before; for the Burmese have been talking so big for the last three years that no one has bought more than would just carry him on, while now they will be more inclined to lay in good stocks of goods. To-morrow we will start for Chittagong. You see I have a considerable store there, and there is a chance of much more serious fighting in that quarter than this little affair we have seen. The governor of Aracan has all along been the source of troubles, and we may expect that he will cross into the province at the head of a large force, and may do an immense deal of damage before we can get enough troops there to oppose him."

Descending the river they coasted along until they arrived, early in March, at Chittagong. They found that great alarm reigned there. In January, Bandoola, the greatest military leader of the Burmese, who was known to have been one of the most strenuous supporters of the war policy at the court of Ava, had arrived at Aracan and taken the command of the troops collected there, and had brought with him considerable reinforcements. A wanton outrage that had been committed by the Burmese showed how intent they were upon hostilities. Owing to the unhealthiness of the islet of Shapuree the sepoys stationed there had been withdrawn, and the Company's pilot vessel *Sophia* was ordered to join the gun-boats off that island. Four deputies from the Burmese court arrived at Mungdoo on the opposite shore, and these invited the commander of the *Sophia* to come on shore in order that they might talk over with him in a friendly way the situation of affairs. He unsuspectingly accepted their invitation and landed, accompanied by an officer and some native seamen. The party were at once seized and sent prisoners to Aracan, where they were detained for a month and then sent back to Mungdoo.

This wanton insult was followed by a formal declaration of war by the government of India, and a similar document was issued by the court of Ava. The force at Sylhet was reinforced, and that in Chittagong increased. It consisted of a wing of the 13th and of the 20th Native Regiments, and a battalion of the 23rd, with a local levy, amounting in all to some 3000 men. Of these a wing of the 23rd, with two guns, and a portion of the native levies were posted at Ramoo, which was the point most threatened by an invasion from Aracan. It was in the north that hostilities first commenced, a force moving into Assam and driving the

Burmese before them; several sharp blows were dealt the enemy, and had it not been for the setting in of the wet season they would have been driven entirely out of Assam.

"I think, Stanley," his uncle said, after he had been a short time at Chittagong, "you had better go up to Ramoo and see about matters there. Of course, until the Burmese move we cannot say what their game is likely to be, but it will be as well to get the stores ready for embarkation in case they should advance in that direction. If they do so get everything on board at once, and you can then be guided by circumstances. As the dhow came in yesterday, I can spare both our boats, and shall, of course, ship the goods here on board the big craft. Even if the Burmese come this way I have no fear of their taking the town, and shall, of course, lend a hand in the defence if they attempt it; you can do the same at Ramoo if you like. I was chatting with Colonel Shatland yesterday; he tells me that a large fleet has been collected, and that an expedition will be sent to capture Rangoon, so in that case it is likely that Bandoola and his force will march off in that direction.

"I think government are wrong. It will be impossible for the troops to move when the wet season once sets in, and they will lose a tremendous lot of men from sickness if they are cooped up in Rangoon. They had very much better have sent a few thousand men down here to act on the defensive and repel any attempted invasion until the rains are over, when they could have been shipped again and join the expedition against Rangoon. It seems to me a madheaded thing to begin at the present time of the year. We have put up with the insults of the Burmese for so long that we might just as well have waited for the favourable season before we began our operations in earnest."

Accordingly, on the following day, Stanley started south for Ramoo, and on arriving there took charge of the trading operations. Shortly after, meeting Captain Noton, who commanded there, in the street, he recognized him as an officer who had been stationed at the same cantonment as his father, and whom he had four years previously known well.

"You don't recognize me, Captain Noton," he said; "I am the son of Captain Brooke, of the 33rd."

"I certainly did not recognize you," the officer said, "but I am glad to meet you again. Let me think; yes, your name is Stanley, and a regular young pickle you used to be. What on earth are you doing here? Of course I heard of your poor father's death, and was grieved indeed at his loss. Where is your mother? She is well, I hope."

"She went back to England with my sisters two months after my father's death. I joined my uncle, her brother. He is a trader, and carries on business in the district between here and Sylhet, trading principally on the rivers, but of course the war has put a stop to that for the present. We saw the fighting up in the north, and then came down to this district. He has remained at Chittagong, and I am in charge of goods here. I speak Burmese fairly now, and if I can be of any use to you I shall be very glad to be so. There is not much business here, and the Parsee clerk, who is generally in charge, can look after it very well. I acted as interpreter with the troops in the north, and have a letter from Mr. Scott, the commissioner, thanking me for my services."

"I remember you used to be able to talk four or five of the native languages, but how did you come to pick up Burmese?"

"From a servant of my uncle's. We thought that there

would be sure to be war sooner or later, and that after it was over there would be a good chance of profitable trade on the Burmese rivers. I had no great difficulty in learning it from my uncle's man, who was a native of Aracan."

"I have no doubt you will find it very useful. What a big fellow you have grown, Stanley; at least as far as height is concerned. Let me see. How old are you now?"

"I am past sixteen," Stanley replied. "I have had several touches of fever, caught, I suppose, from the damp on the rivers, but I think that I am pretty well acclimatized now. I know I don't look very strong, but I have not had much active exercise, and of course the climate is against me."

"Very much so. I wonder that you have kept your health as well as you have in this steamy climate. I am going to the mess-room now. You had better come and lunch with me, and I will introduce you to the other officers. We are very strong in comparison to the force, for, counting the assistant surgeon, there are ten of us."

"I shall be very glad, sir," Stanley said. "I have certainly been feeling rather lonely here, for I know no one, and there is very little to do. During the last year I have often gone up one of the rivers by myself, but there has always been occupation, while at present things are at a stand-still."

"I tell you what, Brooke, if you would like it, I can appoint you interpreter. There is not one of us who speaks this Mug language, which is, you know, almost the same as Burmese, and the officers in charge of the native levy would be delighted to have some one with them who could make the fellows understand. I can appoint you a first-class interpreter. The pay is not very high, you know, but you might just as well be earning it as doing nothing, and it would give you a sort of official position; and, as the son of a British officer and my friend, you would be one of us."

"Thank you very much, Captain Noton. I should like it immensely. Should I have to get a uniform?"

"There will be no absolute necessity for it; but if you get a white patrol-jacket like this, and a white cap-cover, it will establish you in the eyes of the natives as an officer, and give you more authority. Oh, by the way, you need not get them, for one of our lieutenants died the other day of fever. His effects have not been sold yet, but you may as well have his patrol-jackets and belts. We can settle what you are to pay for them afterwards; it will only be a matter of a few rupees, anyhow."

They now arrived at the house that had been taken for the use of the officers. On entering, Captain Noton introduced him to the others, and as several of these had at various times met his father in cantonments or on service, he was heartily welcomed by them, and at luncheon they listened with great interest to his accounts of the fighting in Cachar with the Burmese.

"I fancy we shall find them more formidable here, if they come," Captain Noton said. "Bandoola has a great reputation, and is immensely popular with them. From what you say, a considerable proportion of the fellows you met up there were Assamese levies raised by the Burmese. I grant that the Burmese themselves do not seem to have done much better, but they would never have conquered all the peoples they have come across, and built up a great empire if there had not been good fighting stuff in them. I have no doubt that we shall thrash them, but I don't think we shall do it as easily as our troops did in the north."

The time now passed pleasantly with Stanley; he had, after thinking it over, declined to accept payment for his services, for this would have hindered his freedom of action and prevented his obeying any instructions that his uncle might send him. He therefore joined as a volunteer interpreter, and was made a member of the officers' mess. He was specially attached to the native levy, and, soon acquiring their words of command, assisted its officers in drilling it into something like order.

Early in May a Burmese division, 8000 strong, crossed the Naaf and established itself at Rutnapullung, fourteen miles south of Ramoo. As soon as Captain Noton learned that the Burmese had crossed the river he sent news of the fact to Chittagong, with a request that reinforcements should be at once sent to him, and then moved out with his force from Ramoo to ascertain the strength of the enemy. The Burmese were seen upon some hills, where they were constructing stockades. The small British force advanced against them, drove them off the hills, and, following them, prepared to attack them in the plain beyond. The guns, however, had not come up, partly owing to the cowardice of the elephant-drivers, and partly to the fact that it was found that several of the essential parts of the guns had been left behind.

Without their assistance to clear the way Captain Noton felt that it would be imprudent to attack so great a force, and therefore fell back to Ramoo. Here he was joined by three companies of the 20th Native Infantry, bringing up his force to close upon a thousand, of whom about half were sepoys and the rest native levies. Had any energy whatever been shown by the officer in command of Chittagong in sending up reinforcements,—which he could well have spared, now that the point of attack by the Burmese had been made clear,—Captain Noton might have taken the offensive, in which case serious disaster would have been avoided, and the Burmese would have been driven back across the Naaf. None, however, came, and on the morning of the 13th of May the enemy appeared on the hill east of Ramoo, being separated from the British force by the river of the same name. There was some difference of opinion among the officers as to whether it would be better to maintain a position outside the town or to retreat at once, but the belief that reinforcements might arrive at any hour caused Captain Noton to determine to keep in the open and so to cover the town as long as possible.

On the evening of the 14th, the Burmese came down to the river as if to cross it, but retired when the two six-pounder guns opened fire upon them. That two small guns should produce such an effect confirmed the British officers in their opinion that the Burmese, although they might defend stockades well, were of little use in the open. The next morning, however, the enemy effected the passage of the river farther away, and then advancing, took possession of a large tank surrounded by a high embankment. Captain Noton placed his force in an inclosure with a bank three feet high. His right flank was protected by the river, and a small tank, some sixty paces in front, was occupied by a strong picket. On his left, somewhat to the rear, was another tank, and at this the native levies were placed. The main position was held by the sepoys with the two six-pounders. As the Burmese advanced, a sharp fire was opened upon them, but they availed themselves of every irregularity of the ground and of cover of all kinds, and threw up shelter banks with such rapidity, that the fire was by no means so effective as had been expected.

During the day news came that the left wing of the 23rd Native Infantry had left Chittagong on the 13th, and as it should arrive the next day, Captain Noton determined to hold his ground though the Burmese continued to press forward, and a good many men, as well as two or three officers, had been wounded by their fire. At nightfall, a consultation was held. The reinforcements were expected in the morning, and although the native levies had shown signs of insubordination, and evidently could not be relied upon to make a stand if the Burmese attacked in earnest, it was resolved to retain the position. During the night, the Burmese pushed forward their trenches. A heavy fire was maintained on both sides during the day, but it was with considerable difficulty that the officers in command of the levies kept the men from bolting.

"Things look very black," Captain Pringle said to Stanley, when the firing died away at nightfall. "Reinforcements should have been here to-day; it is scandalous that they should not have been pushed forward at once when we asked for them. Still more so that, when they once started, they should not have come on with the greatest possible speed. I doubt whether we shall be able to hold these cowardly curs together till to-morrow. If they bolt, the sepoys will be sure to do so too; in fact, their position would be altogether untenable, for the Burmese could march round this flank and take them in rear. I wish to Heaven we had two or three companies of white troops to cover a retreat; there would be no fear of the sepoys yielding to a panic if they had British troops with them, but when they are outnumbered, as they are now, one can hardly blame them if they lose heart, when the enemy are ten times their strength, and will be twenty to one against them if our fellows here bolt."

The next morning the Burmese had pushed up their trenches to within twelve paces of the British lines, and a tremendous fire was opened. At nine o'clock, in spite of the efforts of their officers to keep them steady, the native levies bolted, and the officers with them dashed across the intervening ground towards the main body. One of them fell dead, and two others were wounded. Stanley was running when he fell headlong, without a moment's thought or consciousness. The Burmese occupied the tank as soon as the levies had abandoned it, and their fire at once took the defenders of the main position in flank. A retreat was now necessary, and the sepoys drew off in good order, but as the exulting Burmans pressed hotly upon them, and their cavalry cut off and killed every man who fell wounded from their ranks, they became seized with a panic. In vain their officers exhorted them to keep steady. Reaching a rivulet, the men threw down their rifles and accoutrements, as they crossed it, and took to headlong flight.

The little group of officers gathered together and fought to the end. Captains Noton, Truman, and Pringle, Lieutenant Grigg, Ensign Bennet, and Maismore the doctor, were killed. Three officers only made their escape; of these, two were wounded. The fugitives, both natives and sepoys, continued their flight, and when two or three days later they straggled into Chittagong, it was found that the total loss in killed and missing amounted to about two hundred and fifty. Those taken prisoners numbered only about twenty. All these were more or less severely wounded, for no quarter had been given. They had in the pursuit been passed over as dead, and when, after this was over, they were found to be alive, they were spared, from no feeling of humanity, but that they might be sent to Ava as proofs of the victory obtained over the British. The number actually found alive was greater, but only those were spared that were capable of travelling. Among these was Stanley Brooke. He had remained insensible until the pursuit had been discontinued.

A violent kick roused him to consciousness, and sitting up, he found that half a dozen Burmese were standing round him. His first action on recovering his senses was to discover where he was wounded. Seeing no signs of blood on his white clothes, he took off his cap and passed his hand over his head, and found that the blood was flowing from a wound just on the top, where a bullet had cut away the hair and scalp, and made a wound nearly three inches long, at the bottom of which he could feel the bone. Looking up at the Burmese, he said in their own language:

"That was a pretty close shave, wasn't it?"

Two or three of them laughed, and all looked amused. Two of them then helped him to his feet, and the group, among whom there were some officers, then took him some distance to the rear, where he was ordered to sit down with three wounded sepoys who had been brought in.

CHAPTER III.

A PRISONER.

THE little group of prisoners received several additions until the number mounted up to twenty. The spot where they were placed was close to the bank of the river, and as all were suffering severely from thirst, Stanley asked and obtained permission from the guard to fetch some water. He first knelt down and took a long drink, then he bathed his head, and soaking his handkerchief with water, made it into a pad, placed it on the wound, and put his cap on over it, then he filled a flask that he carried, and joined his companions. These were permitted to go down one by one to the river to drink and bathe their wounds. Stanley had already learned from them all they knew of what had happened, after he had been stunned by the bullet. Two of them had crossed the rivulet before being wounded, and these said that they believed all the white officers had been killed, but that they thought most of the troops had got away.

"It is more than they deserved," Stanley said indignantly. "I don't say much about the Mugs; they had very little drill or discipline, and naturally were afraid of the Burmese, who had long been their masters, but if the sepoys had kept together under their officers they might all have escaped, for the Burmese would never have been able to break their ranks."

"Some of the officers had been killed and most of them wounded before the retreat began, sahib," one of the sepoys said apologetically, "and they were ten to one against us."

"Yes, I know that; but you who had fought before should have known well enough that as long as you kept together you could have beaten them off, and they would have been glad enough to have given up the pursuit at last. No doubt they all wanted to have a share in the plunder of Ramoo."

"What do you think that they are going to do with us, sahib?"

"From what they said as they brought me here I think that we shall be sent to Ava or Amarapura; they lie close together, and the court is sometimes at one place and sometimes at the other. What they will do with us when we get there I don't know. They may cut off our heads, they may put us in prison; anyhow, you may be sure that we shall not have a pleasant time of it. All we have to hope for is that the capture of Rangoon by our fleet may lower their pride and bring them to treat for terms. It sailed

STANLEY IS BROUGHT BEFORE BANDOOLA THE BURMESE GENERAL.

nearly six weeks ago from Calcutta, and was to have been joined by one from Madras, and, allowing for delays, it ought to have been at Rangoon a fortnight since, and would certainly capture the place without any difficulty. So possibly by the time we reach Ava we shall find that peace has been made. Still, the Burmese may not consider the loss of Rangoon to be important, and may even try to recapture it, which you may be sure they won't do, for I heard at Chittagong that there were some twenty thousand troops coming, which would be quite enough, if there were but good roads and plenty of transport for them, to march through Burma from end to end."

In the evening food was brought to the prisoners, and talking with some of the Burmese who came up to look at them, Stanley learned that Bandoola himself had not accompanied the force across the Naaf, and that it was commanded by the rajahs who ruled the four provinces of Aracan. Upon the following morning the prisoners were marched away under a strong guard. Six days later they reached the camp of Bandoola. They were drawn up at a distance from the great man's tent. He came down, accompanied by a party of officers, to look at them. He beckoned to Stanley.

"Ask him if he is an officer," he said to an interpreter standing by his side. The man put the question in Hindustani. Stanley replied in Burmese:

"I am an officer, your lordship, but a temporary one only; I served in the Mug levy, and was appointed for my knowledge of their tongue."

"How is it that you come to speak our language?" Bandoola asked in surprise.

"I am a trader, your lordship, but when our trade was put an end to by the outbreak of the war I entered the army to serve until peace was made. I learned the language from a servant in the service of my uncle, whose assistant I was."

The Burmese general was capable of acts of great cruelty when he considered it necessary, but at other times was kindly and good-natured.

"He is but a lad," he said to one of his officers, "and he seems a bold young fellow. He would be useful as an interpreter to me, for we shall want to question his countrymen when we make them all prisoners. However, we must send him with the others to Ava, as he is the only officer that we have taken, but I will send a message to some of my friends at the court asking them to represent that I consider he will be useful to me, and praying that he may be kept for a time and treated well, and may be forwarded to me again when I make my next move against the English."

The following day the prisoners started under the escort of twenty soldiers, commanded by an officer of some rank, who was specially charged to take them safely to Ava. It was a fortnight's march to the Irrawaddy. Until they neared the river the country was very thinly populated, but when they approached its banks the villages were comparatively thick, standing for the most part in clearings in a great forest. On the march the Burmese officer frequently talked with Stanley, asked many questions about England and India, and was evidently surprised and somewhat sceptical as to the account the lad gave him of the fighting strength of the country. He treated him with considerable indulgence, and sent him dishes from his own table. When not talking with him Stanley marched at the head of the little party of prisoners, all of whom were sepoys, no quarter having been given to the native levies. Of an evening Stanley endeavoured to keep up the sepoys' spirits by telling them that probably by this time the British expedition had arrived at Rangoon and captured it, and that peace would most likely follow, and they might be exchanged for any Burmese who fell into the hands of the English. When they reached a village on the banks of the river, the population on seeing them came round and would have maltreated them, had not the officer interfered and said he had Bandoola's orders to carry them safely to the court, and that anyone interfering with them would be severely punished. The head man of the village bent low on hearing the general's name.

"I ask your pardon, my lord; the prisoners shall not be touched. But have you heard the news?"

"I have heard no news," the officer said.

"It arrived here yesterday, my lord. The barbarians have had the audacity to sail up with a great fleet of ships to Rangoon. They had vessels of war with them, and though our forts fired upon them, they had so many cannon that we could not resist them, and they have captured the town. This happened a fortnight since."

The officer stood thunderstruck at what appeared to him to be an act of audacious insolence. However, after a moment's pause, he said wrathfully:

"It is of little matter. The town was weak and in no position for defence, but a force will soon go down to sweep these barbarians away. Now, get ready your war galley as soon as possible."

Each village on the river was compelled by law to furnish a war galley for the king's service, whenever it might be required. These carried from fifty to a hundred men, and some three hundred of these boats were always available for service, and constituted one of the strongest divisions of the fighting force of the Burman empire.

The village was a large one, and in half an hour the crew

of the galley were on board, and, rowing forty oars, started up the river.

"What think you of this news?" the officer said, beckoning to Stanley to take his place in front of him. "These men must be mad to tempt the anger of the Lord of the Golden Stool, the mighty Emperor. Had you heard aught of this?"

"I heard but a vague rumour that a fleet had been collected, but I heard nothing for certain as to its destination."

"It is madness," the officer repeated. "We shall sweep them into the sea. How many of them are there, do you think?"

"As to that I can say little, my lord. I only heard a report that some ships and troops were to sail, some from Madras and some from Calcutta, but of the number of the men and ships I know nothing for certain."

"They have taken evil counsel," the officer said gravely. "I have heard that they gained some slight advantage in Cachar, but there they had but irregular troops to meet, largely Assamese, who are but poor cowards. This little success must have turned their heads. They will now have our regular forces to deal with, and these will number a hundred thousand, or twice as many if necessary. Think you that the handful that would be transported in ships can stand against such a host?"

"There may be more than you think, my lord. Many of the ships will be very big, much bigger than those that trade with Rangoon, and some of them will carry as many as five hundred men."

"Even so," the officer said scornfully; "if there were twenty-five such ships, or even fifty, the force would be as nothing to us. They will have to take to their vessels as soon as our army approaches."

"It may be so, sir; but I think that they will scarce go without fighting. I would represent to you that although much fewer in numbers than your army which attacked us at Ramoo, the troops made a stout fight of it, and that they fought steadily until the Mugs ran away; after that, from what I hear, I admit that they fled shamefully. But the troops that come to Rangoon will be better than those were, for there will be white regiments among them; and though these may, as you say, be overpowered with numbers and destroyed, I do not think that you will see them running away."

"And you think that they will really venture to withstand us?"

"I think that they will endeavour to do so."

"Why, there will scarce be an occasion for fighting," the officer said disdainfully; "they were mad to come, they are madder still to come now. The rainy season is just at hand; in another week it will be upon us: the rivers will spread, the flat country will be a marsh. Even we, who are accustomed to it, suffer. In places like Rangoon fever and disease will sweep them away, and when the dry season comes and our troops assemble to fight them, there will be none left. They will die off like flies; we shall scarce capture enough to send as prisoners to the emperor."

Stanley felt that in this respect the Burman's prophecies were but too likely to be fulfilled. He knew how deadly were the swamp fevers to white men, and that in spite of his comfortable home on board the dhow and boat he had himself suffered, although, during the wet season, his uncle made a point of sailing along the coast, and of ascending only rivers that flowed between high banks and through a country free from swamps. He remembered that his uncle had spoken very strongly of the folly of the expedition being timed to arrive on the coast of Burma at the beginning of the wet season, and had said that they would suffer terribly from fever before they could advance up the country, unless it was intended to confine the operations to the coast towns until the dry season set in.

It would indeed have been impossible to have chosen a worse time for the expedition, but doubtless the government of India thought chiefly of the necessity for forcing the Burmese to stand on the defensive, and of so preventing the invasion of India by a vast army. Unquestionably, too, they believed that the occupation of Rangoon and the stoppage of all trade would show the court of Ava that they had embarked in a struggle with no contemptible foe, and that they would be glad to abate their pretensions and to agree to fair terms of peace.

The Bengal force that had been embarked consisted of two British regiments, the 13th and 38th, a battalion of native infantry, and two batteries of European artillery, amounting in all to 2175 men. The Madras force, of which one division was sent on at once, the other was to follow shortly, consisted of the 41st and 89th Regiments, the Madras European regiment, seven battalions of native infantry, and four batteries of artillery, amounting to 9300 men, making a total of 11,475 fighting men, of whom nearly five thousand were Europeans. In addition to the transports the Bengal force was accompanied by a flotilla of twenty gun-brigs and as many row-boats, each armed with an eighteen-pounder, the *Larne* and *Sophia* sloop, belonging to the Royal Navy, several of the Company's cruisers, and the steamboat *Diana*. General Sir A. Campbell was appointed to the chief command, and Colonel M'Bean, with the rank of Brigadier-general, commanded the Madras force. The Bengal squadron sailed from Saugur in the middle of April, and reached the rendezvous, Port Cornwallis, in the Andaman Islands, at the end of the month. The Madras first division sailed at the same time, and joined them a few days later, and the whole force under the escort of H.M. frigate *Liffey* and the *Slaney* sloop-of-war, left Port Cornwallis on the 5th of May, and arrived on the 9th at the mouth of the Irrawaddy.

Forces were detached for the capture of the islands of Chuduba and Negrais. On the 10th the fleet entered the river and anchored within the bar, and on the following morning proceeded with the flood-tide up to Rangoon, the *Liffey* and the *Larne* leading the way. A few shots were fired as they went up the river, but the Burmese were taken wholly by surprise, the idea that the English would venture to invade them never having entered their minds. There was considerable disappointment on board the fleet when Rangoon came into sight. It was situated on the north bank of the main branch of the river, thirty miles from the sea. It extended about nine hundred yards along the bank, and was six or seven hundred yards wide at its broadest part. Beyond the town were some suburbs outside the palisade that inclosed it. The palisades were ten or twelve feet high, strengthened by embankments of earth thrown up against them on the inner side. One face of the defences ran along the river bank, while the others were protected by a shallow creek communicating with the river. The town itself consisted for the most part of miserable and dirty hovels and of a few official buildings of larger size.

At twelve o'clock the *Liffey* anchored abreast of the principal battery close to the water gate, the transports being ranged in a line in rear of her. A proclamation had been sent on shore on the previous day, giving assurances of protection to the people at large and to all who should offer no resistance. When the guns of the fleet were loaded a pause ensued. The town was evidently incapable of offering resistance, and it was hoped that it would capitulate. The Burmese were seen standing at their guns, but they also remained inactive, apparently paralysed at the appearance of this great fleet of vessels of a size hitherto undreamt of by them, and the threatening guns pointed towards them. However, they were at last goaded by the orders and threats of their officers to open fire upon the ships. The frigate at once replied with a broadside. In a very few minutes every gun on shore was silenced, and the Burmese fled in confusion from their works. As soon as they did so the signal for disembarkation was made. The troops crowded into the boats, which rowed for the shore, and the soldiers entered the town without resistance, and found it completely deserted.

The whole of the population had been driven out by the governor on the previous day, and, according to Burmese custom, the men had all been formed into a levy, while the women and children were held under guard as hostages for their husbands and fathers, their lives being forfeited in case of desertion or cowardice by their male relations. The foreigners in the town had all been seized. They were few in number, consisting of some eight or ten British traders and American missionaries; these, after being fettered, were taken to the Custom House prison. They were brought up and tried early on the morning of the attack, and were accused of having arranged the assault on the town. They naturally urged that if they had had the least knowledge that it was going to be made they would have left the place in time. But the Burmese at once condemned them to death, and they were taken back to the prison to be executed. The sentence was not carried out. The Burmese had intended to execute them on the walls in sight of their countrymen, and the authorities had all assembled at the prison for the purpose, when fortunately a shot from the first broadside fired, passed through the building, causing an instant stampede.

The chiefs at once left the city, and the prisoners, heavily chained, were marched some distance into the country. A party of British troops were, however, pushed forward in advance of the town as soon as it was occupied, and the guard, in alarm for their own safety, placed the prisoners in a house and made off, and a patrol found them there on the following morning and brought them into the town.

The great pagoda, standing two miles and a half from the town, was at once occupied as an advanced position by the British. It stood upon a conical hill rising seventy-five feet above the plain; the area on the top was somewhat over two acres, and in the centre rose the pagoda three hundred and thirty-eight feet high.

Every boat on the river was found to have been removed. In spite of proclamations promising good treatment, none of the inhabitants returned to the town, being prevented from doing so by the Burmese authorities and troops. No stores whatever had been found, and till the end of the wet season the army had to depend entirely upon the fleet for provisions, and remained cooped up in the wretched and unhealthy town, suffering severely from fever and malaria.

The boat in which Stanley and the other prisoners were conveyed was changed at every village going up the river, as the officer was carrying the despatches from Bandoola to the court. A flag was hoisted as the boat came in sight of a village. This was the signal that another was required, and within two or three minutes of their arrival the prisoners, their guard, and officer were on their way again.

Thus they proceeded night and day, and in four days arrived at Ava. Leaving the prisoners in charge of the guard, the officer at once proceeded to the palace. In an hour guns were fired, drums beat, and the bells of the pagodas rung to give notice to the population that a great victory had been won over the English, and their army annihilated, by Bandoola and his valiant troops. This obliterated the impression produced by the news that had arrived a few days previously of the landing at Rangoon, and there were great rejoicings among the population. An officer from the palace presently came down to the boat, and the prisoners were marched through the streets to a jail, amid the jeers of the mob. Stanley was surprised at the meanness of the town; the great majority of the houses being built of bamboo and thatched with grass, and having a very poor appearance. The public buildings and the houses of the great officers were constructed of planks, and tiled, but were heavy and tasteless, and it was only upon the innumerable pagodas in and around the town that any care seemed to have been bestowed. He had wondered much at the numerous pagodas that they had seen near every town and village as they passed up, but the officer had informed him that these were all private property, and that it was considered the most meritorious of actions to erect one, consequently every man who had means to do so built a pagoda, large or small in proportion to the sum that he could bestow upon it. On Stanley's remarking upon the great number that were in ruins, the officer replied that it was considered so much more meritorious an action to build a pagoda than to repair one, that after the death of the founder they were generally suffered to fall into decay.

For some days the prisoners were taken out every day and marched about the town for some time so as to afford the population ocular proof of the victory gained by Bandoola. The place in which they were confined was small and filthy, but at the end of a week Stanley was taken out and placed in a room by himself, and here the officer who had had charge of him paid him a visit an hour or two later.

"I have expressed to the court," he said, "the wishes of the general, and have had permission accorded for you to receive different treatment from the others, partly because you are an officer, but principally because the general thinks that you may be made useful to him. I have informed the officer of the prison that you are to be at liberty to walk about in the city when you please, but that to protect you from violence an officer and two soldiers are to accompany you so long as you may think such a precaution necessary. I have ordered a dress of our fashion to be brought to you, as otherwise you could not go into the streets without being mobbed."

Stanley expressed his gratitude to the officer for obtaining these indulgences, and the latter replied:

"I acted upon the orders of the general, but it has been a pleasure to me, for I see that you are a young man of merit, and I have learned much from you about your people during the journey, and have seen that foolish as they have been to undertake to match themselves against us, there are yet some things that might be learned from them, and that if they had remained in their island, many months' journey away from here, they might have been worthy of our friendship."

A short time after the officer had left, a soldier brought up some food of a very much better nature than that with which Stanley had been hitherto supplied. Half an hour later the dress arrived. It was that of a Burmese officer of inferior grade, and consisted of a tunic of thick cloth coming down to the knees, leathern sword belt, a sort of tippet resembling that of an English coachman, with three layers of cloth thickly quilted, and a leathern helmet going up to a point in the centre with a flap to protect the neck and ears; with it were worn tight-fitting stockings of cloth, and low shoes. Presently an officer came in.

"I am ordered to go out with you once a day at whatever hour you may desire. I am a relative of the officer who brought you here, and he has requested me to look after your safety."

"I am much obliged to you, sir," Stanley said, "and shall be glad indeed to go out to see the city. Your kinsman has kindly sent me a dress; but if I am not to be noticed it will be necessary for me to stain my face and hands somewhat."

"That I have thought of," the officer said, "and have brought with me some dye which will darken your skin. It would be worse than useless for you to dress as a Burman unless you did so, for it would seem even more singular to the people in the streets that a white man should be seen walking about dressed as an officer, than that a white prisoner should be taken through the streets under a guard. I am ready to go out with you now, if you wish it."

"I shall be ready in a few minutes," Stanley replied, and, on being left alone, at once changed his attire and stained his face and hands. He had just finished when the officer returned. He smiled and said:

"There is no fear of your being suspected now, and you might really go about safely without a guard, unless you were to enter into conversation with anyone. You speak the language very well, but your accent is not quite the same as ours here, though in Aracan it would pass unremarked."

As they went out from the prison the officer told two soldiers who were waiting there to follow at a distance.

"Do not approach us," he said, "unless I call you up."

The houses were not constructed in continuous rows, but were very scattered, each house having its inclosure or garden. The population was very small in comparison to the area occupied by the town. This was divided into two parts—the inner and outer town. The whole was surrounded by a brick wall, five miles and a half in circumference, some sixteen feet high and ten feet in thickness, strengthened on the inside by a great bank of earth. The inner town was inclosed by a separate wall, with a deep ditch on two sides, the river Irrawaddy on the third, and a tributary river on the fourth. A considerable portion of the inclosed area was occupied by the royal quarter, containing the palace, the court of justice, the council chamber, arsenal, and the houses of the ministers and chief officials. This was cut off from the rest by a strong and well-built wall, twenty feet high, outside which was a stockade of the same height. The total population of Ava was but 25,000.

The officer did not take Stanley to the royal quarter, observing that it was better not to go there, as, although he had leave to walk in the town, it might give offence were he to show himself near the palace; but after going through the wall, they visited two or three of the markets, of which there were eleven in the town.

The markets consisted of thatched huts and sheds, and were well supplied with the products of the country. Here were rice, maize, wheat, and various other grains; sticks of sugar-cane, tobacco, cotton, and indigo; mangoes, oranges, pine-apples, custard apples, and plantains were in abundance; also peacocks, jungle fowl, pigeons, partridges, geese, ducks, and snipes; but little meat was on sale, as the Burman religion forbids the killing of animals for food. Venison was the only meat allowed to be sold in the markets, but there were lizards, iguanas, and snakes, which were exposed freely for sale, and there were large quantities of turtle and tortoise eggs, which had been brought up from the delta.

Stanley saw that there had really been no great occasion for him to stain his skin, as the people were for the most part lighter in colour than the Hindoos. Many of the men had, however, stained their faces to a darker colour, and all were tattooed more or less. Men, women, and children were all smoking, and frequently, when both hands were required for any purpose, thrust their cigars into the large holes bored in the lobes of their ears. Both men and women were somewhat short in stature, but squarely built and muscular, and in the majority of cases inclined to be fat.

The men wore a sort of kilt, consisting of a double piece of cloth wrapped round the body and falling to the knee; over this was a loose tunic, with sleeves open in front. The head-dress was a scanty white turban. The dress of the women was somewhat similar to that of the Hindoos, consisting of a single garment like a sheet wrapped round the body, fastening under the arms and falling to the ankles. Those of the upper classes were more elaborate. The rank among the women was distinguished, so Stanley's guide pointed out to him, by the manner in which the hair was plaited and twisted, and by the ornaments in it. The men, like the women, wore their hair long, but while the men wore theirs in a knot at the top of the head, the women gathered it in at the back. Their faces were broad at the cheek-bones, but narrowed in sharply both at the forehead and chin. The narrow and oblique eyes showed the relationship between the Burmese and their Chinese neighbours. They seemed to Stanley a light-hearted, merry people, going about their business with much chatter and laughter, and the sound of musical instruments could often be heard inside the houses. Several men in bright yellow garments mingled with the crowds in the market. These were priests, the officer told him, and it would be a mortal act of sacrilege were any one else to wear that colour.

Stanley remarked upon seeing so few soldiers, and the officer told him that there was no regular army in Burma. Every man capable of carrying arms was obliged to serve in case of war, but with the exception of the king's bodyguard and a very small body of men who were police rather than soldiers, there was no force permanently kept up. Every man was expected to know something of military duty, and all were able to build stockades. From the fact that the flesh of wild-fowl formed one of the principal articles of food, the peasantry throughout the country were all accustomed to the use of the gun, and were fair marksmen.

"But you yourself are an officer," Stanley said.

"At present yes, but to-morrow I may return to my land. It is the same with the highest minister; one day he may be a trader, but if recommended to the king as one possessing ability, straightway he is chosen to be a high official. If he does not please the king, or fails in his duties, then the next day he may be selling cloth in the bazaar again. Everything is at the will of the king. Nobody is born with fortune or rank, for everything belongs to the king, and at a man's death all goes back to him. Thus everyone in the land has an equal chance. In war the bravest becomes a general, in peace the cleverest is chosen as a councillor."

Walking about, Stanley soon found that there were a great

variety of dialects talked in the streets, and that the language of the Burmese of the coast, of the natives of Pegu and the central province, and of those from districts bordering on the Shan States or the frontiers of China, differed as widely as those of the most remote parts of Great Britain did from each other. This being so, he was convinced that there would be no difficulty whatever in passing as a native, without attracting any observation or inquiry, so far as the language went. His features, and, still more, the shape of his face, might however be noticed by the first comer in the daytime. He thought indeed that a little tinge of colour in the corner of the eyes, so as to lengthen their appearance and give an oblique cast to them, would make a difference. The general shape of the head was unalterable, but the Burmese nose and mouth did not differ very greatly from the European, except that the nostrils were smaller, and in shape were round rather than oval.

For three weeks he continued the same life, and then the Burmese officer, with whom he had now become very friendly, said when he entered one morning:

"You must not go out to-day; there is news that your people have made two forward marches. The first was against a stockade, which they took, and killed many of our men; the other time they marched out four or five miles, had a fight with our troops, and again killed many. These things have angered the king and the people. Of course it is nothing, for our troops are only beginning to assemble, but it is considered insolent in the extreme, and the king's face is darkened against your countrymen. Four of the prisoners have been taken out this morning and publicly executed, and if the news of another defeat comes, I fear that it will be very dangerous even for you."

"What had I best do, my friend?"

"I would fain save you, for we have come to know each other, and I see that there is much good in your ways, though they differ greatly from ours. Were I to take you out as usual you might be killed in the streets; were you to slip away and escape I should assuredly be put to death; but if in any way I can help you I would fain do so. My relation who brought you up here, left a fortnight since to rejoin Bandoola, so his influence cannot serve you. I do not say that you might not escape from this prison, since you are not, like the others, confined in a dungeon, but I see not what you could do, or where you could go. Were you to disappear, orders would be sent down the river to every village, and every passing craft would be examined, and you would be sure to be detected, while it would be well-nigh impossible to travel the country on foot, for it is but thinly inhabited. There are often very long distances between the villages, and much of the country is swamp and forest without paths, for the village trade goes by the river, and they have little communication with each other. I know that, from what you say, you think that your troops will beat ours even when we assemble in large numbers. Were this so, I fear that there would be little chance of your life being spared. Were it not for that, I should say that, Bandoola having recommended you, you would be in no danger here and had better remain until peace is made. What think you yourself?"

"It is very difficult to reply at once," Stanley said, "but I thank you greatly for your offer to befriend me in any way you can. I do not say that I had not thought of escape, for I have of course done so. But it seemed to me a thing in the distance, and that, at any rate until the rains were over and the rivers had sunk, it would be useless to attempt it. I see now that it will be safest for me to try without delay.

If you will come in again this afternoon I will tell you what I have thought of."

"I will do so, and I myself will try to think how best the matter can be managed. We must remember that the great thing is for you to find concealment for the present. After the search for you has been made for some time, it will die away, and it will then be the easiest plan for you to make your way down the river."

CHAPTER IV.

A RUINED TEMPLE.

AFTER the officer left him, Stanley sat thinking for a long time. He himself inclined strongly towards the river, but he saw that at present the difficulties would be very great. The war boats were passing up and down, and bodies of troops were being carried down in large craft. In every village the men, he knew, were assembling and drilling. Even in Ava he could see the difference in the population, the proportion of men to women having markedly decreased since his arrival. As to the journey by land, it appeared to him impossible. He was, too, altogether without money, and whether by water or land, it would be necessary to go into the villages to buy provisions; indeed, money would have been almost useless, for there was no coined money in Burma, payments being made in lead for small amounts, or in silver for large ones—the quantity necessary being cut off from small sticks or bars, or paid in filings. It seemed to him that the best thing would be to take to the forest for a time, and endeavour to subsist upon wild fruits, or if these were not to be found there, to go out into the fields and orchards at night, and so manage to hold on for a few weeks.

His friend told him that in the forests along the principal lines of route to the capital were many bad characters—persons who had committed crime and fled from justice. Some were cultivators who, having been unable to pay their taxes, had deserted their land and taken to the woods. All committed depredations, and traders coming into the town from the Shan States, or from the country where rubies and emeralds were found, always travelled in caravans for mutual protection. At times levies were called out, and many of these marauders were killed.

Stanley then had hit upon nothing definite when the officer returned in the afternoon, and in reply to the latter's question he acknowledged at once that the only thing he could see was to take to the forest until the active search for him had ceased.

"You would find it difficult to maintain yourself. I have thought of a better way than that. I am acquainted with a Phongee, who lives in a temple in a lonely spot four miles away. He is a good man, though somewhat strange in his habits, and I feel sure that, on my recommendation, he would take you in. There would be little chance of your being discovered there. You could not go dressed as you are, but must disguise yourself as a peasant, though it might be well to retain your present attire, which may be useful to you afterwards. I fear that you will fare badly with him in the way of food; there will be enough to eat, but it will be of the simplest."

"So that there is enough to keep life together it matters little what it is."

"Then that is settled. Now about making your escape from here. Your door is closely barred at night, and there is no window save those four little holes high up in the wall, which scarce a bird could get through."

"I could cut through the thatch above," Stanley said, "if I had but something that I could stand upon to do so. There are some bamboos lying just at the bottom of the steps. With these and some cord I might make a sort of ladder, and should then be able to get at the thatch."

"I will bring you some cord to-morrow for that and to let yourself down to the ground. Then I will arrange where to meet you, and will guide you out of the town and take you to the priest. I will bring a disguise for you, and some stain for your body and arms, for as a peasant you would be naked to the waist. I can think of nothing better."

"I thank you most heartily," Stanley said, "and trust that you may get into no trouble for the kindness that you have shown me."

"There is no fear of that, my friend. No one will know that I have been away from the town. I am greatly afraid that this will be all that I shall be able to do for you, for I am told that I am to go down the river with the next batch of troops, which will start in three days. I have only been informed of it since I saw you this morning. Had it not been for you I should have been glad, for it is in wartime only that one can obtain honour and promotion."

"I am sorry that you are going, sir. I shall miss your kindness sorely; but I can understand your desire to go to the front. It is the same with us; when there is a war every officer and soldier hopes that his regiment will be sent there. However, I shall see you again. Has Bandoola's army moved yet?"

"No; nor do I think that it will do so. It is a long march down to Rangoon from Ramoo, and I believe that he will remain where he is until he sees how matters go at Rangoon. As soon as your people are driven out he will be joined by a great army, and will march to Dacca. There our troops from the north will join him, and then he will go to India, we think."

"I fancy," Stanley said with a smile, "if he waits until we are turned out from Rangoon his stay at Ramoo will be a long one."

The next day the officer brought several yards of strong cloth such as was worn by the peasants, a piece of muslin to make the circular band that was worn by the lower class instead of a complete turban, and a lot of horse-hair to be worn on the top of the head.

"Now," he said, "strip to the waist, and I will dye your body. I have dyes of two colours here, one for the skin and the other to draw lines on the face so as to make you look older, and with this I can also imitate tattoo marks on your chest and shoulders. Here is a long knife such as everyone wears, and here is the cord. As soon as it is getting dark you must carry up two of the bamboo poles, taking care that no one observes you do so; there is seldom anyone in the court-yard. I have had the knife sharpened, and it will cut through the thatch easily enough. When you get away walk straight to the market that lies nearest to us. I will be at its entrance. It will take you, I suppose, two hours to make your ladder and get out. You cannot begin until the guard closes your door. You tell me he never comes in."

"No; he brings the last meal an hour before sunset. I generally sit on the top of the steps till he comes up to lock the door, which is about nine o'clock, and I do not see him again until he unbars the door in the morning. I should not think that it will take as long as two hours to make the ladder and cut the thatch; at any rate, by eleven I ought to join you. I suppose the gates are open."

"Oh, yes! they are never closed, though of course they would be if an enemy were near. There is no guard anywhere."

After staining Stanley's skin the officer waited a quarter of an hour for it to dry thoroughly, and then proceeded to draw lines on his face, across the forehead, and from the corners of his eyes, and then spent nearly an hour in executing rough tattoo marks on his body and arms.

"This dye is very good, and will last for weeks before it begins to fade. I will bring with me another bottle tonight so that you can at least re-dye your skin. Here is some wax, you must turn your hair up from the neck, and plaster it in its place with it. The turban will prevent any one seeing how short the hair is. Here is a little bottle of black dye, with which you had better colour it before fixing it with the wax."

Stanley's hair had not been cut for some time before he had been captured by the Burmese, and in the two months that had since elapsed it had grown very long, and could therefore be turned up as the officer suggested. Putting on his usual garments, he sat at his place, at the door of the cell, until the guard brought up his evening meal. Having eaten this, he dyed his hair, and half an hour later turned it up, plastering it with wax, and tied a bit of fibre round where the turban would come. By this time it was getting dusk. He sat at the door at the top of the steps, until he saw that the court-yard was deserted, the guard at the gate having gone outside to enjoy the coolness of the air. Then he ran down the steps, took two bamboo poles about ten feet in length, and two short pieces of the same wood no thicker than his finger, and hurrying up the steps with them, laid them down against the side of the room. Then he went to the steps again, and sat there until he saw the guard coming across to fasten his door, when he went in, and as soon as he heard the bars put up, began his preparations.

First he lashed the short pieces across the ends of the two bamboos so as to keep them a foot apart, then he put ratlines across, and soon had the ladder completed. He made up his clothes into a bundle, wrapped the rough cloth round his waist, adjusted the knot of horse-hair on the top of his head, and fastened it there with wax. He wound the turban round below, and his disguise was complete. Fixing the ladder against the wall he climbed it, and it was not long before he cut a hole through the thatch of sufficient size to pass out. The work had taken him longer than he had expected, for it had to be done in absolute darkness; however, he was sure that he was well within his time. Fastening the end of the rope to one of the bamboo rafters, he descended the ladder, and picked up his bundle, then climbed up again, got half-way out of the hole and listened intently. Everything was quiet in the street, and in another minute he stood on the ground. When he turned into the principal street there were still many people about. Sounds of music and singing came from the windows, for the Burmese are very fond of music, and often pass the whole night in playing and singing. There was no risk whatever of detection now, and he stepped briskly along until he came to the open space, with its rows of little thatched huts. Here he paused for a minute, and the officer stepped out from behind a house and joined him.

"I was not sure at first that it was you," he said; "your disguise is excellent. You had better follow me now until we get beyond the busy streets."

Keeping some twenty yards behind his guide, Stanley

went on until, after nearly half an hour's walking, they passed through a gate in the city walls. He now closed up to the officer, and after another half-hour's walk across a cultivated country they entered a forest. The ground now rose steadily, and, after keeping on for two miles, they emerged from the trees at the top of a hill. The space had been cleared of timber, but it was nearly covered with bushes and young trees. In the centre were the ruins of a temple that had evidently existed long before the Burmese dynasty occupied the country, and had been erected by some older race. It was roofless, the walls had in places fallen, and the ruins were covered with vegetation. The Burman ascended some broken steps, entered the temple, and crossed to one of the opposite corners. A dim light was burning in a small apartment which had been roofed with thatch. A man was lying dressed on a heap of leaves at one side. He started up as the officer entered.

"Who is it who comes here at this hour?" he asked.

"Thekyn," the officer answered.

"I am glad to see you," the Phongee said, "whatever may bring you here. You have not fallen into trouble, I hope?"

"In no way, good priest. I am starting in two days down the river to fight the barbarians; but before I go I want you to do me a favour."

The Phongee smiled. "Beyond naming you in my prayers, Thekyn, there is but little that a hermit can do for any man."

"Not so in this case," the officer said. "I have one here with me who needs rest and concealment. I would rather that you did not ask who he is. He has done no crime, and yet he is in danger; and for a month maybe he needs a shelter. Will you give it him for my sake?"

"Assuredly I will," the priest said. "Your father was

one of my dearest friends in the days when I dwelt in the city; I would gladly do all in my power for his son, and this is but a small thing that you ask. Let him enter."

Stanley went in. The priest took down the little lamp from a shelf on which it stood and held it near the lad's face. Then he turned with a smile to Thekyn:

"The painting is but clumsily done," he said, "though maybe it would pass without close examination. He is a stranger and comes of a race unknown to me, but, as you said, it matters not to me who he is; suffice that he is a friend of yours. He is welcome to a share of my shelter and my food, though the shelter is rough and the food somewhat scanty. Of late few indeed have sought me, for, as I hear, most of the men have gone down to the war."

"I have brought you some food," the officer said; for Stanley had observed that he also carried a bundle, a larger one than his own. "Here is a supply of rice that will last for some time, and this, with your offerings, will suffice to keep things going. My friend is not, like you, bound by his religion not to take life; and I know that snakes are very plentiful round here."

Snakes had formed a frequent article of his diet since he had been captured, and Stanley had lost the repugnance to them that he at first felt, so the prospect of their forming the staple of his food was not disagreeable to him. It would also afford him some employment to search for and kill them.

"I shall be well content," he said, "with anything that I can get, and trust that I shall be no burden upon you."

"You will assuredly be none," the priest replied. "Here must be at least thirty pounds of rice, which alone would keep two men alive for a month. As regards the snakes, though I may not kill them, I may eat them when killed;

and indeed there are few things better. In truth I should not be sorry to have some of the creatures out of the way, for they swarm round here so thickly that I have to pay great heed when I walk lest I step upon them."

"Have you been troubled with robbers of late, father?" Thekyn asked.

"They trouble me not at all," the priest said. "Men come sometimes, they may be robbers or they may not. I ask no questions. They sometimes bring fruit and other offerings, and I know that I need not fear them. I have nought to lose save my life, and he would be indeed an evil man who would dare to lift his finger against a priest —one who harms not any one, and is ready to share what food he has with any man who comes to him hungry."

"Well, father, I will say good-bye. I must be back to the city before men are about, as I would not that my absence should be discovered."

"Peace be with you, my son; may you come back safe from the wars; my prayers will be said for you night and morning. Be in no uneasiness as to your friend. If any should ask me about my companion I shall reply that he is one who has undertaken to rid me of some of the snakes, who dispute the possession of this place with me."

Thekyn motioned to Stanley to come outside the hut with him, and when he did so handed to him a small but heavy bag.

"This is lead," he said; "you will need it when you start on your journey down the country. There are eight pounds of it, and from what you have seen in the market you will know how much food can be got for a small amount of lead. I would that I could do more for you and assist your flight."

"You have done much indeed, very much, and should I

regain my friends I will endeavour to do as much by one of your countrymen for your sake. I hope that when this war is over I may meet you again."

"I hope so," the Burman said warmly. "I cannot but think that you will succeed in getting away."

"My son," the old priest said when Stanley returned to his cell, "I am going to my prayers. I always rise at this hour and pray till morning, therefore you may as well lay yourself down on these leaves. There is another cell like this in the opposite corner of the temple in the morning you can cut boughs and roof it like this, and make your bed there. There is no room for another here, and it will doubtless be more pleasant for you to have a place to yourself, where you can go and come as you like; for in the day women come up to consult me and ask for my prayers; but mind how you enter it for the first time—as like as not there will be snakes sheltering there."

Stanley lay awake for a time listening to the monotonous voice of the priest as he repeated his prayers, but his senses soon wandered, and he slept soundly till daybreak.

His first step was to cut a stout stick, and he then proceeded to the other cell, which was partially blocked up with stone from the fallen roof. It took him two hours to carry this stuff out, and he killed no less than nine snakes that he disturbed in his work. The prospect of sleeping in a place so frequented was not a pleasant one, especially as the cell had no door to it, and he resolved at once to erect some sort of bed-place where he might be beyond their reach. For this purpose he cut two poles, each three or four inches longer than the cell. One end of each he sharpened and drove in between the interstices of the stone at a distance of some two feet and a half apart and four feet from the ground, the other ends he hammered with a heavy stone against the opposite wall until they would go down no farther. Then he split up some more wood, and lashed strips, almost touching each other, underneath the two poles by the aid of some strong creepers; then he filled up the bed-place between the poles with dry leaves.

One end of the bed was some inches higher than the other. This was immaterial, and he felt satisfied that even the craftiest snake could not reach him. As to the roof he was by no means particular about it. In this part of Burma the rainfall is very small, the inundations being the effect of heavy rains in the distant hill-country, which, as they come down, raise the level of the rivers in some cases as much as eighteen feet, and overflow the low-lying country. Before beginning to construct the bed he had carried the snakes in to the Phongee, after first cutting off their heads, which, as he knew, the Burmans never touch.

"This is good indeed, my son," the priest said. "Here we have our breakfast and dinner. I will boil some rice and fry four of them for breakfast."

The bed was but half completed when he heard the priest sound a bell. It was doubtless used as a call to prayer. However, Stanley rightly conjectured that in this case it was a summons to a meal, and was soon seated on the ground by the side of the priest. Little was said at breakfast, which Stanley enjoyed heartily.

"So my friend Thekyn is starting for the wars. What think you of it, my son, shall we easily overpower these barbarians? We have never met them in war before, and doubtless their methods of fighting are different from ours."

"Quite different. Their men are trained as soldiers, they act as one man, while the Burmese fight each for himself. Then they have cannon with them, which they can drag about quickly and use with great effect. Although they are few in comparison with the armies going down to attack them, the latter will find it very difficult work to turn them out of Rangoon."

"Do you think that they will beat us, then?"

"That I cannot say, but I should not be surprised if it were to prove so."

"The Burmese have never been beaten yet," the priest said; "they have been victorious over all their enemies."

"The Burmese are very brave," Stanley agreed, "but hitherto they have only fought against people less warlike than themselves; now they have to deal with a nation that has made war a study, and which always keeps up a large army of men who are trained to fight, and who spend all their time in military exercises. It is not that they are stronger than the Burmese, for the Burmese are very strong men, but only that men who are trained to act together must necessarily possess a great advantage over those who have had no such training, who simply take up arms for the occasion, and when the trouble is over return to their homes and lay them by until called out to fight again. Besides, their weapons are better than yours; and they have many cannon, which by practice they can load and fire very quickly, and each of which, when the armies are near each other, can fire fifty or sixty bullets at once."

"I have heard a strange story that the barbarians have a ship without sails, with a great chimney that pours out quantities of black smoke, and a wheel on each side, and as the wheels move round the vessel can go straight up the river against the tide, even if the wind is blowing strongly down."

"It is true, father, there are many such ships, but only two or three that have made the long voyage across stormy seas to India."

"It is wonderful how these men can force fire to be their servant. How it can make the wheels of the ship to move round?"

"That I cannot tell you, father. I have never seen one of these vessels, though I have heard of them."

The priest said no more, but evidently fell into a profound meditation, and Stanley, getting quietly up, returned to his work. The priest came in just as he had completed his bed.

"That is well," he said, looking at it approvingly. "I myself, although I know that until my time has come no creature can harm me, cannot resist a shudder when I hear one rustling amid the leaves of my bed, for they come in although some of my friends have had a door placed to exclude their entry at night. I wander but little from my cell, and always close the door after me; but they enter sometimes when I am meditating and forgetful of earthly matters, and the first I know of their presence is the rustling of the leaves in the bed at night. Were I as strong in faith as I should be, I would heed it not. I tell myself so, but my fear is stronger than my will, and I am forced to rise, turn up the leaves with a stick until I find them, and then I open the door and eject them with as much gentleness as may be."

"I should get no sleep at all," Stanley said. "I don't think that even a door would make me feel any safer, for I might forget to shut it sometimes. To-morrow, father, I will wage war with them, and see if I cannot decrease their numbers considerably."

Stanley's first task was to clear the bushes away from the court of the temple, and this, after several days' hard work, he carried out, although he soon saw that by so doing he would not diminish the number of the snakes, for the greater portion of the area was covered with blocks of fallen stone among which the reptiles found an impenetrable shelter. The clearance effected, however, was so far useful that while the creatures were before altogether hidden from sight by the bushes, they could now be killed when they came out to bask in the sun on the uncovered stones, and he could every day destroy a dozen or more without the slightest difficulty. Ten days after he had finished the work he heard the sound of men's voices, and peeping out saw a Burmese officer with a party of eight armed men going to the Phongee's cell. It was possible that they might have come on other business, but it was more probable they had come in search of him. Some of the women who had come up to the hermit had seen him at work, and might have mentioned on their return that the priest had a man at work clearing away the bushes; the matter might have come to the ears of some officer anxious to distinguish himself, and the idea that this was the prisoner for whom a search was being made occurred to him.

Stanley shrank back into his cell, took up the bundle of clothes that served as his pillow, got on to the bed, and standing on it was able to get his fingers on to the top of the wall. He hoisted himself up, made his way through the boughs of the roof, and dropped on to the ground outside. Then he went round by the back of the temple, until he stood outside the priest's cell and could hear the voices within without difficulty.

"Then you know nothing whatever of this man?"

"Nothing whatever," he replied. "As I have told you, he came to me and asked for shelter; I gave him such poor assistance as I could, as I should give it to anyone who asked me. He has been no burden upon me, for he has killed enough snakes for my food and his own."

"You know not of what part he is a native?"

"Not at all; I asked him no questions. It was no business of mine."

"Could you form any idea from his speech?"

"His speech was ours. It seemed to me that it was that of a native of the lower provinces."

"Where is he now?"

"I know not."

"You say that he is away at present."

"Not seeing him in front, I thought he had gone out, for he comes and goes as he pleases. He is not a hired servant, but a guest. He cut down the bushes here in order that he might more easily kill the snakes; for which, indeed, I am thankful to him, not only for the food that they afford, but because they were in such abundance and so fearless that they often came in here, knowing that they had nought to fear from me."

"Then you think that he will return soon?"

"As he told me not of his intention of going out at all, I cannot say. He is away sometimes for hours in the forest."

"Well, in any case, we shall watch here until his return. It may be that he is some idle fellow who prefers killing snakes to honest work; but it may also be that he is the escaped prisoner of whom we are in search."

"I hear little of what passes in the town," the priest said quietly; "news would disturb my meditations, and I never question those who come here to ask for my prayers. I have heard of the escape of no prisoner."

"It was a young English officer who got away. There has been a great stir about it. Every house in the town has been searched, and every guard-boat on the river has been warned to allow no boat to pass without assuring themselves that he is not on board."

"This was a brown man like ourselves, clad only in a petticoat of rough cloth like other peasants."

"He may have dyed his skin," the officer said; "at any rate, we will stay until he returns and question him. Two of my men shall take their places just inside the entrance, and seize him as he enters. Has he arms?"

"None, save his knife and the stick with which he kills the snakes. It may be that he has seen you coming hither, and if he has committed any crime he would flee, and not return here at all."

"If he does not come back before it is the hour when I must return to the town, I shall leave four men to watch for him, and they will wait here, if it is for a week, until he comes back again."

"You can do as you please," the priest said, "only I pray you withdraw your men from the neighbourhood of this cell. I would not that my meditations were disturbed by their talk. I have come hither for peace and quietness, and to be apart from the world and its distractions."

"You shall not be disturbed," the officer said respectfully, and Stanley heard a movement of feet and then the closing of the door. Thinking it probable that the officer might make a search round the temple, he at once made off into the wood behind the temple. As soon as he was well among the trees he exchanged his cloth for the disguise he had worn in the town, and, folding it up to be used as a blanket at night, he went further into the wood, sat down, and proceeded to think what his next step had best be. It was evident that he could not return to the temple for the present, and it was clear also that the search for him was still maintained, and that it would not be safe to attempt to descend the river. He regretted that he had been obliged to leave the place without saying good-bye to the priest and again thanking him for the shelter that he had given him; but he was sure that when he did not return the old man would guess that he had caught sight of the officer and his party entering the temple and had at once fled. Had he not known that the guard would remain there he would have waited until they returned to the town, and would then have gone in and seen the priest, but as they would remain there for some days he thought it was as well to abandon all idea of returning, as the suspicions that he might be the man sought for would be heightened by his continued absence, and the watch might be continued for a long time on the chance of his coming back.

He concluded that at any rate his best course would be to endeavour to make his way for a considerable distance down the country, and then to try and get a boat. He knew that the country near the river was comparatively thickly populated, and that the distances between the villages were not great, so that he would find no great difficulty in purchasing provisions. The dress he had brought with him was not altogether unfavourable for such a purpose, as he could easily pass as a sub-officer, whose duty it was to inquire whether the villages had each sent all their able-bodied men to the war; the only drawback to it would be that if instructions for his arrest had been sent down to the villages along the road, as well as those by the river, they would have probably been directed to specially look for one clad in such attire. However, it would be open to him at any moment to take to his peasant's disguise again.

He at last determined to make a start, and by nightfall had traversed several miles through the great forest stretching along by the side of the Panlaung river. He had asked many questions of his friend the officer as they went up to the temple as to the roads. He was told that there was one running almost due south to Ramuthayn, by which he could travel down to Rangoon, by way of Tannoo. This, however, would take him a long distance from the main river, and he decided that he would presently strike the road that ran about half-way between the hills and the Irrawaddy. He would follow that for a time, and would try and strike the river somewhere between Meloun and Keow-Uan. Below this point there was a network of rivers, and but few villages, and the country was swampy and unhealthy. He infinitely preferred the risks of the descent by the river to those by road, and it seemed to him that if he could but obtain possession of one of the small native fishing-boats he could drop down at night unnoticed, as the width of the river at Ava was upwards of a thousand yards, and below that town often considerably exceeded that breadth.

When it became too dark to proceed further he sat down at the foot of a tree. He regretted that he had no means of lighting a fire, and determined that at any risk he would obtain the means of doing so at the first village that he came to, for he knew that there were both tigers and leopards in the jungles; he thought, however, that they were not likely to be numerous, so near the capital, and the old priest had never alluded to them as a source of danger, though indeed it had never occurred to him to ask. In the morning he continued his way. He had gone but a mile when he heard a sudden scream in the wood a short distance to his left. Feeling sure that it was a human being in great fear or pain, he drew his knife and ran at the top of his speed in the direction of the cry, thinking that it might be some man or woman attacked by the robbers of the forest.

Suddenly he came upon a small open space some twenty yards in diameter. He hesitated when his eyes fell on a group in the centre. Two men were lying on the ground, and a leopard stood with a paw on each of them. They had guns lying beside them, and a fire was burning close by. He guessed that the animal had sprung from a tree, one of whose boughs extended almost as far as the centre of the opening. Probably it had killed one of the men in its spring, for at the moment when he saw the animal, it was licking the blood from the shoulder of the man on whom its right paw rested. The other was, as far as Stanley could see, unhurt. His tread in the light Burmese shoes had been almost noiseless, and the leopard, which was keeping up a low growling, and whose back was towards him, had apparently not noticed it. He hesitated for a moment, and then decided to endeavour to save the man who was still alive. Creeping up stealthily, he gave a sudden spring upon the leopard and buried his knife to the hilt in its body, just behind the shoulder. With a terrible roar, it rolled over for a moment and then struggled to its feet. The time had been sufficient for Stanley to pick up and cock one of the guns, and as the leopard turned to spring at him, he aimed between its eyes and fired. Again the beast rolled over, and Stanley caught up the other gun, thrust the muzzle within a foot of its head, and fired. The leopard gave a convulsive quiver and lay dead.

CHAPTER V.

WITH BRIGANDS.

STANLEY uttered an involuntary hurrah as the leopard expired, and at the sound the Burman, who had been lying motionless, leapt to his feet. He looked at the leopard and then at his rescuer, and exclaimed in a tone of astonishment:

"You have slain the beast alone, and with no weapon but your knife!"

"No," Stanley replied; "I began the fight with my knife only, but caught up one of those guns when I wounded him and fired as he charged me; then I finished him with the other."

"Comrade," the Burman said, "you have done a great deed with courage. I, who am esteemed no coward, would never even have thought of attacking that great leopard with but a knife, and that to save the life of a stranger."

"I saw the guns lying on the ground. Had it not been for that I should not have dared to attack the leopard, for it would have been certain death."

"Certain death indeed. But tell me first how you did it; it seems to me well-nigh a miracle."

"I was passing along not far distant when I heard your cry," Stanley said. "Thinking that it was some person in distress, I ran hither, and saw you both lying with the leopard's fore-paws upon you. The beast's back was turned to me, and, as it was growling, it had not heard my approach. Seeing the guns lying there, and having no doubt that they were loaded, I stole up, sprang suddenly on the leopard, and drove my knife into it behind the shoulder. The blow rolled it over and gave me time to pick up the gun. The rest was easy."

The man without a word examined the body of the leopard.

"It is as you say," he said. "It was well struck, and would probably have been fatal, but the animal would have torn you in pieces before he died, but for the guns. Well, comrade, you have saved my life, and I am your servant so long as I live. I thought all was over with me; the leopard, as it sprang, threw its full weight on my comrade here.

We had just risen to our feet, and the blow struck me also to the ground; I raised that cry as I fell. I lay there immovable; I felt the leopard's paw between my shoulders, and heard its angry growlings, and I held my breath, expecting every moment to feel its teeth in my neck. I had but one hope, namely, that the beast would carry off my comrade—who, I was well assured, was dead—to the jungle to devour him, and would then come back to fetch me. I managed to breathe once very quietly, when I felt a movement of the leopard, and hearing a low sound, guessed that he was licking my comrade's blood; but slightly as I moved, the leopard noticed it, and stood straight up again over me. I dared not breathe again, but the time had come when I felt that I must do so, though I was sure that it would be the signal for my death. Then I knew not what had happened. There was a sharp pain as the leopard's claws contracted, and then there was a loud roar, and its weight was removed from me. Then I heard it snarl as if about to spring, then came the sound of a gun, a fall, and a struggle, and then the sound of another gun; then I heard your shout and knew the beast was dead. Now, sir, what can I do for you? Shall I first skin the leopard?"

"I care not for the skin," Stanley said; "it would be of no use to me."

"Then, with your permission, I will take it off, and keep it as long as I live as a remembrance of the narrowest escape that I have ever had."

"Is your comrade dead?"

"Yes," the man replied. "The leopard struck him between the shoulders as you see, and the force of the blow and the weight of the spring must have killed him instantaneously."

"Then I will take his sword, gun, and cartridges."

So Stanley undid the sword-belt, and buckled it round him, put the bandolier of cartridges over his shoulders, and took up the gun and reloaded it while the man was at work skinning the leopard. This operation the man performed with great speed; it was evidently one that he had done before. As soon as the beast was flayed, he rolled up the skin and placed it on his shoulder.

"You are an officer, sir?" he asked.

"No; I am a fugitive."

While he had been watching the man, Stanley had debated over whether he should confide in him, and thought that after the service he had rendered him he could do so with safety.

"I am an Englishman—I was captured by Bandoola at Ramoo, and sent a prisoner to Ava. I have escaped, and want to make my way down to Rangoon; but I heard that orders had been sent along the river to arrest me, and I do not at present know how to make my way down."

"Come with me," the man said. "I have friends in the forest some distance from here; they will receive you gladly when I tell them what you have done for me, and you will be safe until you choose to go. We are outlaws, but at present we are masters of the forest. The government has its hands full, and there is no fear of their disturbing us."

Stanley thought over the matter for a minute or two. Doubtless it was a robber band that he was asked to join, but the offer seemed to promise safety for a time.

"I agree," he said, "so that you do not ask me to take part in any deeds of violence."

"About that you shall do as you like," the man said; "but I can tell you that we make good hauls sometimes. Our difficulty is not to capture booty, but to dispose of it.

Have you a turban, for that helmet of yours is out of place in the woods? The rest of your dress has nothing peculiar about it, and would attract no attention."

"I have a turban. I have been lately in the dress of a peasant. The cloth I wore lies fifty yards away, I dropped it as I ran; it will be useful to cover me at night, if for nothing else."

Stanley exchanged the helmet for the turban that he had before worn, and fetched the cloth. "Will you bury your companion?" he said.

"It would be useless; he will sleep above ground as well as below, and if we are to reach my comrades to-night it is time for us to be moving."

They at once set out. After five hours' walking they came upon the river Myitnge, the tributary that falls into the Irrawaddy at Ava. It was some four hundred yards across. The Burman walked along its banks for a short distance, and then pulled from a clump of bushes a small boat that was just capable of carrying two. He put it in the water; they took their seats, and paddled across to the other side, where he carefully concealed it as before.

"That is our ferry-boat," he said. "It is not often used, for our head-quarters are in the great forest we shall presently come to, but it is as well, when occasionally parties are sent out to hunt us, to have the means of crossing to the other side."

Another two hours' walking through cultivated fields brought them to the edge of the forest.

"Here you are as safe as if you were in Rangoon," the Burman said. "In another hour we shall reach my comrades. As a rule we change our head-quarters frequently. At present there is no question of our being disturbed, so we have settled ourselves for a time."

"Why were you and your comrade on the other side of the river?"

"His village lies five miles beyond that forest," the man said. "At ordinary times he dared not venture there, but he thought that at present most of the able men would be away, and so he could pay a visit to his friends. He asked me to accompany him, and as I had nothing better to do, I agreed to go. A convoy of traders too strong to be attacked had passed down from the hill country the morning before we started. There was not much probability that anyone would come again for a few days."

"They bring down rubies from there, do they not?"

"The mines are the property of the emperor," the man said, "and the gems are sent down once every two months under a strong guard, but for all that many of the traders bring rubies down from there,—of course secretly. The men who work the mines often conceal stones that they come upon, and sell them for a small sum to the traders; besides, sometimes the peasants pick them up elsewhere, and these, too, make haste to sell them for anything that they can get. We do not care for them much, for it is a risky business going down to Ava to sell them; and the traders there, knowing that at a word from them we should be arrested and most likely executed, will give us next to nothing for them. We prefer silver and lead for money, and garments, arms, and set jewels. Each man takes his share of what is captured, and when we have enough we go home to our villages. A pound of silver, or two or three pounds of lead, are generally quite enough to buy the good-will of the head man of the village. We give out that we have been working on the river or in Ava since we left, and everyone knows better than to ask questions."

In another hour they reached the encampment. It was

now dusk, and some five-and-twenty men were sitting round a great fire. A number of leafy arbours had been constructed in a circle beyond them.

"What, returned so soon!" one of the men said as Stanley's guide came near enough for the firelight to fall on his face; "but where is Ranji, and whom have you brought here—a new recruit?"

"Not exactly, Parnik, but one to whom I have promised shelter for a while. Ranji is dead. I should have been dead, too, and eaten had it not been for my comrade here. Here is the skin of the beast who slew Ranji, and when I tell you that the leopard stood with one paw on me you may guess that my escape was a narrow one."

"The brute was a large one," one of the other men said, as Meinik, for such was the name of Stanley's companion, unrolled and held the skin up. "I see it had a bullet between the eyes, and another just behind the ear, and there is a knife-cut behind the shoulder. It must have been hot work, when it came to knives, with a beast of that size."

"Give us some food and cocoa; we have eaten nothing to-day, and have walked far. When we have fed I will tell you my story."

The Burman's recital of the adventure with the leopard excited great applause and admiration from his comrades. "'Tis wonderful," one said, "not so much that our new comrade should have killed the leopard, though that was a great feat, but that, armed only with a knife, he should attack a beast like this to save the life of a stranger. Truly I never heard of such a thing. Has he all his senses?"

Meinik nodded. He had received permission from Stanley to say who he was. Stanley had consented with some reluctance, but the man assured him that he could trust his companions as well as himself, and that it was much better to tell the truth, as it would soon be seen that his features differed altogether from their own, and that therefore he was some strange person in disguise.

"He is in his senses," he said, "but he does not see things as we do. He is one of those English barbarians who have taken Rangoon, and against whom our armies are marching. He was captured at Ramoo, and sent by Bandoola as a prisoner to Ava. He has made his escape, and will, in a short time, go down the river, but at present the search is too hot for him, so you see that he is, like ourselves, a fugitive."

"What is his age?" one of the men asked after a silence, during which they all gazed at the new-comer.

"He is but a lad, being as he tells me between sixteen and seventeen; but you see his skin is stained, and his face marked so as to give him the appearance of age."

"If the men of his race are as brave as he is, Meinik, our troops will truly have harder work than they think to drive them into the sea. Does he speak our tongue?"

"Yes," Stanley answered for himself. "I have been more than two years in the province of Chittagong, and learned it from one who was in our service."

"And would many of your people risk their lives in the way you did for a stranger?"

"Certainly. Many men constantly run risks as great to save others."

"One life is all a man has," the Burman said. "Why should he give it for a stranger?"

"I don't think that we stop to think of that," Stanley said; "it seems to us natural that if we see another in danger of his life, we should try to save it, whether it is a man or woman, whether it be from fire or from any other fate."

"You must be a strange people," the Burman said gravely, "and I should scarce have credited it had I not heard that you had done it yourself; but it is wonderful, and you, too, a lad who has not yet come to his full strength. We should be glad to have such a man for our comrade, my friends. Whether he be Burman or English matters little. He has risked his life for one of us, and he is our brother as long as he likes to stay with us."

There was a warm exclamation of assent round the circle, and Stanley felt that he had no cause for uneasiness as long as he remained with them. In the evening the men sung many songs, and at their request Stanley sang some English ones, choosing some with lively airs. The Burmese were much pleased and surprised at these, and joined merrily in the chorus. Half a dozen of them then set to work with their knives, cut down some saplings and boughs, and constructed for Stanley an arbour similar to the others, and he lay down well satisfied with the results of his adventure, and feeling that he could remain with these merry fellows, criminals though they might be, until it would be safe to make his way down the river.

In the morning the men started early, leaving him in charge of the fire. They went off in parties of four or five to watch the various roads leading to the capital, two or three of them, dressed as peasants, going to towns where travellers would halt, so as to gain information as to any party coming down. When they gathered again at dusk one party only had had any success. They had met six merchants coming down with horses laden with spices, indigo, and cotton. These had offered no resistance, and they had taken as much as they could carry and then allowed them to go on with the rest of their goods. There was a general feeling of regret that the party had not been more numerous, and some expressions of anger at the spies on the road by which the traders had come, for not letting them know beforehand so that they could have placed their whole force there and carried away all the goods.

"These are the things that suit us best," Meinik said to Stanley. "You see, one can go down with a parcel of cinnamon or pepper, or a bag of dyes, or fifty pounds of cotton into the town and sell it in the market at a fair and proper price. Of course, one dresses oneself as a small cultivator, and there is no suspicion whatever that all is not right. We shall keep a sharp look-out for the men as they come back again and relieve them of the silver or goods they may have taken in exchange, that is, if they come by the same road; but it is more likely that after their adventure to-day they will choose some other, or take a guide and travel by village tracks. No doubt they think that they have got off easily, for they have not lost more than a quarter of their goods. It is war-time now, and there is no fear of a force being sent against us, but usually we do not take so much as a quarter of the merchandise. Were they to lose everything they would make complaints, and then we should have a force sent up against us, and be obliged to move away for a time. But as it is, they are so pleased with getting the greater part of their goods safe to market that they do not care to make a fuss about it, for they might have to pay the court officials and others more than the value of the goods lost."

"They do not often resist, then?"

"Not often. If a man loses his goods he can gather more again; but when his life has gone, everything has gone; besides, as a rule, we take care that we are so strong that they see at once that resistance would be hopeless. Sometimes they bring armed guards with them; these are men who make it their business to convoy traders down when the times are troubled. Sometimes we have fights with these, but, as a rule, we seldom attack them unless we are so strong that they do not dare to oppose us; still we do have fights sometimes, for these Shan guards are brave fellows. Their convoys are generally rich ones, for it would not pay small traders to hire men to protect them. In times of peace we seldom stop long in one neighbourhood, for, when it once becomes known what road we are lying near, they come along in parties too strong to be attacked, and, as it matters little to us where we live, we move away perhaps a hundred miles and then settle on another line of traffic. We have not been here long; we were last down by Tannoo and did well for a long time there, until at last the governor raised all the villagers and hunted the woods, and we found that we had to leave. I expect we shall stay here some time now. There is no fear of troops being sent out, and we can afford not to press too hardly on travellers, for we have done so well of late that we could separate and return to our homes, each with a good store of booty. Half our number did leave when we came up from the south, and more of us would go if it were not for this order that everyone shall join the army. It is much pleasanter to live here free to do as we like than to be driven down like a herd of beasts to fight. Besides, we have no quarrel with your people; it was the officials at Aracan who began it, let them fight if they like."

Stanley remained a fortnight with the band. At the end of that time they heard that a party of thirty traders were coming down together, and that they had with them ten armed guards. This, they no doubt supposed was ample protection, for, as the band generally worked in such small parties, it was believed that there were but a few outlaws in the forest. All the band went out, and returned in the evening laden with spoil; two or three of them were wounded, but not severely.

"So you had resistance to-day, Meinik."

"It lasted only for a minute," the man said. "As soon as they saw how strong we were, the guard were glad enough to put up their swords and let us bind them hand and foot while we searched the merchants. As you see, we have made a good capture, though we have not seized more than a fifth of what they brought down with them, but it will take them some time to pack their bales again, for we searched everything thoroughly, and made all the merchants strip, and searched their clothes and their hair."

"What did you do that for?"

"Well, it was this way. I said to my comrades as we went along this morning, 'The Englishman is going to leave us in a day or two. I have not forgotten what I owe him, and should like to make him a present. I propose that we search all the party thoroughly to-day. From what we heard some of them come from the ruby country, and are pretty sure to have gems concealed about them or in their baggage. I propose that all the stones we find we will give to our friend.' They all agreed at once, for, as you know, they all like you, and rubies, as I told you, are of little use to us, for we cannot dispose of them without great risk. So they did as I proposed, and had good fortune. Twelve out of the number had gems hidden about them, and some of them a good lot. You need not hesitate to take them, for you may be sure that they bought them for next to nothing from poor fellows who had risked their lives to hide them. There they are; we have not looked at them, but just emptied the parcels into this bag as we found them. Of course they are all rough stones. You must take them as a present from all of us, and as a proof that a Burman, even if he is but a robber, is grateful for such a service as that you rendered him."

Stanley felt that he could not refuse a gift so offered, even though the goods were stolen. As Meinik said, the gems were of little use to the robbers, since they were afraid to try and dispose of them, and their owners had themselves broken the law in having purchased them, and had doubtless given sums bearing no proportion to their real value. Therefore he thanked Meinik very heartily, and also, after they had had their meal, the rest of the band, who made very light of the matter.

The things were useless to them, they said. If it had been silver or even lead it would have been different, but to endeavour to sell rubies they had to risk their lives. The goods that they had got that day would fetch them far more money than the rubies, and could be sold without difficulty, and as soon as the war was over and they could go down to their villages, the band would break up. They had enough silver and lead hidden away to keep them for years even if they never did any work whatever.

"What do you do with it when you get back?"

"We hide it. It would never do to enter a village with ten or twelve pounds' weight of silver, and three or four times as much lead, for the head-man might take it into his head to have us searched, so we generally dig a hole at the foot of a tree in some quiet spot, and take, perhaps, a pound of silver and two or three of lead with us; a gift of half that silver is enough to convince the head-man that we are honest fellows who have been working hard since we went away, and from time to time we can go to our store and get what we want from it, and can build a house and marry, and take up a field or two, and perhaps become head-men ourselves before very long."

"Well, I am sure I wish you all well," Stanley said. "You have all been very kind to me since I joined you, and I shall be glad to think of you all as settled quietly down in your villages, rather than as remaining here, when some day or other you might all be captured and harm come to you."

The next morning Stanley started with Meinik, who was a native of a small village on the river some forty miles below Ava, and who had resolved to accompany him down to Rangoon.

"I shall be able to get a boat and some nets for a pound or two of lead. If we are hailed I can do the talking, and can land and buy provisions, if wanted. I have arranged with my comrades to take my share of the silver and lead we have stored up at once, for it is likely that they will also have gone to their homes before I shall have returned, and we have changed everything into money except what we took yesterday."

Before starting, Stanley was again dyed, and the tattoo marks imitated far more carefully than before, three or four of the men operating upon him at once. His face was almost entirely covered with these marks; some liquid was applied that extracted the colour from his eyebrows and left them snow-white, some of his hair was similarly treated; and, looking at himself in a pool of water, Stanley did not in the slightest degree recognize himself, and felt certain that no one would suspect him of being the young English captive. Resuming his peasant's cloth he took a hearty farewell of the band and started with Meinik. The latter carried a bundle slung on his gun; it contained some clothes, and did not look heavy, but in the centre were two parcels that weighed some forty pounds. Stanley carried a bundle with his other clothes, and several pounds of rice. Two days' walking took them to Meinik's village. Once out of the forest they travelled at night, and reached the village just as the people were astir. The place consisted of ten or twelve huts, and Meinik created quite an excitement among the few people who inhabited it. These consisted of two or three old men, some women and children.

"Where have you been for the last year and half, Meinik, if I may ask?"

"Working near Ava," he said; "but as I should have to go to war if I had remained there, I thought that I would come back and see how you all were. I have saved a little money and may settle down, but whether here or elsewhere I have not yet made up my mind."

"You will have to go to the war," one of the old men said. "There is scarce a day that one of the war-canoes does not stop here to see if there are any able-bodied men. They have taken eight, and they will assuredly take you."

"Then I shall get a boat," he said, "and take to fishing. The war cannot last long, and I shall do my best to keep out of the way of the war-canoes until it is over. If any of you have a boat to sell I will buy it."

"I will sell you mine," the old man said. "Both of my sons have been taken to the war, and I am too old to work it myself. It is a good one; my sons made it only last year. Who have you with you?"

Stanley had remained a short distance off while Meinik was talking to his friends.

"He is an old man I joined along the road," he said. "He is a skilful fisherman, and he has agreed to go with me if I can get a boat. Is there an empty hut?"

"Yes, six of them. Of course when the men were taken

they carried off the wives and children, as usual, as hostages for their conduct."

Meinik nodded; he felt no surprise, as it was the custom in Burma to hold the women and children of all the men going to the war as guarantees that their husbands would not desert or show cowardice in battle. In either event their relatives would be at once put to death.

"My companion is tired," he said. "We walked all night, so we will cook some food and he will sleep."

They at once took possession of one of the empty huts, which was just as it was left by its proprietor. One of the women brought a brand or two from her hearth. An earthen cooking-pot was filled with water and placed above it, and a few handfuls of rice dropped in. Two or three snakes cut up into small pieces, and some pepper-pods were added; and then Meinik went out, talked to his acquaintances, and arranged for the purchase of the boat. Stanley watched the fire.

In an hour Meinik returned. "The boat is a good one," he said, "and the nets in fair order. I have bought them for two pounds of lead, and have promised that when the war is over and the man's sons return, it is to be free to them to buy it back at the same price."

After eating their meal they both lay down and slept until late in the afternoon, then Meinik bought an earthenware pot and a flat slab of the same material for making a fire on, some peppers and capsicums, and a little cinnamon and nutmeg, a basket of mangoes, and some tobacco. As soon as it became dusk they took their places in the boat, Meinik carrying down two or three faggots of wood. The boat was a canoe hewn out of a pine log; it would have carried four people comfortably, and there was plenty of room for them both to lie down at full length. It was very light, the wood having been cut away until it was little thicker than cardboard. This was the almost universal method of construction; even the war-canoes that would carry sixty paddlers sitting two by two on a bench, and thirty soldiers, being hewn from great single logs of teak. The nets were stowed one at each end. In the middle was the fireplace, on which the brands of the fire had already been laid. Near it were the faggots and stores.

Meinik and Stanley sat on the nets, each with a paddle; the former had hidden the greater portion of his store of money in the ground before entering the village. As soon as they had fairly started Stanley said:

"Had we not better get rid of the fire, Meinik; its light would draw attention to us."

"That matters little," the Burman replied. "There are not likely to be war-canoes about at night, and I expect that most of them will have gone down the river. People fish either by night or by day, and even if a war-canoe came along they would not trouble about it, for of course many men too old to go to the war remain here and go on fishing. People cannot starve because there is fighting. The old men and women must cultivate the fields and fish, or both they and the people of the towns would starve. Many even of the young men do not go. They keep away from their villages during the day and work in the fields, and the headmen shut their eyes, for they know that if the fields are not cultivated the people cannot pay their share of the taxes. Still it is as well to be on the safe side. When the fire has burnt low we will lay a cloth over the top of the boat so that the glow of the embers will not be seen."

They kept their course near the middle of the river, partly because the current there was stronger, partly because any war-canoes that might be coming up would keep

"THEY FORCED THE CANOE BEHIND BUSHES SO AS TO BE ENTIRELY CONCEALED."

close to one bank or the other. They kept on their way until there was a faint gleam of light in the sky, and then paddled in to the shore, chose a spot where some bushes drooped down into the water, and, forcing the canoe in behind these so as to be entirely concealed from the sight of any passing boat, cooked some food, and, having eaten their breakfast, lay down and slept until evening.

Night after night the journey was continued; their supply of food was ample to last them, and there was therefore no occasion to stop at any village to purchase more. The river at the point where they started was about two miles wide, but at some points it was double that width, while at others it contracted to little over a mile. Its level was much lower now than it had been when Stanley ascended it two months before. Sometimes at night they towed one of their nets behind them and obtained an ample supply of fish for their wants. Each night they made, as Stanley calculated, about forty miles, and after ten days' travel they came to the point where the great river divided, one small arm running down to Rangoon, another descending to Bassein and then falling into the sea at Cape Negrais, while a large proportion of the water found its way down by innumerable branches between the Rangoon and Bassein rivers.

For the last two or three days they had been obliged to observe great caution, for below Prome there were numbers of boats all going down the river laden with men and stores. These, however, only travelled by day, and the canoe was always at that time either floating in the shelter of bushes or hauled up on the bank at spots where it could be concealed from view by thick growths of rushes.

"We shall never be able to get down to Rangoon by water," said Meinik; "the river will be crowded with row-boats near the town, and there will be no chance whatever of making our way through them. At the next village we come to I will go in and learn the news. Your countrymen may have been driven out by this time, and in that case there will be nothing to do but to travel north on foot until we reach Chittagong."

"I have no fear that we shall be driven out, Meinik."

This conversation had occurred on the night when they had passed the point of division of the two arms of the river. They had caught a larger supply of fish than usual; and as soon as the boat was laid up, Meinik started along the bank with a number of them for the nearest village. He returned in two hours.

"It is well I landed," he said, "for the point where the greater portion of our people are gathered is Henzawaddy, only some fifteen miles further on. You were right; your people have not been driven out. A large number of our troops are down near Rangoon, but in the fighting that has taken place we have gained no advantage. Your people marched out at the end of May, carried a stockade, and advanced to Joazoang and attacked some villages defended by stockades and carried them, after having killed a hundred of our men. Then a great stockade on a hill near the river, three miles from Rangoon—which our people thought could not be taken, so strongly was it protected—was attacked. The guns of your people made a great gap in a stockade a mile in front of it, two hundred men were killed, and also the commander. Then your people marched on to the great stockade at Kemmendine. Your troops, when they got there, saw how strong it was and were afraid to attack it. They lay down all night close to it, and we thought we should destroy them all when they attacked in the morning; but their ships that had come up with them opened fire at daybreak. As the stockades were hidden from the sight of those on the river, we had thought that the ships could do nothing, but they shot great balls up into the air, and they came down inside the stockade, where they burst with an explosion like the noise of a big gun, and killed so many that the troops could not remain under so terrible a fire, and went away, leaving it to your people to enter the stockade without fighting."

CHAPTER VI.

AMONG FRIENDS.

"IT certainly seems to me," Stanley said, when he heard the Burman's account of the state of things below, "that it will not be possible for us to go any further by water."

"It would be very dangerous," Meinik said. "It is certain that all the men in this part of the country have been obliged to go with the army; and even were we both natives, and had no special reason for avoiding being questioned, we should be liable to be seized and executed at once for having disregarded the orders to join the army. Assuredly we cannot pass down farther in our boat, but must take to the land. I should say that we had best get spears and shields and join some newly-arrived party."

"But you forget that though my disguise as a native is good enough to mislead anyone passing us on the road, or in the dusk after sunset, I should certainly attract attention if travelling with them by day."

"I forgot that. I have grown so accustomed to seeing you that I forget that to other people your face would seem strange, as it at first did to me in the forest. Indeed you look to me now like one of ourselves; but were we to join a band, someone would be sure to ask questions concerning you ere long. What, then, do you think we had best do?"

"From what I heard of the country from one of your comrades, who is a native of this province, it would be impossible for us after crossing the river to make our way down on the opposite side, since the whole country is swampy and cut up by branches of the Irrawaddy. On this side there are few obstacles of that kind; but on the other hand we shall find the country full of troops going down towards Rangoon. Your comrade told me that the hills that we saw to the east from the forest at Ava extended right down into Tenasserim, and were very high, and could not be traversed, for that no food could be obtained, and that tigers and wild animals and other beasts abounded; but he said that the smaller hills that we crossed on the way to your village, which he called the Pegu Yoma hills, some of whose swells come down to the bank, extend all the way down to the sea, between the Irrawaddy and the Sittang rivers, and that from them streams flowed to one river or the other. Therefore, if we could gain that range we should avoid the swamp country altogether.

"A few miles back we passed a river coming in from the east, and if we follow that up as far as there is water we shall be among the hills. He said that there were no mountains at all there, but just rounded hills, with many villages and much cultivated ground, so there ought to be no difficulty in making our way along. We shall be able to gather food in the fields, or can go into villages and purchase some, for the men will all be away; besides, we can get spears and shields, and can say that having been away from home on a journey, when the men were all ordered to war, we returned too late to go with the rest of the villagers, and are making our way down to join them. Many others must be doing the same, and the story will be likely enough. In that way we can get down till we are close to the troops round Rangoon, and must then take our chance of getting through them."

"That seems better than the other way," Meinik said. "There is such a river as you speak of above Sarawa; we can paddle back to-night and hide near the town, then I can go there in the morning and buy a couple of spears and shields, and get some more rice and other things. We have plenty of ammunition for our guns, which we may want if we meet any wild beasts."

"You don't think that there will be any danger in your going in there, Meinik? Of course, there is no absolute occasion for us to have spears and shields, as we have guns."

"We ought to have shields," Meinik replied, "and it were better to have spears too, and also for us to carry axes—everyone carries an axe in war-time, for we always erect stockades, and though a very poor man may only have his knife, every one who can afford it takes an axe. Most people have such a thing, for it is wanted for cutting firewood, for clearing the ground, for building houses, and for many other things, and a Burman must be poor indeed who does not own one."

"By all means then get them for us, Meinik; besides, we may find them useful for ourselves."

They now lay down and slept until evening, and then started up the river again, keeping close in under shadow of the bank, and two hours before daylight concealed the canoe as usual, at a spot two miles above Sarawa. Meinik started at daybreak and returned three hours later with two axes, spears, and shields. That night they turned into the river running to the east, and for four nights paddled up it. The country was now assuming a different character, and the stream was running in a valley with rising ground, from a hundred to a hundred and fifty feet high, on each side, and was narrowing very fast. Towards morning on the fifth day the river had become a small stream of but two or three feet deep, and they decided to leave the boat, as it was evident that they would be able to go but a short distance further.

"We may as well hide her carefully," Stanley said; "it is certainly not likely that we shall want her again, but there is never any saying, and at any rate there is no great trouble in doing it."

They cooked a meal and then started at once, so as to do a few hours' walking before the sun became high. They determined to keep on eastward until they reached the highest point of the dividing ridge between the two main rivers and then to follow it southward. The country was now well cultivated, and they had some trouble in avoiding the small villages dotted thickly about, as the course they were following was not the one they would take if making straight to join the army. They slept for three or four hours in the heat of the day, and then, pushing on, found themselves before sunset on what seemed to them the highest point of the divide. To the right they could see the flat country stretching towards the Irrawaddy, to the left the ground was more sharply undulating. Two miles away was a stream of fair size, which they judged to be the river that runs down to Pegu and afterwards joins the Rangoon river below the town. Stanley thought that the hill on which they stood was some five hundred feet above the low country they had left. A great part of the hills were covered with trees, although at the point where they had made their way up, the hillside was bare.

They went on until they entered the forest, and there set

to work to chop firewood. Meinik carried a tinder-box, and soon had a fire blazing, and by its side they piled a great stock of wood.

"I do not know that there are any leopards so far south as this," he said, "but at any rate it will be safer to keep a big fire blazing. I never used to think much about leopards, but ever since I had that great beast's foot upon my back I have had a horror of them."

The next morning they continued their journey south, going along boldly and passing through several villages.

"You are late for the war," an old man said as they went through one of them.

"I know we are," Meinik replied, "but we were away with a caravan of traders when the order came, and so, instead of going down the river, we have had to journey on foot; but we shall be there in time. From what we have heard there has not been much fighting yet."

"No; the white barbarians are all shut up in Rangoon. We have not attacked them in earnest, but we shall soon do so, and, moreover, they will soon be all starved, for the country has been swept clear of all cattle for twenty miles round, the villages deserted, and everything laid waste; and we hear that half their number are laid up with sickness, and that a great number have died. I wish that I were younger that I too could help to destroy the insolent foes who have dared to set foot on our sacred soil."

There was no need for haste now, and they travelled by easy stages until, by the smoke rising from different parts of the forest, they knew that they were approaching the spot where the Burmese forces lay around Rangoon, and indeed could see the great pagoda rising above the surrounding country. They had heard at the last villages through which they had passed that there had been an attack made upon the pagoda on the 1st of July. On that day the Burmese in great force had moved down in a line parallel to the road between the pagoda and the town, along which a considerable number of our troops were encamped. They had advanced until within half a mile of Rangoon, then had changed front and attacked the British position near the town. They occupied a hill near our line, and opened fire from there with jingals and small cannon, but two British guns firing grape soon silenced their guns, and a Madras regiment charged the hill and recaptured it.

This entirely upset the plan of the Wongee in command of the Burmese. The signal for the whole of the army to attack was to have been given as soon as their left had broken through the British line, and had thus cut off all the troops on the road leading to the pagoda from the town. Seeing that this movement had failed, the general did not give the signal for the general attack, but ordered the troops to fall back. He had been recalled in disgrace to Ava, and a senior officer, who arrived just after the battle, assumed the command. He at once set to work to make a very strong stockade at Kummeroot, five miles from the great pagoda, and also fortified a point on the river above Kemmendine—the stockade that had been captured by the British—and intended from this point to send down fire-rafts to destroy the British shipping, and at the same time made continuous attacks at night on the British lines.

The rains at this time were falling incessantly, and the Burmese did not think that the British would be able to move out against them. The position on the river was connected with that at Kummeroot by strong stockades, and the Burmese general was convinced that if an attack was made it could be easily defeated. However, eight days after the repulse of the Burmese first attack, the vessels came up the river, while a land column moved against Kummeroot. The position was a strong one; the river was here divided into two branches, and on the point of land between these the principal stockade was erected and was well provided with artillery, while on the opposite banks of both rivers other stockades with guns were erected, so that any attack by water would be met by the direct fire from the great stockade and a cross fire from those on the banks. Four ships came up, and the Burmese guns opened upon them, but the heavy fire from the men-of-war was not long in silencing them, and then a number of boats full of troops had landed and stormed the stockade, and driven out the Burmese. The land column had been unable to take guns with them, owing to the impossibility of dragging them along the rain-sodden paths; and the Burmese chiefs, confident in the strength of their principal post, which was defended by three lines of strong stockades, one above another, and in their immensely superior force, treated with absolute contempt the advance of the little British column, of which they were informed as soon as it started, by their scouts thickly scattered through the woods.

The general, Soomba Wongee, was just sitting down to dinner when he was told that the column had nearly reached the first stockade. He directed his chiefs to proceed to their posts and "drive the audacious strangers away", and continued his meal until the heavy and rapid musketry of the assailants convinced him that the matter was more serious than he had expected. As a rule the Burmese generals do not take any active part in their battles, but Soomba Wongee left his tent and at once went towards the point attacked. He found his troops already retreating, and that the two outer stockades had been carried by the enemy. He rallied his men, and himself led the way to the attack, but the steady and continuous fire of the British rendered it impossible for him to restore order, and the Burmese remained crowded together in hopeless confusion. However, he managed to gather together a body of officers and troops, and with them charged desperately upon the British soldiers. He, with several other leaders of rank, was killed, and the Burmese were scattered through the jungle, leaving eight hundred dead behind them.

The fact that ten stockades provided with thirty pieces of artillery should have been captured in one day by the British had created a deep impression among the villagers of the neighbourhood, from whom the truth could not be concealed, and, indeed, all the villages for many miles round the scene of action were crowded with wounded. They told Meinik that the army was for a time profoundly depressed, many had deserted, and the fact that stockades they had thought impregnable were of no avail whatever against the enemy, whose regular and combined action was irresistible as against their own isolated and individual method of fighting, had shaken their hitherto profound belief in their own superiority to any people with whom they might come in contact.

Since that time no serious fighting had taken place. Occasional night attacks had been made, and all efforts on the part of the invaders to obtain food by foraging parties had proved unsuccessful. The boats of the fleet had gone up the Puzendown river that joined the Rangoon river some distance below the town, and had captured a large number of boats that had been lying there waiting until Rangoon was taken before going up the river with their cargoes of rice and salt fish, but they had gained no other advantage, for although the villages were crowded with fugitives from the town, these were driven into the jungle by the troops stationed there for the purpose, as soon as the boats were seen coming up the river. In some cases, however, the boats had arrived so suddenly that there had not been time to do this, and the fugitives had been taken to Rangoon, where it was said they had been very well treated.

Great reinforcements had now come down from the upper provinces. Two of the king's brothers had arrived to take command of the army; one had established himself at Donabew, the other at Pegu. They had brought with them numbers of astrologers to fix upon a propitious time for an attack; and the king's Invulnerables, several thousands strong, a special corps, whom neither shot nor steel could injure, were with them.

About the 6th of August a strong position, that had been taken up by a force sent by the prince at Pegu, in the old Portuguese fort of Syriam, had been attacked, with orders that the channel of the Rangoon river should be blocked, so that none of the strangers should escape the fate that awaited them. The position was a very strong one; the trees and brushwood round the fort had been cleared away, wherever there were gaps in the old wall stockades had been erected, and great beams suspended from the parapet, in order that if an attack was made the ropes could be cut and the beams fall upon the heads of the assailants.

The British had, however, thrown a bridge across a deep creek, pushed on against the place, and carried it in a few minutes, the garrison flying, as soon as the assailants gained the ramparts, to a pagoda standing on a very steep hill, defended by guns, and assailable only by a very steep flight of steps. The troops, however, pressed up these fearlessly, and the garrison, discouraged and shaken by the reports of the fugitives from the lower fort, had fled as soon as the British arrived at the top of the steps. Notwithstanding this and other as successful attacks upon their stockades, the Burmese troops now felt confident that with their numerous forces they would be victorious whenever the astrologers decided that the favourable moment had arrived.

Meinik had ascertained from the villagers the name of the leader, and the locality to which the corps belonged that was posted nearest to Rangoon. As soon as it was dark, he and Stanley entered the forest. The smoke had served as a guide to them as to the position of the different corps, and they were able to make their way between these without being questioned. Presently, however, they came upon a strong picket.

"Where are you going?" the officer in command asked.

"To join the corps of the Woondock Snodee," Meinik replied. "We were away at Bhanno when the order came, and the rest had gone down the river before we got to Mew, so we came on by ourselves, not wishing to fail in our duty."

"You are just in time," the officer said. "The Woondock is a quarter of a mile away on the left."

They moved off in that direction, but soon left the track, and, avoiding the camp, kept away until they reached the edge of the forest. Then they crept forward through the jungle and brushwood, pausing to listen from time to time, and three times changing their course to avoid parties of the Burmese acting as outposts. On issuing from the jungle they crawled forward for three or four hundred yards, so as to be beyond musket-shot of the outposts, and then remained quiet until morning broke. Then they could perceive red coats moving about in a small village before which a breastwork had been thrown up, some four hundred yards away from them, and, getting up to their feet, ran towards it. Several shots were fired at them from the jungle behind, and some soldiers at once appeared at the breastwork. Supposing that the two figures approaching were Burmese deserters they did not fire, and Stanley and his companion were soon among them. They were soldiers of one of the Bengal regiments, and Stanley, to their surprise, addressed them in their own language.

"I am an Englishman," he said. "I am one of the prisoners whom they took at Ramoo, and have escaped from their hands. Are there any of your officers in the village?"

"I will take you to them," a native sub-officer said, and Stanley in a minute or two entered a cottage in which four English officers were just taking their early breakfast preparatory to turning out on duty.

"Who have you got here, jemadar?" one of them asked in Bengalee.

Stanley answered for himself. "I am an Englishman, sir, and have just escaped from Ava."

The officer uttered an exclamation of surprise. "Well, sir," the senior of them said as he held out his hand to Stanley, "I congratulate you on having got away, whoever you are, but I am bound to say that if it were not for your speech I should not have believed you, for I have never seen anyone look less like an Englishman than you do."

"My name is Stanley Brooke, sir. I am the son of the late Captain Brooke of the 15th Native Regiment."

"Then I should know you," one of the other officers said, "for I knew your father, and I remember seeing your name in the list of officers killed at Ramoo, and wondered if it could be the lad I knew five or six years ago."

"I recollect you, Captain Cooke," Stanley said; "your regiment was at Agra when we were there."

"Right you are; and I am heartily glad that the news of your death was false," and he shook hands cordially with Stanley.

"And who is your companion?" the major asked. "Is he an Englishman also?"

"No, sir; he is a native. He is a most faithful fellow. He has acted as my guide all the way down from the point we started from, twenty miles from Ava. I could never have accomplished it without his aid, for, although I speak Burmese well enough to pass anywhere, my face is so different in shape from theirs that if I were looked at closely in the daylight I should be suspected at once. I could never have got here without his aid."

"How was it that he came to help you, sir?" Major Pemberton asked. "As far as we can see the Burmese hate us like poison. Even when they are wounded to death they will take a last shot at any soldiers marching past them."

"I happened to save his life from a leopard," Stanley said, "and truly he has shown his gratitude."

"Jemadar," the major said, "take that man away with you, see that he is well treated; give him some food, of course. He will presently go with this officer to the general."

Stanley said a few words in Burmese to Meinik, telling him that he was to have food and would afterwards go with him to the general, and he then, at the invitation of the officers, sat down with them to breakfast. While eating it, Stanley told them something of his adventures. After the meal was over the major said:

"You had better go with Mr. Brooke to the general, Captain Cooke. I cannot well leave the regiment. We can let you have an outfit, Mr. Brooke, though we are most of us reduced pretty well to our last garments. What with the jungle and what with the damp, we have nearly all arrived at the last state of dilapidation; but I am sure the general would like to see you, in your present disguise."

"It makes no difference to me, sir," Stanley said with a laugh. "I am so accustomed to this black petticoat now that I should almost feel strange in anything else. I am afraid this dye will be a long time before it wears itself out. It is nearly three weeks since I was dyed last, and it has faded very little yet."

"You need not take your arms anyhow," Captain Cooke said. "You will attract less attention going without them, for it will only be supposed that you are one of the natives who have been brought in by the boats."

Meinik was sitting on the ground contentedly outside the cottage, the jemadar standing beside him.

"Have you had any food, Meinik?" Stanley asked.

The man nodded. "Good food," he said.

"That is all right. Now come along with us; you can leave your weapons here—they won't be wanted."

Meinik rose and followed Stanley and Captain Cooke. There were houses scattered all along the roadside. These were now all occupied by officers and troops; and there were so many of them that it had not been necessary to place any of the men under canvas—an important consideration during the almost continuous rain of the last three months.

"Why, Cooke, I did not know that you talked Burmese," an officer standing at one of the doors remarked, as the officer came along chatting with Stanley.

"You don't know all my accomplishments, Phillipson," the captain laughed, for the idea that there existed such a thing as a Burmese peasant who could talk English had not occurred to the other. "I am taking him to the chief to show off my powers," and passed on, leaving the officer looking after him with a puzzled expression on his face.

On their arrival at Sir Archibald Campbell's head-quarters, Captain Cooke sent in his name, and as the general was not at the moment engaged he was at once shown in, followed by Stanley, Meinik remaining without.

"Good morning, sir. I see you have brought in a deserter," the general said.

"He is not a deserter, sir; he is an escaped prisoner who has made his way down from Ava through the enemy's lines. This is Mr. Brooke. He was serving as an officer with the native levy at Ramoo, and was reported as killed. However, he was fortunately only stunned, and being the only officer found alive was sent by Bandoola as a prisoner to Ava. I may say that he is a son of the late Captain Brooke, of the 15th Native Infantry."

"You are certainly wonderfully disguised," the general said; "and I congratulate you heartily on your escape. I should have passed you by as a native without a second glance, though now that I am told that you are an Englishman I can see that you have not the wide cheek-bones and flat face of a Burman. How did you manage to make your way down?"

"I travelled almost entirely by night, sir, and I had with me a faithful guide. He is outside. I don't think that I should ever have got down without him, though I speak Burmese well enough to pass—especially as the language differs so much in the different districts."

"Is he a Burman?"

"Yes, general."

"Have you arranged with him for any particular sum for his services? If so, it will of course be paid."

"No, sir; he came down simply in gratitude for a service

I rendered him. I do not know whether he intends to go back; but I hope that he will remain here with me."

"I have brought Mr. Brooke here, sir," Captain Cooke said, "at the request of the major, thinking that you might like to ask him some questions as to the state of things in the interior."

"I should like to have a long talk with Mr. Brooke," the general said; "but unless he has any certain news of the date they intend to attack us I will not detain him now. The first thing will be for him to get into civilized clothes again. By the way, poor young Hitchcock's effects are to be sold this morning. I should think that they would fit Mr. Brooke very well. Let me see. Of course your pay has been running on since you were taken prisoner, Mr. Brooke."

"I am afraid, sir, that there is no pay due," Stanley said. "I happened to be at Ramoo at the time, looking after some goods of my uncle, who carries on a considerable trade on the coast; and as I talk the language, and there were very few who did so, I volunteered to act as an officer with the native levy; I preferred to act as a volunteer in order that I might be free to leave at any time if I received an order from my uncle to join him at Chittagong. I could give an order on him, but I do not know where he is to be found. I have with me some uncut rubies, though I have no idea what they are worth, for I have not even looked at them yet, but they should certainly be good security for £50."

"We can settle that presently, Mr. Brooke. I will write an order on the paymaster for 500 rupees, and we can talk the matter over afterwards. I am afraid that you will have to pay rather high for the clothes, for almost everyone here has worn out his kit, and Mr. Hitchcock only joined us a fortnight before his death, so that his are in very good condition. Of course they are all uniform—he was on my staff—but that will not matter. You could hardly be going about in civilian clothes here. I shall be very glad if you will dine with me at six o'clock this evening. Have a talk with your man before that, and see what he wants to do. If he is a sharp fellow he might be very useful to us."

The general wrote the order on the paymaster, and Captain Cooke took Stanley across to the office and obtained the cash for it. Making inquiry, he found that the sale was to come off in a quarter of an hour.

"I will do the bidding for you if you like, Brooke," Captain Cooke said. "I dare say you would rather not be introduced generally in your present rig."

"Much rather not, and I shall be much obliged by your doing it."

"All right. I will make your money go as far as I can. Of course the poor fellow brought no full-dress uniform with him or anything of that sort."

"You will find me here with my Burman," Stanley said. "We will stroll round the place for half an hour, and then come back here again."

There was very little to see in the town. Meinik was astonished when they mounted the river bank and had a view of the ships lying at anchor. For a time he was too surprised to speak, never having seen anything larger than the clumsy cargo-boats which made a voyage once a year up the river.

"It is wonderful!" he said at last. "Who would have thought of such great ships? If the emperor could but see them, I think that he would make peace. It is easy to see that you know many things more than we do. Could one go on board of them?"

"Not as I am at present, Meinik; but when I get English clothes on again and rid myself from some of this stain, I have no doubt I shall be able to take you on board one of the ships-of-war. And now, will you let me know what you are thinking of doing. I told the general what service you had rendered me, and he asked me what you were going to do. I told him that as yet I did not know whether you were going to stay here or go back again."

"Are you going to stay here?"

"I think so—at any rate for a time. I do not know where the uncle I have told you about is at present. At any rate, while this war is going on he can do very little trade, and can manage very well without me."

"As long as you stay here I shall stay," the Burman said. "If I went back I should have to fight against your people, and I don't want to do that. I have no quarrel with them, and from what I see I am not so sure as I was that we shall drive you into the sea. You have beaten us whenever you have fought, and I would rather stay with you than be obliged to fight against you. Not many men want to fight. We heard that in the villages, and that those who have not got wives and children held as hostages for them, get away from the army and hide in the woods. You will be a great man now, and if you will let me stop, I will be your servant."

"I will gladly keep you with me, Meinik, if you are willing to stay, and I am sure that you will be better off here than out in the woods, and a good deal safer. At any rate stay until after your people make their next attack. You will see then how useless it is for them to fight against us. When we can attack them in their stockades, although they are ten to one against us, and drive them out after a quarter of an hour's fighting, you may be sure that in the open ground without defences they will have no chance whatever. I hope they will soon get tired of fighting, and that the court will make peace. We did not want to fight with them—it was they who attacked us, but now that we have had all the expense of coming here we shall go on fighting till the emperor agrees to make peace; but I don't think that we shall ever go out of Rangoon again, and believe that we shall also hold the ports in Tenasserim that we have captured."

"The emperor will never agree to that," Meinik said, shaking his head positively.

"Then if he does not he will see that we shall go up the river to Ava; and in the end if he goes on fighting we shall capture the whole country, and rule over it just as we have done the greater part of India."

"I think that would be good for us," the man said philosophically. "It would not matter much to us to whom we paid our taxes—and you would not tax us more heavily than we are now—for as we came down you saw many villages deserted and the land uncultivated because the people could not pay the heavy exactions. It is not the king—he does not get much of it, but he gives a province or a district or a dozen villages to someone at court, and says, you must pay me so much, and all that you can get out it besides is for yourself; so they heap on the taxes, and the people are always in great poverty, and when they find that they cannot pay what is demanded and live, then they all go away to some other place where the lord is not so harsh."

"I am sure that it would be a good thing for them, Meinik. The people of India are a great deal better off under us than they were under their native rulers. There is a fixed tax, and no one is allowed to charge more or to oppress the people in any way. But now we must be going. I said that I would be back at the place we started from in half an hour."

CHAPTER VII.

ON THE STAFF.

CAPTAIN COOKE had done his best previous to the beginning of the auction to disarm opposition by going about among the officers who dropped in with the intention of bidding, telling them something of Stanley's capture, adventures, and escape, and saying that the general had himself advised him to obtain an outfit by buying a considerable portion of the young officer's kit.

"I have no doubt that he will put him on his staff," he said. "From his knowledge of the country and the fact that he speaks the language well he would be very useful; and as he has gone through all this from serving as a volunteer without pay, I hope you fellows won't run up the prices except for things that you really want."

His story had the desired effect; and when Captain Cooke met Stanley, he was able to tell him that he had bought for him the greater portion of the kit, including everything that was absolutely necessary.

"Are there any plain clothes?" Stanley asked, after thanking him warmly for the trouble he had taken.

"No. Of course he left everything of that sort at Calcutta. No one in his senses would think of bringing mufti out with him, especially to such a country as this."

"Then I shall have to go in uniform to the general's," Stanley said, in a tone of consternation. "It seems to me that it would be an awfully impudent thing to go in staff uniform to dine with the general when I have no right whatever to wear it."

"Well, as the general advised you himself to buy the things, he cannot blame you for wearing them, and I have not the least doubt that he is going to offer you a staff appointment of some sort."

"I should like it very much as long as the war lasted, Captain Cooke, but I don't think that I should care about staying in the army permanently. You see my uncle is working up a very good business; he has been at it now seven or eight years, and he was saying the last time that I was with him, that as soon as these troubles were over, and trade began again, he should give me a fourth share of it, and make it a third share when I got to twenty-one."

"Then you would be a great fool to give it up," Captain Cooke said heartily. "A man who has got a good business out here would have an income as much as all the officers of a regiment together. He is his own master, and can retire when he likes, and enjoy his money in England. Still, as trade is at a stand-still at present, I think that it would be wise of you to accept any offer that the general might make to you. It might even be to your advantage afterwards. To have served on Campbell's staff will be an introduction to every officers' mess in the country, and you may be sure that not only shall we hold Rangoon in future, but there will be a good many more British stations between Assam and here than there now are, and it would be a pull for you even in the way of trade to stand on a good footing everywhere."

"I quite see that," Stanley agreed, "and if the general is good enough to offer me an appointment I shall certainly take it."

"You have almost a right to one, Brooke. In the Peninsula lots of men got their commissions by serving for a time as volunteers; and having been wounded at Ramoo, and being one of the few survivors of that fight, and having gone through a captivity at no small risk of being put to death the first time that the king was out of temper, your claim is a very strong one indeed; besides, there is hardly a man here who speaks Burmese, and your services will be very valuable. Here are fifty rupees," he went on, handing the money to Stanley. "It is not much change out of five hundred, but I can assure you that you have got the things at a bargain, for you would have had to pay more than that for them in England, and I fancy most of the things are in very good condition, for Hitchcock only came out about four months ago. Of course the clothes are nothing like new, but at anyrate they are in a very much better state than those of anyone who came here three months ago. I have ordered them all to be sent to my quarters, where, of course, you will take up your abode till something is settled about you, which will probably be this evening. In that case you will have quarters allotted to you to-morrow."

"Thank you very much. I shall devote the best portion of this afternoon to trying to get rid of as much of this stain as I can, at least off my face and hands; the rest does not matter one way or the other, and will wear off gradually, but I should like to get my face decent."

"Well, you are rather an object, Stanley," he said. "It would not matter so much about the colour, but all those tattoo marks are, to say the least of it, singular. Of course they don't look so rum now in that native undress, but when you get your uniform on the effect will be startling. We will have a chat with the doctor; he may have something in his medicine chest that will at least soften them down a bit. Of course if they were real tattoo marks there would be nothing for it, but as they are only dye or paint of some sort, they must wear themselves out before very long."

"I will try anything that he will give me. I don't care if it takes the skin off."

On returning to the quarters of Captain Cooke, Stanley was introduced to the other officers of the regiment, among them the doctor, to whom he at once applied for some means of taking off the dye.

"Have you asked the man you brought down with you?" the surgeon said. "You say that he put it on, and he may know of something that will take it off again."

"No; I have asked him, and he knows of nothing. He used some of the dye-stuffs of the country, but he said he never heard of anyone wanting to take the dye out of things that had been coloured."

"If it were only cotton or cloth," the doctor said, "I have no doubt a very strong solution of soda would take out the greater portion of the dye, but the human skin won't stand boiling water. However, I should say that if you have water as hot as you can bear it, with plenty of soda and soap, it will do something for you. No doubt if you were to take a handful or two of very fine sand, it would help a great deal, but if you use that I should not put any soda with the water, or you will practically take all the skin off, and leave your face like a raw beef-steak, which will be worse than the stain, and indeed in so hot a sun as we have, might be dangerous, and bring on erysipelas. So you must be very careful; and it will be far better for you to put up with being somewhat singular in your appearance for a bit, than to lay yourself up by taking any strong measures to get rid of it."

After an hour spent in vigorous washing, and aided by several rubs with very fine sand, Stanley succeeded, to his great satisfaction, in almost getting rid of the tattoo marks on his face.

The general dye had faded a little, though not much, but that with which the marks had been made was evidently of a less stable character, and yielded to soap and friction. Before he had concluded the work two trunks arrived, and finding that his face was now beginning to smart a good deal, he abstained for the time from further efforts, and turned to inspect his purchases with a good deal of interest. The uniforms consisted of two undress suits, one with trousers, the other with breeches and high boots for riding. There was also a suit of mess jacket, waistcoat, and trousers, three suits of white drill, half a dozen white shirts for mess, and as many of thin flannel, and a good stock of general underclothes, a pair of thick boots, and a light pair for mess. There was also the sword, belt, and other equipments—in fact, all the necessaries he would require for a campaign. Before beginning to dress, he began to free his hair from the wax with which it had been plastered up. He had obtained from the doctor some spirits of turpentine, and with the aid of this he found the task a less difficult one than he had expected, and the regimental barber being sent for by Captain Cooke, his hair was soon shortened to the ordinary length.

"You will do very well now," the major said as he went down into the general room. "You have certainly succeeded a great deal better than I thought you would. Of course you look very brown, but there are a good many others nearly as dark as you are; for between the rain-showers the sun has tremendous power, and some of the men's faces are almost skinned, while others have browned wonderfully. I am sure that many of them are quite as dark as yours. So you will pass muster very well."

Before beginning to wash and change, Stanley had given Meinik the clothes he had carried down with him, and when he went out to take a short look round before tiffin, for which the servants were already laying the cloth, he found the man, now looking like a respectable Burman, standing near the door. He walked slowly past him, but the man did not move, not recognizing him in the slightest degree in his present attire. Then Stanley turned and faced him.

"So you don't know me, Meinik." The Burman gave a start of surprise.

"Certainly I did not know you, my lord," he said. "Who could have known you? Before you were a poor Burmese peasant, now you are an English lord."

"Not a lord at all, Meinik. I am simply an English officer, and dressed very much the same as I was when your people knocked me on the head at Ramoo."

"I know your voice," Meinik said; "but even now that I know it is you, I hardly recognize your face. Of course the tattoo marks made a great difference, but that is not all."

"I think it is the hair that has made most difference, Meinik. You see it was all pulled off the brow and neck before, and it will be some time before it will grow naturally again. I had great trouble to get it to lie down, even when it was wet, and it will certainly have a tendency to stick up for a long time. The dress has made a good deal of alteration in you too."

"They are very good clothes," Meinik said. "I have never had such good ones on before. I have had money enough to buy them, but people would have asked where I got it from, and it never does to make a show of being better off than one's neighbour. A man is sure to be fleeced if he does. What can I do for my lord?"

"Nothing at present, Meinik. I am going to lunch with the officers here, and to dine with the general, and sleep here. To-morrow I daresay I shall move into quarters of my own. You had better buy what you want for to-day in the market. I don't know whether it is well supplied, but as we saw some of your people about there must be food to be obtained."

"They gave me plenty to eat when I came in," he said, "but I will buy something for supper. No, I do not want money, I have plenty of lead left."

"You had better take a couple of rupees anyhow. There are sure to be some traders from India who have opened shops here, and they won't care to take lead in payment. You must get some fresh muslin for your turban, and you had better close it up at the top this time; it will go better with your clothes."

Meinik grinned. "I shall look quite like a person of importance. I shall be taken for at least the head-man of a large village."

He took the two rupees and walked off towards the town, while Stanley went in to luncheon. There were a good many remarks as to his altered appearance.

"Do you know, Brooke," one of the young lieutenants said, "I did not feel at all sure that Cooke was not humbugging us when he introduced you to us, and that you were not really a Burman who had travelled and had somehow learned to speak English extraordinarily well."

"Clothes and soap and water make a wonderful difference," Stanley laughed, "but I shall be a good many shades lighter when the rest of the dye wears off. At any rate, I can go about now without anyone staring at me."

After tiffin, Stanley had to tell his story again at a very much greater length than before.

"You certainly have gone through some queer adventures," the major said when he had finished his relation; "and there is no doubt that you have had wonderful luck. In the first place, if that bullet had gone half an inch lower you would not have been one of the four white survivors of that ugly business at Ramoo; then you were lucky that they did not chop off your head, either when they first took you or when they got you to Ava. Then again it was lucky that Bandoola sent a special message that he wanted you kept as an interpreter for himself, and that the official in charge of you turned out a decent fellow and aided you to make your escape. As to your obtaining the services of the man you brought down with you, I do not regard that as a question of luck. You saved the man's life by an act of the greatest bravery, one that not one man in ten would perform or try to perform, for the life of a total stranger. I hope that I should have made the effort had I been in your place, but I say frankly that I am by no means sure that I should have done so. The betting was a good twenty to one against its being done successfully. If the brute had heard your footstep it would have been certain death, and even when you reached him the chances were strongly against your being able to strike a blow at the animal, that would for a moment disable him and so give you time to snatch up one of the guns, which might not, after all, have been loaded. It was a wonderfully gallant action, lad. You did not tell us very much about it yourself; but while you were getting the dye off I got hold of one of the traders here, who happened to be passing, and who understood their language, and with his assistance I questioned your fellow and got all the particulars from him.

I say again it was as plucky a thing as I have ever heard of."

A few minutes later an orderly came in with a note from the general, asking the major and Captain Cooke also to dine with him that evening. Stanley was very pleased that the two officers were going with him, as it took away the feeling of shyness he felt at the thought of presenting himself in staff uniform at the general's. Sir Archibald Campbell put him at ease at once by the kindness with which he received him. Stanley began to apologize for his dress, but the general stopped him at once.

"I intended, of course, that you should wear it, Mr. Brooke. I am sure that you would not find a dress suit in the camp. However, we will make matters all right to-morrow. Judging from what you said that, as you cannot join your uncle at present, you would be willing to remain here, your name will appear in orders to-morrow morning as being granted a commission in the 89th pending the arrival of confirmation from home, which of course in such a case is a mere form. You will also appear in the orders as being appointed my aide-de-camp in place of Mr. Hitchcock, with extra pay as interpreter. No, do not thank me. Having served as a volunteer, taken part in a severe action, and having been wounded and imprisoned, you had almost a right to a commission. After dinner I hope that you will give us all a full account of your adventures; it was but a very slight sketch that I heard from you this morning."

The general then introduced Stanley to the other members of his staff.

"If you had seen him as I saw him this morning," he said with a smile, "you certainly would not recognize him now. He was naked to the waist, and had nothing on but the usual peasant attire of a piece of black cloth reaching to his knees. I knew of course that the question of costume would soon be got over, but I own that I did not think that I should be able to employ him for some little time. Not only was his stain a great deal darker than it is now, but he was thickly tattooed up to the eyes, and one could hardly be sending messages by an aide-de-camp so singular in appearance; but I see that somehow he has entirely got rid of the tattoo marks, and his skin is now very little, if at all, darker than that of many of us, so that I shall be able to put him in harness at once."

After dinner was over and cigars lighted, Stanley told his story as before, passing over lightly the manner in which he had gained the friendship of the Burman. When he had finished, however, Major Pemberton said:

"With your permission, general, I will supplement the story a little. Mr. Brooke has told me somewhat more than he has told you, but I gained the whole facts from his guide's own lips."

"No, major, please," Stanley said colouring, even under his dye. "The matter is not worth telling."

"You must permit us to be a judge of that, Mr. Brooke," the general said, with a smile at the young fellow's interruption of his superior officer.

"I beg your pardon, Major Pemberton," Stanley stammered in some confusion. "Only—"

"Only you would rather that I did not tell about your struggle with the leopard. I think it ought to be told, and I am pretty sure Sir Archibald Campbell will agree with me," and Major Pemberton then gave a full account of the adventure in the forest.

"Thank you, major. You were certainly quite right in telling the story, for it is one that ought to be told, and if Mr. Brooke will forgive my saying so, is one of those cases in which it is a mistake for a man to try to hide his light under a bushel. You see it cannot but make a difference in the estimation in which we hold you. Most young fellows would, as you did, have joined their countrymen when threatened by a greatly superior enemy; and, again, most would, if prisoners, have taken any opportunity that offered to effect their escape. Therefore in the brief account that you gave me this morning, it appeared to me that you had behaved pluckily and shrewdly, and had well earned a commission, especially as you have a knowledge of the language. You simply told me that you had been able to render some service to the Burman who travelled down with you, but such service might have been merely that you assisted him when he was in want, bound up a wound, or any other small matter. Now we find that you performed an act of singular courage, an act that even the oldest shikaree would have reason to be proud of. Such an act, performed, too, for a stranger, and that stranger an enemy, would of itself give any man a title to the esteem and regard of any among whom he might be thrown, and would lead them to regard him in an entirely different light to that in which they would otherwise have held him. I think that you will all agree with me, gentlemen."

"Certainly." There was a chorus of assent from the circle of officers. His narrative had, as the general said, shown that the young fellow was possessed of coolness, steadiness, and pluck; but this feat was altogether out of the common, and, as performed by a mere lad, seemed little short of marvellous.

"You will of course have Hitchcock's quarters," the quartermaster-general said to Stanley as the party broke up. "It is a small room, but it has the advantage of being water-tight, which is more than one can say of most of our quarters. It is a room in the upper story of the next house. I fancy the poor fellow's card is on the door still. The commissariat offices are in the lower part of the house, and they occupy all the other rooms upstairs, but we kept this for one of the aides-de-camp, so that the general could send a message at once night or day."

"Of course I shall want a horse, sir."

"Yes, you must have a horse. I will think over what we can do for you in that way. There is no buying one here, unless a field-officer is killed or dies. By the way, Hitchcock's horses are not sold yet; they were not put up yesterday. I have no doubt that some arrangement can be made about them and the saddlery."

"That would be excellent, sir. As I told the general this morning, I have some rubies and other stones. I have no idea what they are worth. They were given me by those men I was with in the forest. They said that they were very difficult to dispose of, as the mines are monopolies of government, so when my man Meinik proposed it, they acceded at once to his request and handed a number of them over to me. I have not even looked at them. There may be some one here who could tell me what they are worth."

"Yes, I have no doubt some of those Parsee merchants who have lately set up stores could tell you. I should only take down two or three stones to them if I were you. If they are really valuable you might be robbed of them; but I am rather afraid that you will not find that they are so. Brigand fellows will hardly have been likely to give you anything very valuable."

"I don't think that they looked at them themselves; they were the proceeds of one day's attack on a number of merchants. They found them concealed on them, and they were so well satisfied with the loot they got in merchandise that they could dispose of, that I doubt whether they even opened the little packages of what they considered the most dangerous goods to keep, for if they were captured and gems found upon them, it would be sufficient to condemn them at once."

"Do you speak Hindustani? If not, I will send one of the clerks with you."

"Yes, sir; and three or four other of the Indian languages."

"Ah! then you can manage for yourself. When you have seen one of these Parsees, come round to my office. I shall have seen the paymaster by that time, and have talked over with him how we can arrange about the horses. I should think that the best way would be to have a committee of three officers to value them and the saddlery, and then you might authorize him to receive your extra pay as interpreter, and to place it to Hitchcock's account. You will find your own staff-pay more than ample here, as there are no expenses whatever except your share of the mess."

"Thank you very much indeed, colonel."

In the morning Stanley took one of the little parcels from the bag and opened it; it contained thirty stones, of which twenty were rubies, six sapphires, and four emeralds. They seemed to him of a good size, but as they were in the rough state he had no idea what size they would be when cut. There were three of the Parsee merchants. The first he went to said at once that he did not deal in gems; the next he called on examined the stones carefully.

"It is impossible to say for certain," he said, "how much they are worth until they are cut, for there may be flaws in them that cannot be detected. Now, if I were to buy them like this I could not give more than a hundred rupees each.

If they are all flawless they would be worth much more; but it would be a pure speculation, and I will not go beyond that sum."

Stanley then visited the third store. The trader here inspected them a little more carefully than the last had done, examined them with a magnifying-glass, held them up to the light, then he weighed each stone and jotted down some figures. At last he said, "The stones are worth five thousand rupees. If they are flawless they would be worth double that. I will give you five thousand myself, or, if you like, I will send them to a friend of mine at Madras. He is one of the best judges of gems in India; he shall say what he will give for them, and you shall pay me five per cent commission. He is an honest trader; you can ask any of the officers from Madras."

"I will accept that offer if you will make me an advance of fifteen hundred rupees upon them, and will pay you at the rate of ten per cent per annum interest till you receive the money for them."

The Parsee again took the gems and examined them carefully.

"Do you agree to take the jeweller's offer whatever it is?"

"Yes; that is to say, if it is over the five thousand; if it is under the five thousand I will sell them to you at that sum."

"I agree to that," the man said. "But do not fear; if the two largest stones are without a flaw, they alone are worth five thousand."

"Let us draw up the agreement at once," Stanley said. And accordingly the terms were drawn up in Hindustani and were signed by both parties. The Parsee then went to a safe, unlocked it, and counted out the rupees to the value of £150. These he placed in a bag and handed them to Stanley, who, delighted at the sum that he had obtained for but a small portion of the gems, went to the quartermaster-general's office."

"We have just finished your business," Colonel Adair said as he entered. "Major Moultrie, the paymaster, Colonel Watt, and myself have examined the horses. I know that Hitchcock paid sixty pounds apiece for them at Calcutta. They are both Arabs and good ones, and were not dear at the money. Our opinion is that if they were put up to auction here they would fetch £40 apiece, and that the saddle and bridle, holsters, and accoutrements would fetch another £20. There are also a pair of well-finished pistols in the holsters, they were overlooked or they would have been put up in the sale yesterday, they value them at £8 the brace; in all £108. Will that suit you? The major will, as I proposed, stop the money from your pay as a first-class interpreter, that is, two hundred and fifty rupees a month, so that in four months and a half you will have cleared it off."

"I am very much obliged to you, colonel, but I have just received an advance of fifteen hundred rupees on some of my gems which the Parsee is going to send to a jeweller of the name of Burragee at Madras."

"I congratulate you, for I hardly hoped that they would turn out to be worth so much. Burragee is a first-rate man, and you can rely upon getting a fair price from him. Well, that obviates all difficulty. By the way, I should recommend you to get a light bedstead and bed and a couple of blankets at one of the Parsee stores. Of course, you did not think of it yesterday or you might have bought Hitchcock's. However, I noticed in one of the Parsees' shops a number of light bamboo bedsteads, which are the coolest and best in a climate like this. If you lay a couple of blankets on the bamboos you will find that you don't want a mattress."

"I don't know what my duties are, sir, or whether the general will be wanting me."

"He will not want you to-day. Anyhow he will know that you will be making your arrangements, and moving into your quarters. By the way, Hitchcock brought a syce with him. You must have a man for your horses, and I have no doubt he will be glad to stay on with you."

Two hours later Stanley was installed in his quarters— a room some twelve feet long by eight wide. A bed stood in one corner. There was a table for writing on, two light bamboo chairs, and an Indian lounging chair. In the corner was a small bamboo table, on which was a large brass basin, while a great earthenware jar for water stood beside it, and a piece of Indian matting covered the floor. He learned that the staff messed together in a large room in the next house, and that he would there get a cup of coffee and a biscuit at six in the morning, breakfast at half-past eight, lunch and dinner; so that he would not have to do any cooking whatever for himself. He had given Meinik a small sum to lay out in cooking-pots and necessaries for his own use. The syce had gladly entered his employ. Stanley had inspected the horses, which, although light to the eye, would be well capable of bearing his weight through a long day's work. They were picketed with those of the general and staff, in a line behind the house devoted to the head-quarters. After lunch he went into the general's, and reported himself as ready for duty.

"I shall not want you this afternoon, Mr. Brooke. Here is a plan showing the position of the different corps; you had better get it by heart; when it gets cooler this afternoon I should advise you to ride out, and examine the position and the roads, so that even at night you can, if necessary, carry a message to any of the regiments. The Burmese are constantly creeping up and stabbing our sentries, and sometimes they attack in considerable force. When anything like heavy firing begins it will be your duty to find out at once what is going on, and bring me word, as it may be necessary to send up reinforcements.

"In the morning it will be your duty to examine any prisoners who have been taken during the night, and also natives who have made their way in to the town, in order to ascertain whether any date has been fixed for their next attack, and what forces are likely to take part in it. You can make your man useful at this work. By the way, I will tell Colonel Adair to put him down on the list of the quartermaster's native followers. He need not do anything else but this. But it is likely that the natives will speak more freely to him than they would to a white officer, and he may as well be earning thirty rupees a month and drawing rations as hanging about all day doing nothing."

Thanking the general, Stanley took the plan, and going back to his quarters studied it attentively. He told Meinik of the arrangement that had been made for him, with which the Burman was much pleased. Thirty rupees a month seemed a large sum to him, and he was glad that he should not be costing Stanley money for his food. Three hours later one of his horses was brought round, and he started on his ride through the camp. There were two roads leading through the town to the great pagoda. Both were thickly bordered by religious houses and pagodas, the latter, for the most part, being in a state of dilapidation. Houses and pagodas alike had been turned into quarters for the troops, and had been invaluable during the wet season.

The terrace of the great pagoda was occupied by the

89th Regiment and the Madras Artillery. This was the most advanced position, and was the key of the defence. Leaving his horse in charge of his syce at the foot of the pagoda hill, Stanley went up to the terrace and soon entered into conversation with some of the British officers, who at once recognized him as having been that morning put in orders as the general's aide-de-camp. As he was unknown to every one, and no ship had come in for some days, there was naturally much curiosity felt as to who the stranger was who had been appointed to a commission and to the coveted post of aide-de-camp in one day. After chatting for two or three minutes, they conducted Stanley to the colonel's quarters, a small building at the foot of the pagoda.

"This is Mr. Brooke, colonel, the gentleman who was gazetted to us this morning."

"I am glad to see you, Mr. Brooke, but I should be more glad still if you had been coming to join, for we have lost several officers from sickness, and there are others unfit for duty. When did you arrive?"

"I arrived only yesterday morning, sir. I came here in disguise, having made my way down from Ava."

"Oh, indeed! We heard a report that a white man had arrived in disguise at the lines of the 45th Native Infantry, but we have had no particulars beyond that."

"I was captured at Ramoo, sir, while I was acting as an officer of the native levy. Fortunately I was stunned by the graze of a musket-ball, and being supposed dead, was not killed, as were all the other officers who fell into the hands of the Burmese. Their fury had abated by the time I came to myself, and I was carried up to Ava with some twenty sepoy prisoners. After a time I made my escape from prison and took to the forest, where I remained some weeks till the search for me had abated somewhat. Then

I made my way down the country, for the most part in a fishing-boat, journeying only at night, and so succeeded in getting in here. Fortunately I speak the Mug dialect, which is very closely akin to the Burmese."

"Well," the colonel said, "I hope that you will consider the regiment your home, though I suppose that, until the campaign is at an end, you will only be able to pay us an occasional visit. You are lucky in getting the staff appointment. No doubt your being able to talk Burmese has a great deal to do with it."

"Everything, I think, sir. The general had no one on his staff who could speak the language, and, unless he happened to have with him one of the very few men here who can do so, often had to wait some time before a prisoner could be questioned."

He remained chatting for half an hour, and then rode back to the town, taking the other road to that which he had before traversed.

CHAPTER VIII.

THE PAGODA.

TWO days later a prisoner was captured when endeavouring to crawl up the pagoda hill, having slipped past the outposts, and was sent into head-quarters. Stanley questioned him closely, but could obtain no information whatever from him. Telling him to sit down by the house he placed a British sentry over him.

"Keep your eye," he said, "on the door of the next house. You will see a Burman come out. You are to let him talk with the prisoner, but let no one else speak to him. Don't look as if you had any orders about him, but stand carelessly by. The fellow will tell us nothing, but it is likely enough that he will speak to one of his own countrymen."

"I understand, sir." Stanley went into his house and told Meinik what he was wanted to do.

"I will find out," Meinik said confidently, and a minute or two later went out and strolled along past the prisoner. As he did so he gave him a little nod, and returning again shortly, saluted him in Burmese. The third time he passed he looked inquiringly at the sentry, as if to ask whether he might speak to the prisoner. The soldier, however, appeared to pay no attention to him, but stood with grounded musket leaning against the wall, and Meinik went up to the man.

"You are in bad luck," he said. "How did you manage to fall into the hands of these people?"

"It matters not to you," the Burman said indignantly, "since you have gone over to them."

"Not at all, not at all," Meinik replied. "Do you not know that there are many here who, like myself, have come in as fugitives, with instructions what to do when our people attack? I am expecting news as to when the soothsayers declare the day to be a fortunate one. Then we shall all be in readiness to do our share as soon as the firing begins."

"It will be on the fourth day from this," the Burman said. "We do not know whether it will be the night before or the night after. The soothsayers say both will be fortunate nights, and the Invulnerables will then assault the pagoda and sweep the barbarians away. The princes and woongees will celebrate the great annual festival there two days later."

"That is good!" Meinik said. "We shall be on the look-out, never fear."

"What are they going to do to me; will they cut off my head?"

"No, you need not be afraid of that; these white men never kill prisoners. After they are once taken, they are safe. You will be kept for a time, and when our countrymen have destroyed the barbarians and taken the town they will free you from prison. There are some of the white officers coming; I must get away, or they will be asking questions."

As he walked away the sentry put his musket to his shoulder and began to march briskly up and down. A moment later the general stepped up to him.

"What are you doing, my man? who put you on guard over that prisoner?"

"I don't know his name, sir," the sentry said, standing at attention. "He was a young staff officer, he came to the guard-tent and called for a sentry; and as I was next on duty the sergeant sent me with him. He put me to watch this man."

"All right; keep a sharp look-out over him. I wonder what Brooke left the fellow here for, instead of sending him to prison," the general said to Colonel Adair. "We examined him, but could get nothing out of him even when I threatened to hang him."

"I will just run up to his quarters and ask him, sir."

Just as he entered the house Stanley was coming down the stairs.

"The general wants to know, Mr. Brooke, why you placed a prisoner under a guard by his house, instead of sending him to the prison, as usual."

"I was just coming to tell him, sir."

"Ah, well, he is outside; so you can tell us both together."

"Well, Mr. Brooke, what made you put a sentry over the man and leave him here? The men are hard enough worked without having unnecessary sentry duty."

"Yes, sir; I only left him for a few minutes. I was convinced the man knew something by his demeanour when I questioned him, and I thought I might as well try if my man could not get more out of him than I could; so I put a sentry over him and gave him instructions that he was to let a Burman who would come out of this house speak to the prisoner, but that no one else was to approach him. Then I instructed my man as to the part that he was to play. He passed two or three times, making a sign of friendship to the prisoner. Then, as the sentry had apparently no objection to his speaking to him, he came up. At first the man would say nothing to him, but Meinik told him that he was one of those who had been sent to Rangoon to aid when the assault took place, and that he was anxiously waiting for news when the favourable day would be declared by the astrologers, so that he and those with him would be ready to begin their work as soon as the attack commenced. The prisoner fell into the snare and told him that it would be made either on the night before or on the night of the fourth day from this, when the Invulnerables had undertaken to storm the pagoda. It seems that the date was fixed partly because it was a fortunate one, and also in order that the princes and head officials might properly celebrate the great annual festival of the pagoda, which falls, it seems, on the sixth day from now."

"Excellent indeed, Mr. Brooke. It is a great relief to me to know when the assault is going to take place, and from what point it will be delivered. But what made you think of the story that the Burman was one of a party that had come in to do something?"

"It was what Colonel Adair mentioned at dinner last evening, sir. He was saying how awkward it would be if some of these natives who have come in were to fire the town just as a strong attack was going on, and most of the troops engaged with the enemy. It was not unlikely that if such a plan had been formed the prisoner would know of it, and that he might very well believe what my man said, that some men had been sent into the town with that or some similar intention."

"True enough; the idea was a capital one, Mr. Brooke, and we shall be ready for them whichever night they come. Will you please go across to the guard-tent and tell the sergeant to send a corporal across to the man on sentry with orders to take the prisoner to the jail, and hand him over to the officer in command there. When you have done that, will you ride out to the pagoda and inform your colonel what you have discovered. It will be a relief to him and to the men, for as the date of the attack has been uncertain, he has been obliged to largely increase his patrols, and to keep a portion of his force all night under arms. He will be able to decrease the number, and let the men have as much sleep as they can for the next two nights. The clouds are banking up, and I am very much afraid that the rain is going to set in again. They say that we shall have another two months of it."

After seeing the prisoner marched away, Stanley rode to the pagoda, and saying that he had come with a message from the general, was at once shown into the colonel's quarters.

"Any news, Mr. Brooke?"

"Yes, colonel; the general has requested me to inform you at once of the news that I have obtained from a prisoner, namely, that either on the night of the 30th or 31st your position will be attacked by the men who are called the Invulnerables."

"We will give them a chance of proving whether their title is justified," the colonel said cheerfully. "That is very good news; the men are getting thoroughly worn out with the extra night-duty caused by this uncertainty. You think that there is no doubt that the news is correct."

"None whatever, sir. I could do nothing with the prisoner; but my Burman pretended to have a mission here to kick up a row in the town when the attack began, and the man, believing his story, at once told him that the attack will be made on the pagoda by the Invulnerables on the early morning of the fourth day from this, or on the next night, the astrologers having declared that the time would be propitious, and also because they were very anxious to have the pagoda in their hands, in order that the princes might celebrate the great annual festival that is held, it seems, two days after."

The colonel laughed. "I am afraid that they will have to put it off for another year. The general gave no special orders, I suppose?"

"No, sir; he had only just received the news, and ordered me to ride over at once to you, as he was sure that you would be glad to know that it would not be necessary to keep so many men on night duty for the next two days."

"Thank you, Mr. Brooke. Will you kindly tell the general that I am very pleased at the news? No doubt he will be up here himself this afternoon or to-morrow."

Stanley rode back fast, and was just in time to escape a tremendous downpour of rain which began a few minutes after he returned. He went in at once to the general's, but was told that he was engaged with the quartermaster and adjutant generals. He therefore went into the anteroom where Tollemache, his fellow aide-de-camp, was standing at the window looking out at the rain.

"This is a beastly climate," he grumbled. "It is awful to think that we are likely to get another two months of it, and shall then have to wait at least another before the country is dry enough to make a move. You were lucky in getting in just now before it began."

"I was indeed," Stanley agreed, "for I had ridden off without my cloak, and should have been drenched had it begun two minutes earlier."

"I saw you gallop past, and wondered what you were in such a hurry about. Was it like this when you were out in the woods?"

"Not in the least. There is very little rain near Ava, though the country is a good deal flooded, where it is flat, from the rivers being swollen by the rains in the hills. We had lovely weather all the time."

"I should like to see a little lovely weather here. The last week has been almost worse than the rain—the steamy heat is like being in a vapour bath. If it were not that I am on duty I should like to strip, and go out and enjoy a shower bath for half an hour."

Stanley laughed. "It really would be pleasant," he said. "I don't think that I gained much by hurrying back, for the gallop has thrown me into such a perspiration that I might almost as well be drenched by the rain, except that my clothes won't suffer so much."

"Ah, it is all very well for you," the other grumbled. "Of course after once having wandered about in the forest painted up like a nigger you feel cheerful under almost any circumstances, but for us who have been cooped up doing nothing in this beastly place, it is impossible to look at things cheerfully."

"Have you heard that the enemy are going to attack on Tuesday or Wednesday night?"

"No," the other exclaimed with a sudden animation. "The general only came in a quarter of an hour ago, and as he had the two big-wigs with him of course I did not speak to him. Is it certain? how did you hear it?"

"It is quite certain—that is, unless the Burmese change their mind, which is not likely. The princes want to celebrate the great annual festival at the pagoda on Friday, and so the Invulnerables are going, as they think, to capture it either on Tuesday or Wednesday night. I have just been up there to tell the colonel. As to your other question, how did I learn it,—I got it, or rather my Burman did, from that prisoner we were questioning this morning. He would not say anything then, but my man got round him, and, believing that he was a spy or something of that kind, the prisoner told him all about it."

"Are they only going to attack at the pagoda?"

"That I cannot say; that is the only point that the man mentioned. I should say that it would only be there."

"Why should it only be there?"

"Because I should imagine that even the Burmese must be beginning to doubt whether they could defeat our whole force, and as they particularly wish to occupy the pagoda on Friday, they would hardly risk an attack on other points which might end in disaster, while what with the propitious nature of the day and the fact that the Invulnerables have undertaken to capture the pagoda, no doubt they look upon that as certain."

"I suppose that you are right, Brooke. Well, I do hope that the general will let us go up to see the fun."

"What, even if it is raining?"

"Of course," the other said indignantly. "What does one care for rain when there is something to do. Why, I believe that if it was coming down in a sheet, and the men had to wade through the swamps waist-deep, they would all march in the highest spirits if there was the chance of a fight with the Burmans at the end of the day. However, I am afraid that there is no chance of our getting off unless the chief goes himself. There may be attacks in other places. As you say, it is not likely; but it is possible. Therefore, of course, we should have to be at hand to carry orders. Of course if he takes his post at the pagoda, it will be all right, though the betting is that we shall have to gallop off just at the most interesting moment."

Presently the two officers left the general. The latter's bell rang, and Stanley went in.

"You saw the colonel, Mr. Brooke?"

"Yes, sir; and he begged me to say that he was extremely glad to get the news, and much obliged to you for sending it so promptly."

"There is no occasion for you and Mr. Tollemache to stay here any longer now, but at five o'clock I shall ride out to the pagoda. At any rate, should I want you before then, I shall know where to send for you."

This was the general order, for in the afternoon there was, when things were quiet, a hush for two or three hours. The work of the aides-de-camp was indeed generally very light, for, as there were no movements of troops, no useless parades, and very few military orders to be carried, they had a great deal of time on their hands, and usually took it by turns to be on duty for the day, the one off duty being free to pay visits to acquaintances in the various camps or on board ship. During the rainy season, however, very few officers or men went beyond shelter unless obliged to do so, and from two till four or five no small proportion passed the time in sleep.

Stanley had intended to pay a visit to the *Larne*, as Captain Marryat, who had dined at the staff mess on the previous evening, had invited him to go on board whenever it might be convenient to him. The *Larne* had performed good service in the operations against the stockades, and her boats had been particularly active and successful. Her captain was one of the most popular as well as one of the most energetic officers in the service, and was to become as popular with future generations, as the brightest of all writers of sea stories. However, the day was not favourable for an excursion on the water; Stanley therefore went back to his room, where, divesting himself of his jacket, he sat down at the open window and read up a batch of the last newspapers from England that had been lent him by Colonel Adair.

At five o'clock Meinik came in to say that his horse was at the general's door. Stanley hastily put on his jacket and cloak, and sallied out. The general came down in a few minutes, followed by Tollemache, and, mounting, they rode to the pagoda. Here Sir Archibald had a talk with the colonel of the 89th and the officer commanding the battery of the Madras Artillery. Both were of opinion that their force was amply sufficient to resist any attack. The only approach to it from the forest was a long road between two swamps, which, a short distance away, had become lakes since the wet weather set in.

"Had they taken us by surprise," the colonel said, "some of them might have got across before we were quite ready for them, and might have given us some trouble; but as we shall be prepared I don't think that any of them will reach the foot of this hill, and if they did, none of them would reach this terrace. If an attack were made from the other side, it would of course be a good deal more serious, as the ground is firm and they could attack all along the foot of the hill; but, as they cannot get there until they have defeated the rest of the army, I consider that, even without the assistance of the guns, we could hold the hill with musket and bayonet against any force that they are likely to bring against us."

"Very well, then; I shall not reinforce you, colonel. Of course we shall keep a considerable number of troops under arms, in case they should attack all along the line, at the same time that they make their principal effort here. I rather hope that the rain will keep on until this affair is over." The colonel looked surprised.

"I am much more afraid," the general went on, "of fire in the town than I am of an attack without. The number of natives there is constantly increasing. No doubt the greater number of those who come in are natives of the place who have managed, since we cleared out their war-galleys from some of the creeks and channels, to escape from the authorities and to make their way in, either on foot or in fishermen's boats; but some of them may be sent in as spies, or to do us harm. I have been having a long talk over it with Colonel Adair this afternoon, and he quite agrees with me that we must reckon on the probability of an attempt to fire the town. It would be a terrible blow to us if they succeeded, for the loss of our stores would completely cripple us. They would naturally choose the occasion of an attack upon our lines for the attempt, for in the first place most of the troops will be under arms and drawn up outside the town, and in the second place the sight of the place on fire would cause much confusion, would inspirit our assailants, and necessitate a considerable force being withdrawn from the field to fight the fire. If the rains continue we need feel no uneasiness whatever, for there would be no getting anything to burn; whereas, in dry weather, a man with a torch might light the thatch as fast as he could run along, and a whole street would be in a blaze in two or three minutes, and if a wind happened to be blowing it might make a sweep of the whole place in spite of all our efforts."

"I see that, sir. I own that I had never given it a thought before."

"I shall come up here, colonel, unless we obtain sure news before the time arrives that the attack is going to be a general one; indeed it is in any case the best place to post myself, for I can see over the whole country, and send orders to any point where the enemy may be making progress, or where our men can advance with advantage. The line of fire flashes will be as good a guide at night as the smoke by day."

"I will get a cot rigged up for you, general, as we don't know which night it is to be."

"Thank you. Yes, I may just as well turn in, all standing, as the sailors say, and get a few hours' sleep, for in this climate one cannot keep at it night and day as we had to do in Spain."

The two aides-de-camp were kept in suspense as to what the general's intentions were, and it was not until the morning of Tuesday that he said to them:

"I am going up to the pagoda this evening, Mr. Tollemache, and you had better, therefore, put some provisions and a bottle of brandy into your holsters."

At nine in the evening they rode off. The rain had ceased; the moon was shining through the clouds.

"It will be down by twelve o'clock," Tollemache said. "I should think most likely they will wait for that; they will think that we shall not be able to take aim at them in the darkness, and that they will manage to get to the foot of the hill without loss."

When they reached the platform in front of the pagoda, their syces took their horses. Meinik had begged Stanley to let him take his groom's place on this occasion, and laying aside the dress he ordinarily wore, assumed the light attire of an Indian syce, and had run behind the horses with the others. He had a strong desire to see the fighting, but his principal motive in asking to be allowed to accompany Stanley was that, although greatly impressed with what he had seen of the drill and discipline of the white and native regiments, he could not shake off his faith in the Invulnerables, and had a conviction that the pagoda would be captured, and therefore wished to be at hand to bring up Stanley's horse at the critical moment, and to aid him to escape from the assailants. Fires were burning, as usual, at several points on the terrace. Two companies were under arms, and were standing well back from the edge of the platform so as to be out of sight of those in the forest. The rest of the men were sitting round the fires; their muskets were piled in lines hard by.

When he alighted, the general proceeded to the battery.

"Have you everything in readiness, major?" he asked the officer in command.

"Yes, sir. The guns are all loaded with grape, and as it will be very dark when the moon has set, I have pegged a white tape along just under each gun, so that they can be trained upon the causeway however dark it may be."

"That is a very good idea," the general said. "There is nothing more difficult than laying guns accurately in the dark."

The colonel now arrived, a soldier having brought the news to him as soon as the general reached the platform.

"I see that you are well prepared to give them a hot reception, colonel."

"I hope so, sir. I have a strong patrol out beyond the causeway. My orders are, that they are to resist strongly for a minute or two, so as to give us time to have the whole of our force in readiness here. Then they are to retreat at the double to the foot of the hill, and then to open fire again, so that we may know that they are out of the way, and that we can begin when we like. We have been making some port-fires this afternoon, and I have a dozen men half-way down the hill, and directly the outposts are safely across they are to light the port-fires, which will enable us to take aim. These white tapes will be guide enough for the artillery, but my men would make very poor shooting if they could not make out the muzzles of their guns. Anyhow I don't think that it is likely that the enemy will get across the causeway however numerous they may be."

"I don't think they will, colonel. Certainly, so far, they have shown themselves contemptible in attack, and have never made a successful stand, even for a minute, when we once entered their stockades, though they defend them pluckily enough until we have once got a footing inside. Still, these fellows ought to fight well to-night, for if they are beaten it will be a death-blow to their reputation among their countrymen. Besides, many of them do believe in the power they claim, and, as we have found before now in India, fanatics are always formidable."

After taking a look round with the colonel, the general accompanied him to his quarters, while the two aides-de-camp remained on the terrace chatting with the officers, and then, after a time, went with some of them to the mess-tent, where they sat smoking and talking until midnight, when all went out. The troops were formed up under arms, and all listened impatiently for something that would show that the long-delayed assault would take place that night. At half-past twelve there was the sound of a shot, which sent an electrical thrill through the troops. It was followed almost immediately by others. The troops were at once marched forward to the edge of the platform. A babel of wild shouts went up at the sound of the first shots, followed by a burst of firing.

The two aides-de-camp had taken their places close to the general, who was standing in the gap between the infantry and the guns, and was looking intently through his night-glasses at the forest.

"They are in a dense mass," he said; "I cannot see whether they are in any regular order, but they are certainly packed a great deal closer than I have ever before seen them. Those in front have got lanterns. They are coming along fast."

As yet the enemy were half a mile away, but the lanterns and the flash of their guns showed their exact position, while the fire of the outposts was kept up steadily. As the latter fell back along the causeway the interval between the two forces decreased, and then the fire of the outposts ceased as, in accordance with their orders, they broke into the double. The uproar of the advancing crowd was prodigious. Every man was yelling, at the top of his voice, imprecations upon the defenders of the pagoda, who were standing in absolute silence waiting eagerly for the word of command. Suddenly the firing broke out again at the foot of the hill, and immediately a bright light shot up from its face. The edge of the dense mass of Burmese was now but some fifty yards from the wall that surrounded the foot of the hill, and the causeway behind was occupied by a solid mass of men. Then came the sharp order to the artillerymen, and gun after gun poured its charge of grape into the crowd, while at the same moment the infantry began to fire by companies in steady volleys.

THE BURMESE MAKE A GREAT EFFORT TO CAPTURE PAGODA HILL.

For an instant the din of the assailants was silenced, then their shouts rose again, and after a moment's hesitation they continued their advance. But not for long; none but the most disciplined soldiers could have advanced under that storm of grape and bullets, and in ten minutes they fled in wild confusion, leaving the causeway thickly covered with the dead. Again and again the British cheers rose loud and triumphant, then the infantry were told to fall out, but the guns continued their fire until the fugitives were well in the forest. Between the shots the general listened attentively, and examined the country towards the town through his glasses.

"Everything is quiet," he said. "It is probable that if those fellows had carried the hill they would have made a signal, and there might have been a general attack. As it is, the affair is over for the night, and the Invulnerables will have some difficulty in accounting for their failure and loss. Now, gentlemen, we may as well have up the horses, and ride back. We hardly expected to get away as soon as this."

"Well, Meinik, what do you think of your Invulnerables now?" Stanley said, as the Burman, after picketing his horse, came up to his room to see if he wanted anything before lying down on his bed in the passage.

"I don't know," the Burman replied gravely. "They may be holy men, and proof perhaps against native weapons, but they are no good against your cannon and muskets. I understand now how it is that you beat us so easily. Your men all stood quiet and in order; one only heard the voices of the officers, and the crash as they fired together. Then, your guns are terrible. I have seen ours firing, but though our pieces are smaller than yours, your men fire five shots to our one. I stood by while they were loading. It was wonderful. Nobody talked, and nobody gave orders; each man knew what he had to do—one did something, and directly another did something; and almost before the smoke of the last shot was out of the gun, it was ready to be fired again. It is clear to me that we have not learnt how to fight, and that your way of having only a few men, well taught and knowing exactly what they have to do, is better than ours of having great numbers, and letting everyone fight as he pleases. It is bad every way. The brave men get to the front and are killed, and then the others run away. You were right. We shall never turn you out of Rangoon till Bandoola comes. He has all our best troops with him, and he has never been beaten. All the troops know him, and will fight for him as they will not fight for these princes, who know nothing of war, and are chosen only because they are the king's brothers. When he comes, you will see."

"No doubt we shall, Meinik; and you will see that although they may make a better fight of it than they have done to-night, it will be just the same in the end."

For the next two months the time passed slowly. No attacks were made by the enemy after the defeat of the assault upon the pagoda. Peasants and deserters who came in reported that there was profound depression among the Burmese troops. Great numbers had left the colours, and there was no talk of another attack. The troops being therefore relieved of much of their arduous night-duty, the

English took the offensive. The stockades on the Dalla river, and those upon the Panlang branch, the principal passage into the main stream of the Irrawaddy, were attacked and carried, the enemy suffering heavily, and many pieces of artillery being captured.

The rains continued almost unceasingly, and the troops suffered terribly in health. Scarce three thousand remained fit for duty, and the greater portion of these were so emaciated and exhausted by the effects of the climate that they were altogether unfit for active operations. Three weeks after the fight at the pagoda a vessel came up the river with a letter from the officer in command of the troops assembled to bar the advance of Bandoola against Chittagong, saying that the Burmese army had mysteriously disappeared. It had gone off at night so quietly and silently that our outposts, which were but a short distance from it, heard no sign or movement whatever. The Burmese had taken with them their sick, tents, and stores, and nothing but a large quantity of grain had been found in their deserted stockades.

The news was received with satisfaction by the troops. There was little doubt that the court of Ava, finding that their generals had all failed in making the slightest impression upon our lines, and had lost vast numbers of men, had at last turned to the leader who had conquered province after province for it, and had sent him orders to march with his whole army to bring the struggle to a close. The soldiers rejoiced at the thought that they were at last to meet a real Burmese army. Hitherto they had generally stood on the defensive, and had to fight the climate rather than the foe, and it seemed to them that the campaign was likely to be interminable.

The march of the Burmese from Ramoo to Sembeughewn, the nearest point of the river to the former town, must have been a terrible one. The distance was over two hundred miles, the rains were ceaseless, and the country covered with jungles and marshes, and intersected by rivers. No other army could have accomplished such a feat. The Burmans, however, accustomed to the unhealthy climate, lightly clad, and carrying no weight save their arms and sixteen days' supply of rice, passed rapidly over it.

Every man was accustomed to the use of an axe and to the formation of rafts, and in an incredibly short time rivers were crossed, deep swamps traversed on roads made by closely-packed faggots; and but a few days after hearing that Bandoola had started, the general learned from peasants that the news had come down that he and a portion of his army had arrived at Sembeughewn. Almost at the same time other parties who travelled down along the coast reached Donabew, a town on the Irrawaddy, some forty miles in direct line from Rangoon. This had been named as the rendezvous of the new army, and to this a considerable proportion of Bandoola's force made their way direct from Ramoo, it being the custom of the Burmese to move, when on a march through a country where no opposition was to be looked for, in separate detachments, each under its own leader, choosing its own way, and making for a general rendezvous.

Travelling in this manner they performed the journey far more rapidly than they could have done moving in one body, and could better find shelter and food. Other forces from Prome, Tannoo, and other quarters were known to be marching towards Donabew. It was soon reported that the dejected forces around Rangoon had gained courage and confidence at the news that Bandoola and his army were coming to their aid, and that the deserters were returning in large numbers from their villages. The British sick were sent away in the shipping to Mergy and Tavoy, two coast towns of which we had taken possession, and both of which were healthily situated. The change had a marvellous effect, and men who would have speedily succumbed to the poisonous exhalations of the swamps round Rangoon, rapidly regained their strength in their new quarters.

CHAPTER IX

VICTORIES.

IN the meantime negotiations had been going on with Siam, between which state and Burma there was the bitterest enmity. It had been thought that Siam would have willingly grasped the opportunity to revenge itself for the many losses of territory that it had suffered at the hands of Burma. This there was no doubt that it would have been glad to do, but our occupation of several points on the coast of Tenasserim roused the fears of Siam, and inclined it to the belief that we might prove an even more dangerous neighbour than Burma. The court of Ava had on its part also sent urgent messages to the king of Siam when misfortunes had to some extent lowered its pride, calling upon him to make common cause with Burma, and to join it in repelling an enemy who would doubtless be as dangerous to him as to Burma. Siam, however, determined to steer a middle course. An army was assembled in readiness for any contingency, but Siam believed as little as Burma itself that the British could possibly be victorious over that power, and feared its vengeance if she were to ally herself with us; while upon the other hand, Siam had a long seacoast, and feared the injury our fleet might inflict upon it were it to join Burma. The king, therefore, gave both powers an assurance of his friendship, and marched his army down to the frontier of the province of Martaban, which bordered on the great Salween river on the Tenasserim coast, and lay some two hundred miles from Rangoon across the Gulf of Martaban. The intentions of the king being so doubtful, the advance of the Siamese army in this direction could not be regarded with indifference by the British. The town of Martaban was the centre of the Burmese military power in Tenasserim, and the advance towards it of the Siamese army would place it in direct communication with that of Burma. On the 13th of October, therefore, a force, consisting of a wing of the 41st Regiment and the 3rd Madras Infantry, sailed from Rangoon against the town. The expedition was delayed by light winds, and when it arrived at the mouth of the river found that every preparation had been made for an obstinate defence. They learned from a peasant that strong works had been erected on every eminence round the town, and that the road from the coast had been cut and stockaded.

Approach by this route was impossible, for there were twenty miles of country to be traversed, and much of this was under water from the inundations. It was, therefore, determined to go up the river, although this was so shallow and full of shoals that the navigation was extremely difficult. At last, after great labour, incurred by the ships constantly getting ashore, they succeeded in making their way up to Martaban and anchored off the town. A heavy cannonade was carried on for some time between the ships and the enemy's works, then the troops were embarked in boats, which rowed for the shore under a very heavy fire from the enemy. As soon as they landed, and advanced to attack the stockades, the Burmese lost heart and hastily retreated, while the inhabitants received the troops as they entered with the warmest welcome, for they were for the most part natives of Pegu, and still entertained a deep hatred for the Burmese because of the long oppression that they had suffered at their hands. Throughout the rest of Tenasserim, however, and indeed throughout the whole country traversed by the troops later on, the inhabitants appeared to have entirely forgotten their ancient nationality and the conquest of their country by the Burmans, and to have become completely absorbed by them. Throughout the whole time that we occupied Martaban the people gave no trouble whatever, and indeed offered to raise a force for service with us if we wished it.

At the end of October the rain ceased, to the intense delight of the troops, and the cold season set in. November was, however, an exceptionally deadly month, the occasional days of fine weather drawing up the exhalations from the swamps, and the number of deaths was greater than they had been at any previous time. There was, too, no prospect of a forward movement at present. The expedition had come unprovided with boats or other means of transport, making sure that an abundant supply would be obtained in a country where the whole trade was carried on by the rivers. The promptness with which the native authorities had, on the first appearance of the fleet, sent every boat away, had disappointed this anticipation, and although the opening of some of the other rivers had enabled the local fishermen to bring their boats to Rangoon, where fish were eagerly purchased, the British troops were still, up to the end of November, without the means of sending a hundred men up the river save in the boats of the fleet. The Indian authorities, believing that when the Burmese found themselves impotent to turn us out of Rangoon, the court of Ava would be glad to negotiate, had not until the autumn was drawing to a close thought of making any preparations to supply the army with water-carriage. They now, however, began to bestir themselves.

Five hundred boatmen were sent from Chittagong, bringing many boats down with them, and building others at Rangoon. Transports with draft cattle sailed from Bengal, and a considerable reinforcement of troops was on its way to join at the end of December, for all the natives agreed that no movement could be made by land until the end of January. In November, even Bandoola's army was obliged to make its approach by water. Early in that month it was learned that the Burmese general had given orders for the advance, and preparations were at once begun to meet what none doubted would be a very serious attack. The reinforcements had not yet arrived, and the greatly diminished force was far too small for the length of the line that had to be defended. Redoubts were therefore thrown up, pagodas and other buildings were fortified, and two complete lines of works constructed from the great pagoda to the city, one facing east and the other west. The post at Kemmendine was strengthened, and was supported by H.M. sloop *Sophie*, a Company's cruiser, and a strong division of gun-boats. The retention of this post was of great importance, as it barred the river approach to Rangoon, and prevented the enemy sending down a huge fleet of war-galleys and fire-rafts to attack the town and set fire to the merchant shipping lying off it.

In the last week of November, smoke was seen to rise from many points in the forest. Many fugitives came in from their villages, and reported that Bandoola's army were all on their way down the river, and by the end of the month some sixty thousand men, with a large train of artillery and a body of cavalry, were assembled round our position. Of this force, thirty thousand were armed with muskets. They had with them, too, a great number of jingals; these little guns carried ball of from six to twelve ounces, and were mounted on a light carriage, which two men could wheel with ease; the cannon were carried to the scene of action on elephants. The cavalry were seven hundred strong, drawn from the borders of Manipur. The rest of the army were armed with swords and spears, and carried implements for stockading and intrenching. The force was accompanied by a number of astrologers, and by the Invulnerables, who had doubtless satisfactorily explained their failure to capture the pagoda.

A great semicircle of light smoke rising from the trees showed that the position taken up by Bandoola extended from the river above Kemmendine to the neighbourhood of Rangoon. On the night of the 31st, the troops at the pagoda heard a loud and continuous stir in the forest. It gradually approached, and by morning great masses of troops had gathered at the edge of the jungle within musket-shot of the post. The garrison there were drawn up in readiness to repel a sudden rush, but just as the sun rose, a din made by thousands of men engaged in cutting down the trees began, and it was evident that the Burmese were going to adopt their usual plan of intrenching themselves behind stockades.

During the time that had elapsed between the repulse of the Invulnerables and the arrival of Bandoola's army, Stanley's work was light and the life dull and monotonous. An hour was spent every morning in examining the fugitives who had, by the retreat of the Burmese, been enabled to make their way back to the town, and of women who had escaped from the vigilance of the Burmese police, and had come in from the villages where they had been held as hostages for their husbands.

Once or twice a week he went off with the general to the hospital-ship to inquire into the state of the sick and to pay a visit to the long line of cots along the main and lower deck. Almost every day he rode, in spite of the weather, to one or other of the regimental camps, and soon came to know most of the officers of the force. His previous experience on the rivers had done much to acclimatize him, and his health continued good. On the evening of the 30th he had, at the general's order, ridden up to the pagoda. It was considered likely that the attack would be delivered there in the first place; and at three o'clock in the morning, when it became evident that a large body of men were approaching through the forest, he galloped back to Rangoon with the news, and at five rode out again with Sir A. Campbell. Among the garrison there was much disappointment when the sound of wood-chopping announced that the Burmese did not intend to attack; but the general, who had been watching the edge of the jungle through his glasses, lowered them and put them into their case with an expression of satisfaction.

"I don't want them to attack, colonel," he said. "If they do, and we beat them off, we are no nearer the end than before. That sort of thing might be carried on for months, as long, in fact, as there remains a man to bring up. What we want is to inflict such a heavy blow upon them that even the court at Ava may become convinced that they cannot hope to drive us out of Rangoon; in which case they may consent to negotiate, and we may bring the war to an end. Heaven knows that we have suffered enough loss at present, and I don't want to have to undertake such a difficult operation as an advance against Ava. I am glad to see that they have begun to construct stockades. I do not intend to interfere until they have completely finished their work, and gained sufficient confidence to make a general attack on us; then we shall be able to give them a heavy lesson. Ah, there they are at work!"

As he spoke a roar of musketry and artillery broke out suddenly from Kemmendine, and all eyes were turned in that direction. The spot was two miles distant, but the forest shut out alike the view of the river and of the works held by us. The exact position, however, was indicated by the masts of the two war-vessels rising above the trees. Soon great wreaths of heavy white smoke rose above the forest in and around Kemmendine, shutting out all view. The fire continued without abatement, and it was evident that the attack was a hot and determined one. Confident as all felt that the little fort would be able to defend itself successfully, the great smoke clouds were watched with some feeling of anxiety, for the garrison was, after all, but a handful. In momentary intervals of the firing the yells and shouts of the natives could be distinctly heard, and once or twice, after a heavy broadside from the ships of war, the cheers of the British sailors could be plainly recognized. After two hours' fighting the din gradually ceased; the clouds of smoke rolled away, and the masts of the ships became visible, and the garrison of the pagoda raised three hearty cheers to tell the defenders that their successful defence had been watched and welcomed.

Presently some heavy columns of the enemy issued from the forest on the other side of the river and marched across the plain to Dalla, which faced Rangoon. They moved with great regularity and order, led by their chiefs on horseback, their gilded umbrellas glittering in the rays of the sun. On reaching the bank of the river opposite Rangoon they began intrenching themselves and throwing up stockades and batteries with the evident intention of opening fire on the shipping. Soon afterwards large bodies of men issued from the forest facing the pagoda, and marching along a slight ridge that extended from that point to the creek below Rangoon, took up their position there, and began intrenching themselves all along the line. Thus the British position was now completely surrounded; there was, however, no doubt that the main body of the enemy was still facing the pagoda.

"We must see what they are doing," the general said. "This is too important a point for us to allow them to erect a strongly fortified position close at hand."

Accordingly, Tollemache was sent down with an order to the 18th Madras Infantry, supported by a detachment of the 13th Regiment under Major Sale, to advance against the enemy in the jungle. The movements of this force were eagerly watched from the terrace of the pagoda. At a rapid pace they crossed the intervening ground, and a rattle of musketry broke out from the jungle as they approached. The British made no response, but charged with a cheer and were soon lost to sight in the trees. Their regular volleys could be heard at short intervals above the scattered rattle of the Burmese musketeers, and their cheers frequently rose loud and triumphant. In half an hour the red line emerged again from the jungle, having destroyed the stockades the Burmese had erected, captured several guns, a quantity of muskets and intrenching tools thrown away by the Burmese, and killed a large number of the enemy.

During the day the enemy made repeated efforts to send fire-rafts down the river from above Kemmendine. These rafts were constructed of bamboos, upon which were placed great numbers of earthenware pots filled with petroleum. These rafts were skilfully constructed, and made in sections, so that when they drifted against an anchor-chain they would divide, those on each side swinging round, so as to envelop the ship on both sides with fire. The sailors from the sloops and gun-boats rowed up to meet the rafts, and although a heavy fire was kept up by the enemy from the jungles lining the banks, they succeeded in towing most of them safely to shore, while the rest grounded on a projecting spit off Kemmendine.

So diligently did the Burmese work at all points throughout the day that by the afternoon their whole line of circumvallation was covered with earth-works, behind which they lay entirely hidden from sight.

"If they could fight as well as they dig and build stockades," Sir A. Campbell remarked, "they would be one of the most formidable enemies in the world. No European army ever accomplished the work of intrenching themselves so speedily as they have done. Their arrangements have been admirable; everything has been done without confusion, and each body has taken up the position allotted to it, as is evident by the fact that there is no gap in their lines. As to Bandoola's tactics, I cannot say so much for them. In the first place, he has divided his force into two parts, separated by a river, and incapable of helping each other. In the next place, great as are his numbers, his lines are far too extended. Well, we will let them go on for a time, and then show them the mistake that they have committed."

Major Sale's report of the intrenchments were, that they consisted of a long line of holes, each capable of containing two men. The earth was dug out on one side so as to form a sort of cave. In this was a bed of straw or brushwood, on which one man could sleep while the other watched. Each hole contained a sufficient supply of rice, water, and even fuel for its inmates. One line of these holes had been completed and another was being dug a short distance in advance. The Burmese do not relieve their men in the trenches; those who occupy the line first made remain there; fresh men dig and occupy the next line, and so the advance is continued until close to the work to be attacked. The system has the great advantage that a shell falling into one of these holes only kills its two occupants instead of destroying many, as it might do if it fell in a continuous trench.

In the afternoon the general returned to Rangoon, leaving Stanley at the pagoda with orders to ride down should there be any change of importance. In the evening a considerable force of Burmese issued from the jungle and prepared to intrench themselves near the north-east angle of the pagoda hill. Major Piper therefore took two companies of the 38th, and, descending the hill, drove the Burmese in confusion back to the jungle.

In the morning it was found that the enemy had intrenched themselves upon some high and open ground, within musket-shot of the north gate of the pagoda. It was separated from the gate by a large tank, but as their jingals and musketry were able from the point they occupied to sweep the plateau and the huts occupied by the troops, a party of the 38th and the 28th Madras Infantry went out and drove them off. As soon, however, as our troops fell back the Burmese reoccupied the position, and for the next few days a constant skirmishing went on at this point, while an artillery fire was maintained by the assailants and defenders along the whole line down to Rangoon, and the enemy's batteries at Dalla kept up an incessant fire on the shipping. Kemmendine was attacked time after time, and many attempts made to launch fire-rafts down the river.

The work was very harassing for the troops. Night and day they were expecting an attack in force, and there was a general feeling of delight when, on the evening of the 4th, orders were issued for a general movement against the enemy.

The latter had by this time brought the greater portion of their guns up from the jungle, and placed them in their intrenchments, and it was therefore in the power of the British to strike a heavy blow. A division of the flotilla of gun-boats was ordered up the creek by the town. These opened a heavy fire upon the enemy's flank, thus attracting their attention to that point, and after the cannonade had continued for some little time the two columns of attack, the one eight hundred strong, under Major Sale, the other five hundred, under Major Walker of the Madras army, issued out. The latter was to attack the enemy facing the town, the former to force his way through the centre of the their position. He had with him a troop of horse that had landed only the previous day. Major Walker's force was the first to encounter the enemy. Their resistance was for a time obstinate. Major Walker and several other officers fell in the attack on the first line of intrenchments, but the soldiers carried it at the point of the bayonet, and as the enemy broke and retreated, followed them so hotly that the works in the rear fell into their hands with but slight opposition.

Major Sale's column now began its attack on the enemy's centre. Here the resistance was more feeble, and, bursting through the enemy's lines, the British drove them before them in headlong flight. Then, turning, they swept along the line of intrenchments, carrying all before them until they effected a junction with the other column, which was advancing to meet them. They then drove the Burmese from every part of their works into the jungle, leaving the ground behind them covered with dead and wounded. Except at the point first attacked by Major Walker, the resistance of the Burmese was very feeble, and the British loss inconsiderable, and a large number of guns, intrenching tools, and muskets fell into the hands of the victors. The next day Bandoola rallied the troops that had been driven from the plain, and gathered the greatest part of his force in the forest round the pagoda, where they continued to push forward their works with unabated energy.

The British had a day of rest given them, and on the 7th prepared to attack the enemy at this point. Four columns of attack were formed, composed of detachments drawn from all the corps of the army. In the morning a heavy cannonade was opened upon the jungle, the artillery being assisted by several heavy guns, which had with great labour been brought up by the sailors from the ships to the pagoda. The enemy returned it with a steady fire of light artillery, jingals, and musketry. While the firing was still going on the four columns were already in motion; one had entered the jungle on the enemy's left, and another on the right. One of the central columns advanced from the foot of the pagoda hill, while the 38th Regiment descended the stairs from the north gate, and advanced, one wing on each side of the tank, against the enemy's intrenchments on the high ground. As the four columns approached the enemy our artillery fire ceased. The Burmese appeared for a moment bewildered at the sight of their foes advancing against them from so many directions, but they soon opened a very heavy fire upon the assailants, and kept it up with undiminished steadiness until our troops, advancing at the charge, dashed into their intrenchments, and drove them headlong before them into the thick forest behind, where pursuit, which would at any time have been difficult, was now impossible, the troops, exhausted by their seven days' and nights' watching, being wholly incapable of following their active and lightly-armed enemies.

There now remained but the force at Dalla to cope with, and in the evening a force composed of the 89th and 43rd Madras Infantry, under Colonel Parlby, embarked in boats. The night was dark, and the troops crossed unobserved. The alarm was not given until the British actually entered the intrenchments and opened fire upon the enemy, who were sitting, unsuspicious of danger, round their fires. Scarcely any opposition was encountered, and the whole of the works, with the guns and the stores, were soon in our hands, while the enemy were flying towards the forest. In the actions during these three days the Burmese lost some 5000 men, 240 pieces of artillery of every kind, and a great number of muskets, and vast supplies of ammunition, while the British had but 50 killed and 300 wounded.

Great numbers of Bandoola's men never rejoined the army, and the whole force was dispersed through the country. Bandoola himself was retiring towards Donabew with but a remnant of his army when he met considerable reinforcements on their way to join him. During his operations he had left a reserve corps at the village of Kokein, four miles from the pagoda, and these had been busily intrenching the position, which commanded the road leading from Rangoon to Donabew. The ground was elevated, and on his arrival there Bandoola set his troops, now some 25,000 in number, to aid in the work. In a marvellously short time the heights were completely stockaded with trunks of trees, and with a broad, deep ditch in front. Beyond this were lines of felled trees, their heads pointing outwards and each branch sharpened, forming a very formidable abattis, and, believing this to be impregnable, Bandoola awaited the attack of the British.

As soon as his army had been dispersed great numbers of deserters and of the inhabitants of the villages poured into Rangoon. With the deserters were mingled a good many of the troops sent in by Bandoola himself with instructions to fire the town. In order to lull the suspicions of the British he caused a report to be spread that an imperial commissioner from the court of Ava would arrive in the course of a few days to treat for terms of peace.

The general, however, determined to attack Bandoola before the commissioner could arrive, as it was evident that better terms could be obtained after the total dispersion of the Burmese, than if their famous general remained, with 25,000 men, in a formidable position close at hand. He was uneasy at the presence of so large a number of natives in the town, and the precautions that had been taken against fire some time before were now redoubled. Were one to break out not only might the whole of the stores collected for the advance of the army be destroyed, but if Bandoola had his force gathered in readiness at the edge of the jungle, he might take advantage of the confusion that would be caused by the fire, and rush forward to the attack of the town. Numbers of troops and of sailors from the fleet patrolled the streets in every direction at night, but, in spite of their efforts, a week after the retreat of Bandoola the dreaded cry of fire was raised.

At a dozen points on the windward side of the town fires had been lighted by incendiaries, and as there was a brisk wind blowing the danger was extreme. The drums beat to arms along the whole of the British lines. Orders had already been issued as to what was to be done in such an emergency, and while a portion of the troops lined the trenches, the rest were marched at once to the town and formed up between it and the jungle to repel any attack that might be made there, leaving the troops quartered in the town and the sailors of the fleet to battle with the flames. For a time it seemed as if the whole place would be swept away, but by levelling lines of huts and beating out the flames at the barrier so formed, their progress was at length checked, but not until more than half the town had been destroyed. Fortunately this was the half farthest from the river, and with the exception of the commissariat stores for the supply of the troops of the Madras Presidency, the buildings containing the food, ammunition, and necessaries for the army escaped unharmed. What had happened once might, however, happen again in spite of all precautions. The general therefore determined to attack Bandoola at once, as, were his force once scattered, the motive for these incendiary fires would cease to operate.

The difficulties were formidable. One or two light fieldpieces could at the most be taken with the column. They would have to march by a narrow and winding footpath through a thick forest, exposed at any moment to a desperate attack by the enemy. Moreover, it would be necessary to leave a strong force for the defence of Rangoon, as Bandoola would be sure to learn from his spies of the intended movement, and having with him men intimately acquainted with every forest track, could make a rush down upon the town during the absence of so many of its defenders.

The general felt it imperative, however, to attack without delay, and early on the morning of the 15th he moved out with a force of 1500 men against Kokein. They marched without molestation through the forest, and on reaching its confines could see the truly formidable nature of the works that they were to attack.

The moment they issued from the forest a dropping fire was opened upon them by parties of the enemy in flank and rear, and no time was lost in preparing for the assault.

The 13th Light Infantry and the 18th Madras with 60 cavalry, under Brigadier-general Cotton, were ordered to move round the stockade and assault it on the left rear, while the rest of the troops, some 800 strong, with 100 cavalry under the general himself, were to attack in front. The enemy's works consisted of a central intrenchment connected with two large intrenched stockades on its flank, but somewhat advanced in front of it. As soon as the force under General Cotton had gained its position in the rear of the enemy, a gun was fired, and the whole force moved forward to the assault. The Burmans regarded the attack by so insignificant a force upon their works with such contempt that they did not for some time fire a shot, but continued chanting a war-song, swaying themselves to its cadence, stamping and beating time with their hands on their breasts. This delay proved fatal to them. When they opened fire their assailants were already close to the ditch, and leaping down into this were sheltered from the fire of the defenders. Scaling-ladders were speedily placed, and the troops running up them, leaped down into the intrenchment.

Astounded at this sudden entry into the works they had deemed impregnable, the Burmese hesitated; and the assailants being joined by their comrades from behind, rushed impetuously upon the enemy. The column in the rear had greater difficulty, for they had several strong stockades to carry before they reached the central work, and lost four officers, and eight men killed, and forty-nine officers and men wounded, in the 13th Regiment alone. Fifteen minutes after the first shot was fired the whole of the works were in our possession, and the Burmese, who gathered in a confused mass, had been decimated by our volleys. They were now in full flight, many being cut down by the cavalry before they reached the shelter of the woods. The British troops marched back to Rangoon, while the Burmese retreated to Donabew, leaving strong posts on the two rivers leading in that direction.

Their retirement left it free to the country people to return to Rangoon, and very large numbers came in, including very many of the villagers who had been forced to fight against us. All had alike suffered from famine and hardship, even the women had been compelled to labour in the work of stockading, and the sufferings of all had been terrible. The work of rebuilding the town began at once, and the wooden huts sprang up with great rapidity; markets were opened, and in a short time supplies of fish, fruit, game, and vegetables poured in, sufficient not only for the native population, but to effect a most welcome change in the diet of the troops. As most of the natives were accustomed to the construction and management of boats, the work of preparing the flotilla, by which the troops were to proceed up the rivers, went on rapidly, and numbers of men were hired as servants and drivers for the commissariat, with which the force was very insufficiently supplied, as the natives of India of that class for the most part refused, on account of their caste prejudices, to engage themselves for service across the sea. Reinforcements arrived, and Rangoon, which but six weeks before presented a miserable and deserted appearance, was towards the beginning of January a cheerful and bustling town.

Preparations were being made in other quarters to assume the offensive. Some 3000 men were driving the Burmese out of Assam, and a force 7000 strong was marching from

Sylhet to expel them from Cachar and capture Manipur, while 11,000 men were assembled at Chittagong, and were advancing into Aracan with the intention of driving the Burmese from that province, and they meant if possible to cross the mountains and effect a junction with Sir Archibald Campbell's force. The first part of the operations were conducted with complete success, and Aracan wrested from Burma, but it was found impossible to perform the terrible journey across mountain and swamp or to afford any aid to the main expedition.

CHAPTER X.

THE ADVANCE.

WHILE the preparations for the advance were being made, the general's aides-de-camp had been kept at work from morning until night. There were constant communications between the military and naval authorities, for the expedition was to be a mixed one. Transports were daily arriving with troops and stores, innumerable matters connected with the organization, both of the land and water transport required to be arranged, and the general himself was indefatigable in superintending every detail of the work. It had been settled that the advance could not take place until the second week in February, as the roads would be impassable until that time, and the 11th was fixed for the commencement of operations.

Upon the day after his arrival at Rangoon, Stanley had written a letter to his uncle, giving him a brief account of

THE ADVANCE. 177

his adventures, and stating that he had been appointed one of the general's aides-de-camp. He said that he should of course be guided by his uncle's wishes, but that now that he had entered on the campaign as an officer, he should certainly like to remain till the end, when he would at once resign his commission and rejoin him.

He sent this to his uncle's agent at Calcutta, but received no answer until the end of December. After expressing his delight at hearing that Stanley had not, as he had supposed, been killed at Ramoo, but was now safe and well in the British camp, he went on:

"I only received your letter this morning, for I have been moving about from point to point, and owing to the falling off of trade, had no occasion to go to Calcutta until now, and was indeed astounded at finding your letter lying for me here, as they had not forwarded it, having no idea where I was, and knowing that the chance of any letter sent on reaching me was extremely small. By all means, lad, stop where you are; trade is improving again, for now that Bandoola's army has marched away from Ramoo, the scare among the natives has pretty well subsided. Still, I can manage very well without you, and it will certainly be a great advantage to you to serve for a year in the army; and to have been one of Campbell's aides-de-camp will be a feather in your cap, and will give you a good position at all the military stations. I am very glad now that I abstained from writing to your mother after the battle at Ramoo. I thought it over and over, and concluded that it was just as well to leave the matter alone for a time; not that I had the slightest idea, or even a hope, that you were alive, but because I thought that the cessation of letters from you would to some extent prepare her mind for the blow when it came.

"It would be very improbable that she would see the gazette with the list of killed and wounded at Ramoo, and even if she did so, she would not associate the death of Ensign Brooke in any way with you. When we have been trading up country, there have been, once or twice, no means of sending off a letter for a couple of months, and therefore she could not have begun to feel seriously anxious about you before she received your letter from Rangoon.

"Every one says that you will not be able to advance until February, so that no doubt this letter will reach you long before you leave. I hear the losses have been very heavy from fever, but I am not anxious about you on that score, for I think that you are thoroughly acclimatized. I am trying to get a contract for the supply of a couple of thousand bullocks for the use of the army, and as I know all the country so well, from Chittagong to Sylhet, and can buy below Indian prices, I think that I shall not only get the contract, but make a very good thing of it, and it may lead to other matters."

After this, Stanley was hardly surprised when in the last week of January his uncle walked into his quarters. After the first pleasure of meeting was over, Stanley said:

"I suppose you have got the contract, uncle?"

"I have, lad. I have come down from Ramgur with six

dhows packed full. I have brought a thousand head down, and directly I land them am going back for the remainder, which will be ready for me by the time I get there. I have got hold of an uncommonly good fellow. He was established as a small trader at Chittagong. His business was ruined there, and he was glad to accept my offer of a berth, and he has turned out a very energetic and pushing fellow; he will come down with the next consignment. I myself am going to work my way up along the edge of the Tipperah forest, and shall pick up another thousand head by the time that I get to the Goomtee, and shall send them by water up to Sylhet, and then go up by land, picking up more on the way. I have a contract for five thousand, to be sent in, a thousand a month, for the force that is to move against Manipur, while Johnson is to send another two thousand down here, so you see for the present the store business can wait. It is a good line that I have got into; I shall make a big profit out of it, and have hopes that it will be to some extent permanent, for I can get the cattle so cheap in the interior, on the rivers we know, that I can ship them to Calcutta at lower terms than they can buy them in India, and I was as much as told that if I carried out my present contracts satisfactorily I should get the supply of the troops there. Of course, that would not be a very great thing of itself, but as I could work it without trouble in connection with my own business, it would make a handsome addition to the profits."

"But how about money, uncle?"

"That is all right, lad. I had no difficulty whatever in getting an advance at Calcutta on the strength of my contract and upon the guarantee of my agents, so that I am all right in that respect."

"I asked, uncle, because I can let you have eighteen hundred pounds if you want them."

Tom Pearson looked at him in astonishment:

"Why, what on earth have you been doing—robbing the treasury of the king of Ava?"

"No, uncle. I had a bag of gems given me by some Burmese bandits. When I got down here I took a few of them to a merchant. He advanced fifteen hundred rupees on them, and sent them to Burragee, the jeweller at Madras, and six weeks afterwards he paid me another three thousand five hundred. I sent up another batch, and last week I got an order from the jewellers for fifteen hundred pounds, so that I have more than eighteen hundred in hand now, and I don't think that I have sent more than a third of the gems away."

"Well, that is a piece of luck, Stanley! Why on earth did the brigands give you the gems?"

"Well, uncle, they are things that, from what they told me, there is great difficulty and risk in trying to dispose of. They are a royal monopoly, and nobody dare buy them; or if they do will give next to nothing for them, because of the risk of the transaction, and because they know that the vendors are in a fix and must sell. Besides, there is a strong chance of their handing over anyone who offers such things to the authorities. That was one reason why they gave them to me. Then, too, they had made a good haul of merchandise which was to them a great deal more valuable, as there was no difficulty in disposing of it. Lastly, they had taken a fancy to me because I saved one of their comrades' life—the man who showed you up here."

"Well, lad, you shall tell me all about it this evening. I must be going down to the commissariat yard to arrange the landing of my beasts. I came straight to see you directly I landed. We dropped anchor here at daybreak."

"I will go with you, uncle. I will run in and see the chief first and get leave off for the day. I have earned a holiday, for I have been at work pretty well morning, noon, and night for the last two months. You see I have not only the duties of aide-de-camp, but of interpreter, and have helped both the quartermaster's department and the commissariat in making their arrangements with the natives. I daresay I shall be able to help to hurry your business on quicker than you would be able to get it done alone."

The general at once granted Stanley leave, and he went with his uncle down to the commissariat office and introduced him to the senior officer.

"We shall be glad to do all in our power to help you, Mr. Pearson," the officer said. "We have been expecting your arrival for the last week. Of course, we heard from Calcutta that you had the contract for two thousand head; at least half of these were to be delivered by the tenth of February. We were getting rather anxious about it. The force will probably want to start before that time, and we shall have to victual both the land and water columns. Of course, I did not know that you were a relation of Mr. Brooke, or I should have mentioned to him that you were likely to come."

"I should like to get off as soon as possible," Tom Pearson

said; "for by the time that I get back to Ramgur the rest of the cattle will be in readiness for me."

"I will write you an order for four large boats at once. If you had come three weeks sooner you might have been kept waiting some days; but such a number of native craft have of late come down the rivers that we are enabled to get sufficient for our work."

The officer gave him a note to the one in charge of the landing arrangements.

"It is lucky that you have come just at this moment," the latter said. "We have just made our last trip with the baggage of the 47th, and I have six boats disengaged. You may as well take them all."

The craft in question were some of those that had been captured—unwieldy craft, that took fish and salt up the river. They were almost as large as the dhows in which the cattle had been brought down, but drew very much less water. They were towed off to the dhows, one by one, by two captured war-canoes, each having thirty rowers. One was taken to each dhow, and the work of transhipping the cattle began at once. These were in good condition, for although closely packed they had been well supplied with food and water on the way down, and a herdsman with four men under him had been sent in each boat to take care of them, as Tom Pearson was very anxious that his first consignment should be reported upon favourably. The animals were all landed in the course of the afternoon, and with the acknowledgment of their receipt in excellent order, in his pocket, the contractor went off again with Stanley to his own dhow.

"I have told them to have everything in readiness to drop down the river with the tide to-morrow morning. It will turn just about sunrise. That is a rare bit of business, Stanley; and I doubt if a contractor ever got his work through so quickly before. Of course it is principally due to you; they would never have pushed things through so quickly had you not gone with me. I thought that very likely I might be detained here a week before I could get all the cattle on shore—and by that time, if all goes well, I shall be at Ramgur again. Now we can have a comfortable evening's talk, which is very much better than my going to dine with you at mess, for there is a great deal to hear about, and I dare say that I can give you as good a dinner as we should have had on shore."

"A good deal better," Stanley said. "Things have improved immensely during the last month, still our mess cook is certainly not so good as your man; and, at any rate, the quiet of your cabin makes a very pleasant change after always sitting down with a large party."

After dinner was over, Stanley gave a full account of his adventures from the time that he was taken prisoner.

"You have done wonderfully well for yourself, lad, wonderfully well. Certainly when you picked up Burmese from my man we had no idea that it was ever likely to turn out so useful. I thought that it would have been an assistance among the Mugs on the coast, and I had, too, some idea that the war might lead to the opening of a trade up the Irrawaddy; but it has turned out infinitely more useful than that. If you could not have spoken Burmese Bandoola would never have thought of asking for you to be spared as an interpreter, and if he had not done so you would have had your head chopped off at Ava. Of course that leopard business was the turning-point of your fortunes; but, though it has turned out so well, I must say that I hardly think that you were justified in risking your life in such a desperate act for a native, who might, for aught you know, be already dead. Of course, it was a most gallant action, but the betting was ten to one against your succeeding. However, as it turned out, it was a fortunate business altogether. I don't say that you might not have made your way down to Rangoon unaided, but the odds would have been very heavily against it. However, these rubies were a windfall indeed."

"Will you take the rest of them, uncle, and sell them at Calcutta—or shall I send them to Madras, or home to England?"

"I will take them with me to Calcutta if you like, Stanley. I don't say that there are better men there than the one you sent to at Madras, but I think some of them do a larger business up country with the native princes, who don't care what they give for good gems. At any rate I will take them there and get them valued by an expert, and then try two or three of the leading firms and get their offers. If these are as high as the value put on them by the expert, I would send them to England through my agents, who would do the best they could for you."

"For us, uncle. Of course it is all in the partnership business. You have just got some contracts that will pay well, and while you have been doing that I have been getting hold of these rubies.'

"I don't think that that is fair, Stanley," his uncle said gravely.

"It seems to me perfectly fair; and, besides, the money put into the business will make a lot of difference, and will certainly pay me a great deal better than it would in any other way. I sent home £100 for my mother directly the money came from Calcutta, and told her that I hoped to be able to send home at least as much every year."

"A good deal more, lad, if you like. I calculate these contracts that I have got will bring in a pound a head, so that by the time that the war is over I hope to have cleared £8000, which will be about what you will make by your rubies, and when trade begins again we shall be in a position to do it on a big scale; but I still think that it will not be fair to take that money."

"Well, uncle, if you won't take it I certainly won't have anything to do with the money that you make while I am away, so please don't let us say anything more about it. Shall I give you that eighteen hundred now, or will you have an order upon the paymaster in Calcutta?"

"That would be the best way, if you will have it so, lad. I have left money with Johnson at Ramgur for the next herd that is to come down here, and have orders from my agent on their agents at Dalla for those that I am going to buy for the Manipur column, so I don't want the money now, and suppose the dhow were to be lost going up, the cash might go with it. So do you get the order; you had better send it straight to Bothron, and tell him to collect it and credit it to my account. How long do you think that this business is going to last?"

"It depends how far we have to go before the Burmese decide that they have had enough of it. At present the general hope is that as soon as we arrive at Prome they will give in; if they don't we may have to go up to Ava, and in that case we may not finish it until this time next year, for I suppose operations will have to come to a stop when the wet season begins again, and we could hardly reach Ava before that."

"I expect some day we shall have to take the whole country, Stanley. You may frighten the court into submission when you approach the capital, but I fancy they will never keep to the terms that we shall insist upon, and that there will have to be another expedition. That is generally our way—it was so at Mysore, it has been so in a dozen other places; when we have done all the work and have got them at our mercy we give them comparatively easy terms. As soon as they recover from the effects of their defeat they set to work again to prepare for another tussle, and then we have all the expense and loss of life to incur again, and then end by annexing their territory, which we might just as well have done in the first place. It may be all very well to be lenient when one is dealing with a European enemy, but magnanimity does not pay when you have to do with Orientals, who don't care a rap for treaty engagements, and who always regard concessions as being simply a proof of weakness. There would not be half the difficulty in annexing Burma that there would be in the case of a large province in India, for all the towns, and most even of their villages, lie on rivers, and a couple of dozen gun-boats would suffice to keep the whole country in order. You will see that that is what we shall have to do some day, but it will cost us two or three expeditions to do what might just as well be done now."

"Well, uncle, it is nearly twelve o'clock, and as I shall be on duty at six, I think I had better be going. I wish that you could have stayed for another two or three days, and paid a visit to the pagoda and camps. I am very glad that I have had a sight of you again, though it's a very short one."

"I should be glad to stay another day or two, Stanley, but it is really of importance for me to get down to Ramgur as soon as I can, and send Johnson off with the cattle, for I want to set about buying the herds for the other column as quickly as possible. I think I have left myself a fair margin of time, but there is nothing like promptitude in delivery, and I want to get a good name, for future business; and if this affair here is going to last another twelvemonth, regular supplies must be sent up, for as beef is forbidden by the Burmese religion, they keep no cattle except for draught purposes, and the army must get their bullocks by sea."

Five minutes later Stanley was rowed ashore. The next morning he accompanied the general, and went down to inspect the newly-arrived cattle.

"They are a capital lot," he said to Stanley; "decidedly the best that we have had yet. You see it is a good deal shorter voyage from Ramgur than from either Calcutta or Madras, and the animals probably had a much shorter land journey before they were shipped. Then, too, as your uncle came down himself, they were no doubt much better looked after than usual on the voyage. However, I will take care to mention when I write next to Calcutta that the cattle are far above the average, and I shall be glad if they will arrange for such further supplies as we may require, from the same source."

"Thank you, sir; that will be a great help to my uncle. Hitherto he has had very uphill work of it, though he was beginning to get on very well when the war put a stop to trade; he knows the whole country so thoroughly that he can certainly buy up cattle at many places where no European trader save himself has ever penetrated."

"No doubt, Brooke; and I hope for your sake that he will succeed well in this contracting business. He has certainly made an excellent start, and as he is first in the field in the country between Assam and Ramgur he ought to make a good thing of this opportunity that has fallen in his way. I know that it takes a long time to build up a business, but when the foundation is laid, and a man is quick in taking advantage of an opportunity, he can do as much in a year as he might do in twenty without it. Now, I am going over to the lines of the 47th, to see how they have shaken down into them."

This regiment had brought out tents, for, as every building was already occupied, it was necessary that they should be put under canvas. The general found that everything was arranged in order, and the encampment certainly presented a pleasing contrast to the irregular and often crowded quarters of the troops who had passed the wet season there. The colonel and three of his officers dined with the general that evening, the party being made up of the military staff, including the two aides-de-camp. Two days later, Stanley, with some of the other members of the staff, dined at the 47th mess. Stanley was introduced to several of the officers, and these were specially desirous of making his acquaintance, as they had learned that he had been a prisoner at Ava, and could therefore tell them much more than they had hitherto learned of the country into which they were about to advance. Among them was a young lieutenant, also of the name of Brooke. Stanley had three weeks before attained the same rank; at the time that he was appointed to the 83rd there were already several death vacancies in the regiment, and disease and fighting had carried off six more officers, the whole of the ensigns had consequently obtained their step. At dinner he found himself placed next to his namesake.

"It is curious our having the same name," the other remarked as he sat down. "It is not a very common one."

"No, I have not met anyone of the same name before," Stanley said. "Indeed, until the affair at Ramoo I was nearly three years trading with an uncle of mine up the rivers, and was not much in the way of falling in with white men. But, before that, I had been with my father in a good many stations in India, but I do not, as far as I can remember, recollect meeting anyone of the same name."

"Then your father was in the service too?"

"Yes. He was a captain in the 15th Native Infantry."

"Indeed," the other said in surprise. "Then we are connections. But I had no idea that Captain Brooke was ever married."

"He was married just after he came out to India," Stanley said; "so it is likely enough that you would never have heard of it. He died three years ago, and my mother and sisters are now in England. What is the connection between us? I have never heard my father speak much of his family."

"Your father was a cousin of mine—second cousin, I think. I fancy there was some row between your grandfather and the rest of the family. I don't know anything about the right or wrongs of it, for it was of course many years before we were born; and I never heard of your father's existence until a fortnight before I left England. Then there were some inquiries made about the family owing to various deaths that took place in it. Do you know that your father was related, distantly of course, to the Earl of Netherley?"

"I do remember his mentioning it once. I know he said that it was a distant connection, and that he knew nothing whatever about the earl or his family."

"Well, curiously enough, it is not so distant now," the other said. "I was a pretty distant connection of his; he was childless, and the family generally don't seem to have been prolific. A good many of them died, and the result was, that the year before I left England, an uncle of mine succeeded to the title. He has no son, and my father was his next brother. My father died two years ago, and the result is that, to my astonishment, I found that I was next heir to the title. They wanted me to leave the army when my regiment was ordered out to India, but of course I was not going to do that, for my aunt may die and my uncle marry again and have children. Besides, I was not going to leave anyhow just as the regiment was ordered abroad and might see service. However, there was a great hunting by the lawyers in the genealogical tree, and I know it was decided that in case anything happened to me your father would have been the next heir had he been alive. I don't know whether any further inquiries were made, or whether they ever ascertained that he had married. I don't suppose there were, for of course as long as I live the matter is of no importance. So that as things stand now, if a Burmese bullet puts an end to my career you are the next heir to the title."

"You surprise me, indeed," Stanley said. "From the way my father spoke of the matter I am sure that he had not the slightest idea there was any likelihood whatever that he would have any chance of succeeding to the title."

"That I can well imagine, for it was not until a few years ago, when the deaths of several who stood between him and the succession occurred, that my uncle regarded his coming into it as a matter worth thinking about, and of course all our family stood between it and your father. However, as you see, we have dwindled away, and if I do not get safely through this business you are the next heir."

"It is curious news to hear at a dinner in Burma," Stanley said thoughtfully. "At any rate, I can assure you honestly that the news gives me no particular satisfaction. I suppose it would be a nice thing to come in for a peerage, but my prospects out here are good. I have no intention of staying in the army after the end of the war, and am really in partnership with my uncle, with whom I have been for the last three years in business, which is turning out very well. I like the life, and have every chance of making enough to retire on, with ample means. Certainly I should not like to come into the title by the death of anyone that I know."

"That is the fortune of war," the other said smiling. "We get our steps by death vacancies. We are sorry for the deaths, but the steps are not unwelcome. By the way, my name is Harry. I know that yours is Stanley. I vote that we call each other by them. We are cousins, you know, and I suppose that as you are my heir, you must be my nearest male relation at present, so I vote that we call each other by our Christian names instead of Brookeing each other always."

"I shall be very glad to do so," Stanley said cordially. "I hope that we shall be close friends as well as distant relations."

Then, as there was a momentary lull in the conversation, Harry raised his voice and said to the colonel:

"A very curious thing has just happened, colonel. Brooke and myself have just discovered that we are cousins, and what is still more curious, that if anything happens to me he takes my place as next heir to my uncle, a fact of which he was entirely ignorant."

"That is certainly a very curious coincidence, Brooke; very singular. Then you have not met before?"

"I did not even know of his existence, colonel, and had indeed no idea that Captain Brooke, his father, had been married. The cousinship is a distant one, but there is no question whatever as to his being next in succession to myself to the peerage."

The discovery excited general interest, and quite turned the conversation for the time from the subject of the war and of their approaching advance. After dinner was finished many of the officers gathered round Stanley asking him questions about the nature of the country, and his experiences as a captive in the hands of the Burmese. Presently Colonel Adair, who had also dined at the mess, joined the group.

"I suppose, Mr. Brooke," he said, "your newly-found cousin has told you about his adventure with the leopard."

"No, colonel, he has not said anything about a leopard."

"He is grievously afflicted with modesty," the colonel went on, "and so I will tell it for him, for I think you ought to know that he is not only able to speak half a dozen languages, but that he is capable of doing deeds of exceptional gallantry. You can go and chat with the colonel, Brooke; he is anxious to hear your report as to the country, and I will be your trumpeter here."

Stanley gladly moved away, and entered into conversation with the colonel of the 47th, while Colonel Adair related his adventures with the leopard to his cousin and the officers standing round.

"By Jove, that was a plucky thing!" Harry Brooke said admiringly.

"It was indeed!" the colonel agreed, as similar exclamations went round the circle. "I don't think one man in a hundred would have attacked a leopard with no weapon but a knife, except to save the life of a comrade; even then it would be a most desperate action. I have done a good deal of big-game shooting in India, but I am certain that nothing but a strong affection for a comrade in the grasp of a leopard would induce me to risk almost certain death in the way your cousin did. We should never have heard of it if we had not got the details from the man he saved, and who has since attached himself to him as a servant, and is the man who, as I daresay he did tell you, served as his companion and guide in making his way down here. At any rate you see, Brooke, your cousin is an uncommonly fine young fellow, and you have reason to be proud of the relationship."

"I feel so, colonel, and it is really a pleasure to know that, if one does go down, a thoroughly good fellow will benefit by it, instead of some unknown person who might be a very objectionable representative of the family."

For the next three or four days the bustle of preparations went on, and on the fifth a detachment was sent up with a sloop and gun-boats to attack an advanced position of the enemy on the Lyne river. Although the 3000 Burmese, who were posted in a strong stockade, were supported by thirty-six guns, the works were carried by storm with little loss. The two branches of the Pellang or Rangoon River, by which the force were to advance against Donabew, were on the following day reconnoitred for some distance. A number of fire-rafts were destroyed, but the Burmese were too disheartened to offer any resistance.

To the disappointment of the troops, the general was able to take with him only a limited force, for the difficulties of carriage were enormous, and as experience had shown that the country was likely to be deserted and devastated on their approach, it was therefore impossible for the bulk of the army to be taken on by land.

There were other points, however, where the troops left

behind could be profitably employed; the capture of the important town of Bassein on the main branch of the Irrawaddy would open the river to the passage of our ships, and put an entire stop to the trade of Ava.

The force told off for the advance against Donabew was divided into two columns. The first, 2400 strong, consisting of the 38th, 41st, and 47th Regiments, three native battalions, the troop of body-guard, a battery of Bengal horse artillery, and part of the rocket company, was to march by land. The second column, which was to proceed by water, was 1169 strong, and it consisted of the 89th Regiment, the 10th Madras Europeans and 250 of the 18th Native Infantry, a body of dismounted artillery, and the rest of the rocket company.

This force was commanded by Brigadier-general Cotton. It was to be carried in a flotilla of sixty-two boats, each armed with one or two guns, and the boats of all the ships of war at Rangoon under the command of Captain Alexander, R.N. Major Sale was, at the same time, to advance against Bassein with 600 men of the 13th Regiment and the 12th Madras Native Infantry, with some artillery. After occupying the town he was to cross the country lying between the two main arms of the Irrawaddy, and to join the general's force near Donabew. The rest of the force—nearly 4000 men, chiefly native regiments and Europeans who had not as yet recovered sufficient strength to take part in field operations—was to remain at Rangoon, under Brigadier-general M'Creigh, who was to form a reserve column, in readiness to move as directed as soon as sufficient transport was collected

It was to the water force that the capture of Donabew was intrusted, as it lay upon the opposite bank of the Irrawaddy, while the general's force was directed against Tharawa, at the junction of the two main branches of the river. Here they were to be joined by General Cotton's force after the capture of Donabew; then, unless the court of Ava sued for peace, a united advance was to be made on the important town of Prome.

CHAPTER XI.

DONABEW.

STANLEY BROOKE did not accompany the land column, as the general said to him two days before, " I have been speaking with General Cotton, and he said that he should be glad if I would attach you to his staff until the force unites again. Not one of his staff officers speaks Burmese, and although he has two or three interpreters with him, it will be better, if Bandoola sends in an officer offering to surrender, that he should be met by a British officer. In the next place, it may be necessary for him to communicate with me, and assuredly, with your experience of the country, you would be able to get through better than any one else. I do not apprehend that there would be any great danger, for we know that every available fighting man has been impressed by Bandoola, and the passage of our column will completely cow the villagers lying between us and the river. I suppose," he said with a smile, "that you have no objection, since it will save you a long, and, I have no doubt, a very unpleasant march, and you will also obtain a view of the affairs at the stockades at Pellang and Donabew."

The land column started on the 13th of February, the water column on the 16th, and the detachment for Bassein sailed on the following day. Stanley was delighted at being appointed to accompany the boat column. The march through the country would present no novelty to him, and it was probable that the land column would encounter no serious resistance until, after being joined by General Cotton's force, it advanced against Prome. His horses went with those of General Cotton and his staff, under charge of the syce and Meinik. The one steam-boat kept at the start in rear of the great flotilla of boats, so that in case of any of them striking on a sand-bank, it could at once move to her assistance and pull her off.

The scene was a very bright one, as in all upwards of a hundred craft of various sizes proceeded together. In front were half a dozen gun-boats, next to these came the two sloops of war, followed by the rest of the boats, proceeding in irregular order. There was very little stream, for the rivers were now quite low, and although the flat country was still little more than a swamp, the rains in the hills that supplied the main body of water to them had long since ceased. The ships' boats were, of course, rowed by the blue-jackets. The other craft were, for the most part, manned by natives, though the soldiers on board occasionally lent a hand. Two days after starting the boats destroyed three newly-erected stockades that were found unoccupied, and on the 19th reached Pellang, where three very strong stockades had been erected. A battery was thrown up next day, from which, as well as from the steam-boat and sloops of war, shells were thrown into the stockade with such effect that two of the enemy's works were evacuated as soon as the troops took the offensive, and the main Pellang stockade was also abandoned without resistance. The two smaller works were destroyed, and a portion of the 18th Madras Infantry was left here to maintain communication with Rangoon.

On the 27th the flotilla entered the main stream, and the next day the advance came in sight of Donabew. It was another five days before the whole force was in position, for several of the most heavily laden craft stuck fast on the sand-banks at the fork of the river. The next day Donabew was summoned to surrender. Bandoola, who was at the head of 15,000 men, returned a refusal which was given in courteous terms, differing very widely from the haughty and peremptory language in which all previous communications had been couched. The next day a party of the 89th landed on the low-lying ground between the main stockade and the river, and, in spite of the heavy fire, succeeded in ascertaining the strength and nature of the defences. The main work was in the form of a parallelogram, about a mile long, and stood on ground rising above the general level, and fifty pieces of cannon of various sizes were in position on the river face. Two outworks, constructed of square beams of timber, with an outer ditch, and a thick abbatis, defended the southern face against an attack from an enemy landing below it. It was necessary to leave a strong guard on board the flotilla, lest an attack should be made by war-canoes and fire-rafts; the general, therefore, had not more than 600 men available for the assault.

As the enemy's guns completely commanded the river, it was necessary to land below it, and on the morning of the 7th the troops were disembarked, with two six-pounder guns and a rocket detachment. Forming in two columns they advanced against the lower of the two covering stockades, and after an exchange of fire with the enemy rushed forward and forced an entrance into it, although the enemy resisted with more resolution than they had for some time shown. 280 prisoners were taken, and the rest of the defenders fled to the second work. Two more guns and four mortars were landed and placed in position, and after the stockades had been shelled for a short time, a storming party, under Captain Rose, advanced to the assault. So heavy a fire was opened upon them that the little column was brought to a stand-still and forced to fall back, with the loss of its commander and of Captain Cannon of the 89th, while most of the seamen with the storming-party were either killed or wounded.

This want of success against a mere outwork showed General Cotton that, with the small force at his disposal, it would be worse than useless to renew the attack, for were the outwork carried the loss would be so great that it would be hopeless to think of attacking Bandoola's main position. He therefore determined to abstain from further attack until reinforced.

"Now, Mr. Brooke," he said, as soon as the troops had

been taken on board the boats again, "I must bring your services into requisition. This is just the contingency that we thought might possibly occur. I cannot advance up the river until Donabew is taken, and I cannot attack the place with the force at my command. Therefore I will at once write a despatch to General Campbell for you to carry. You will be accompanied by the two men of the body-guard who have come with me as orderlies. I shall have no use for them here, and three of you together need not fear any molestation from the few people remaining in their villages, and may be able to cut your way through any of the bands of deserters or beaten troops dispersed over the country."

"Very well, general. I shall also take my Burman on my second charger; he may be useful in getting news as to roads from the natives, who will as likely as not fly into the jungle when they see us approaching. However, there is not much fear of our losing our way, as it will be along the river as far as Tharawa."

A boat was at once sent off to the craft carrying the two orderlies, and the horses of the staff. As soon as the despatch was written, Stanley, after shaking hands with his companions, was also rowed to the horse-barge. This was, at a signal of the general, taken in tow by the steamer and piloted to the opposite bank. A boat sounding ahead presently found a spot where there was enough water for the barge to get alongside the bank. The horses were led ashore, and Stanley, the two troopers, and Meinik mounted.

The Burmese are poor riders, but during the wet season Stanley had often taken Meinik on his spare horse when riding about in the camp, partly because he could trust him to look after the horses carefully, and in the second place to accustom him to ride on horseback so as to act, if required, as an orderly. Meinik was quite of opinion that there would be no risk whatever in passing through villages, but thought it probable that they might fall in with disbanded troops, as it was known that the land column had, soon after starting, captured the fort of Mophi, and that its garrison, between two and three thousand strong, had taken to the jungle and dispersed.

"Still, master," he said, "I don't think it likely that they will attack us. They will be expecting no one, and we shall come upon them by surprise; then they will run into the bushes, thinking that you must have many more troops behind you. No, it is not likely that they will have many guns; they would throw them away when they fled, partly to run faster through the forest, partly because most of them will be making off to the villages, hoping to lie concealed until the war is over; while if they had guns in their hands it would be known that they were deserters, and they might be seized and sent across the river to Bandoola or up to Prome."

They rode some fifteen miles before dark, and then took up their quarters in a village. The few old men, women, and children inhabiting it fled at their approach; but when Meinik went to the edge of the jungle and shouted out loudly that they need not fear, for that no harm would be done to any of them, and good prices would be given for food, two or three returned, and, finding the statements to be true, one of them went into the jungle again and brought the others back. Fowls and eggs were brought into the hut that Stanley occupied, and a good supply of grain for the horses was also purchased. Thus Stanley was able to avoid breaking into the small stock of provisions they had brought with them. The inhabitants of this part of Burma were a tribe known as Carians. They were the tillers of the soil, and were an industrious and hardy race. The country was so rich that they not only raised sufficient for their own wants, but sent large supplies of grain and rice to Ava. They were very heavily taxed, but, as a rule, were exempt from conscription. Nevertheless they had on the present occasion been forced to labour at the stockades, and in transporting food for the troops.

Their forest villages were small. They consisted of little huts erected either in trees shorn of their branches, or upon very strong poles; these abodes were only accessible by rough ladders, formed by nailing pieces of wood across the trees or poles. This was absolutely necessary on account of the number of tigers that infested the forest. The village where they had halted was, however, built upon the ground, but was surrounded by a strong stockade. The people assured Stanley that none of the fugitives from Mophi had come that way.

There had, they said, been many after Bandoola's defeat, but they had seen none of late. They declared that they had far greater fear of these than they had of the English, for that they plundered wherever they went, and if they could not obtain enough to satisfy their expectations, burnt the houses and often killed many of the inhabitants. The villagers volunteered to keep watch all night at the gate of the stockade, although they said that there was no fear of anyone approaching, as strangers could not find their way through the forest in the dark; and even could they do so the fear of tigers would prevent them from making the attempt. Stanley agreed to pay some of them to watch, but also stationed one of his own men as sentry, relieving him every three hours. An hour after they reached the village they saw one of the war-boats rowing rapidly up the stream, and had no doubt that it was bearing a message from Bandoola, saying that he had repulsed the attack of the British. Beyond hearing the howling of tigers in the forest Stanley passed the night undisturbed, except when he went to change the sentry; Meinik took his share of watching, and Stanley himself relieved him an hour before daybreak.

By the time the sun rose the horses had been fed and breakfast taken. After riding some miles the country became more open; cultivated fields succeeded the dense forest; the ground was higher, and little groups of huts could be seen wherever a small elevation rose above the general level. The change was very welcome, for they were able to travel faster, and there was less chance of their coming suddenly upon a party of the disbanded troops. Presently, just as they reached a larger village than usual by the river bank, a thick smoke arose from one of the houses, and they could hear female screams.

"Come on!" Stanley shouted to the three men riding behind him. "See that your pistols are ready to hand, and draw your swords."

This village was not, like the last, stockaded, being some miles away from the forest. As they dashed into it they saw some twenty Burmese. Two women lay dead in front of one house, and one of the men with a torch was about to fire another. Absorbed in their own doings the Burmese did not notice the coming of the horsemen until the latter were close to them, then, with a cry of consternation, they turned to fly, but it was too late. Stanley cut down the man who was about to fire the hut, and he and the others then fell upon the Burmans with sword and pistol. Six of them were killed, the rest were pursued, but dashing down to the river they plunged in, pistol shots being sent after them. Stanley remained on the bank until he saw that they had fairly started to cross the river, then he re-entered the village. Two or three frightened people came out from their hiding-places when Meinik shouted to them that all was safe.

"They have all gone," he said, "you need not fear being disturbed by them again. See, there are six guns lying in the road, and you will find plenty of ammunition on those fellows that have fallen. There are some spears and swords, too. Of course you can do nothing if a number of these fellows come, but if there are only two or three, you and the women ought to be able to dispose of them. Now we must ride on."

On the third day they arrived at Tharawa, and found that Sir A. Campbell, who had been assured by the natives that Bandoola had retreated, had continued his march the day before. The place was so large that Stanley thought it unsafe for them to sleep there, and they rode on to a little village two miles away. Here they were received with great deference, the passage of the troops the day

"STANLEY CUT DOWN THE MAN WHO WAS ABOUT TO FIRE THE HUT."

SCYLLA

before having profoundly impressed the villagers. After waiting three hours to rest the horses, they again mounted, and, riding all night, arrived in the morning at Yuadit, a village twenty-six miles from Tharawa, and found the force on the point of starting.

"No bad news, I hope, Mr. Brooke?" the general said as he rode up to him.

"I am sorry to say, sir, that my news is not good. Here is the brigadier's despatch."

"This is unfortunate indeed," the general said when he had run his eye over the document. "Mr. Tollemache, please to ride along the line and say that the column is not to get into motion until further orders."

Colonel Adair and the other officers of the staff had been on the point of mounting when Stanley rode up. The general called two or three of the senior officers to him.

"Cotton can neither take Donabew nor get past it," he said. "Here is his despatch. You see he has lost several officers and a good many men, and that in the assault on an out-lying work only. I am afraid that there is nothing for us to do but go back to his assistance."

"I am afraid not, sir," Colonel Adair said. "Our supplies are running short already, and you see we decided upon filling up all the carts at Tharawa, where we made sure that we should be met by the boats. The country round here has been completely stripped, and it would be a very serious matter to endeavour to advance to Prome without supplies. Moreover, we might expect a much more serious resistance than we have bargained for. The news that Bandoola has repulsed his assailants—and you may be sure that this has been exaggerated into a great victory—will restore the spirit of the Burmese. It is evident that we must turn back and finish off with Bandoola before we advance further."

Orders were accordingly sent to the officers commanding the various corps that the column was to retrace its steps, and while they passed through the village, Stanley related in much greater detail than had been given in the despatch, the events of the attack and the nature of the defences at Donabew.

The troops marched along with a cheerful mien. It was of course an annoyance to have to plod back along the road they had before traversed, but upon the other hand there was a general satisfaction that they were after all to take part in the capture of Bandoola's last stronghold. Colonel Adair rode on with the little troop of cavalry. He was to push forward to Tharawa, and was to offer rewards to the natives there for every boat brought in. There was little doubt that many of the fishermen had hauled up their craft into clumps of bushes and brush-wood to prevent their being requisitioned by Bandoola, and although it was not likely that a large number would now be obtained, yet even if but a dozen were found it would be of assistance. The rest of the force reached Tharawa on the following evening, with the exception of a party left to protect the slow-moving wagons. They found that nine canoes had been obtained, and that a considerable portion of the scanty population had been all day employed in cutting bamboos and timber for rafts.

The next morning the troops were all engaged on the

same work, and in the construction of rafts, and at nightfall three hundred men of the 49th were taken across the river to the town of Henzada, in case Bandoola, on hearing of the preparations for crossing, should send a force to oppose the passage. It took four days' continuous labour to get the little army across, as it was necessary to make large timber rafts to carry the carts, horses and bullocks, guns and stores. Hearing that a force was posted some fifteen miles away to intercept the detachment that was marching from Bassein, Colonel Godwin with a party was sent off that night to endeavour to surprise it. The Burmese, however, took the alarm before they were attacked, and scattered in all directions without firing a shot. The army marched along the right bank, and arrived before Donabew on the 25th of March. Communications were opened with General Cotton's force below the town, and both divisions set to work to erect batteries.

The Burmese made several sorties to interrupt the work, and one of these was accompanied by Bandoola's seventeen elephants. The troop of cavalry, horse artillery, and the rocket company charged close up to the elephants, and opened fire upon the howdahs filled with troops that they carried. In a short time most of these and the drivers were killed, and the elephants, many of which also had received wounds, dashed off into the jungle, while the infantry fled back into the stockade, into which a discharge of shells and rockets was maintained all day. The next morning—the 1st of April—the mortar batteries were completed, and these and others armed with light guns kept up a continuous fire into the enemy's camp. At daybreak on the 2nd the heavy guns of the breaching batteries also opened fire, and in a very short time the enemy were seen pouring out in the rear of their works and making their way into the jungle. As there had been no idea that they would so speedily evacuate the stockade, no preparations had been made for cutting them off, and the garrison therefore effected their escape with but little loss.

The troops at once occupied the work, and found large stores of grain and ammunition there as well as a great number of guns. From some of the wounded Burmans it was ascertained that the evacuation of the fort was due to the death of Bandoola, who had been killed by the explosion of a shell while watching the operations from a look-out that had been erected for him at the top of a lofty tree. His death had caused the most profound depression among the garrison; their leaders in vain endeavoured to reanimate their courage, the opening of the fire with the heavy guns completed their discomfiture, and they fled without thought of resistance. Indeed, the greater part had stolen away during the night.

A portion of the fleet had already passed up beyond the fort under a heavy fire, and the rest now came up. The supplies of grain were renewed, and a guard being left to hold the works, which would now serve as a base, the army again started up the river, the water column proceeding to Tharawa, the land force marching back to Henzada, whence they were carried across the river in the boats. Here the force was joined by the reserve column from Rangoon, consisting of several companies of the Royals and the 28th Native Infantry, with a supply of elephants and carriage cattle which had arrived from Calcutta. On the 14th Yuadit was again reached. No opposition whatever was encountered, indeed the whole country was deserted, the inhabitants having been ordered away by the Burmese authorities as soon as the fall of Donabew was known. When within four days' march of Prome, two native officials came in with a communication to the effect that the Burmese were ready to treat for peace. As it was known, however, that reinforcements were on their way down from Ava, it was evident that this was merely a pretext to gain time, and the general sent word that when he arrived at Prome he would be ready to open negotiations for peace.

The country through which the army was now passing was very beautiful. In the far distance on the left the mountains of Aracan could be seen, while on the right the country was undulating, richly cultivated, and broken by clumps of timber, with a background of the range of hills running along near the Pegu River. On the 24th the heights of Prome, eight miles away, were visible, and the flotilla could be seen lying at anchor a short distance below the town. Messengers came out that afternoon to endeavour to induce the general not to enter it, but a reply was sent that this was out of the question, that no harm would befall the inhabitants, and that as soon as he entered, the general would be ready to receive any persons qualified to treat for peace.

Some hours before daybreak the army marched forward, and by sunrise were close to the town. The position was found to be extremely strong. Every hill commanding the place had been fortified to the very summit, strong stockades ran in every direction, and it was evident that a great number of men must have been engaged for a long time in attempting to render the place impregnable.

Not a soldier, however, was to be found. A native of the place presently met them with the news that the governor and troops had evacuated it, with the exception of a small party who were firing the town. This story was corroborated by wreaths of smoke rising at various points. The troops pressed forward at the top of their speed; on entering the town they found that the native population had all been forced to leave, and piling their arms, they set to work to extinguish the flames, which they did not, however, succeed in doing until nearly half the town was destroyed. Fortunately the fire was checked before it reached the great magazines of grain and other stores for the army.

The belief that the negotiations had been only pretexts to arrest the advance of the troops against the town until the expected reinforcements arrived was confirmed by the natives, who presently came in from hiding-places where they had taken refuge until their army retired. They said that as soon as the news came of the fall of Donabew, fresh levies were ordered to be collected in every part of Upper Burma, while the whole population of the province had been employed in adding to the defences of the town, which had been already very strongly stockaded.

It was a disappointment to the force, which had hoped that the occupation of Prome would bring about the submission of the court of Ava, and enable them to be taken down the river in boats, and embark before the rainy season again set in. Nevertheless the prospect of passing that season at Prome was vastly more pleasant than if it had to be spent at Rangoon. They were now inland beyond the point where the rains were continuous. The town was situated on high ground, and the country round was open and healthy. Although for some little distance round the cattle had been driven off and the villages destroyed, it was certain that flying columns would be able to bring in any amount of cattle before the wet season began.

For a short time it was thought that the occupation of Prome would show the king and court that it was useless to continue the struggle any longer, but these hopes were dissipated when it was known that a further levy of 30,000 men had been called out. The court, however, was apparently conscious that its commands would no longer be obeyed with the alacrity before manifested. The early levies had obeyed the call with cheerfulness, believing in their invincibility, and confident that they would return home laden with spoil, after driving, without difficulty, the audacious strangers into the sea. Things, however, had not turned out so. The troops that had left Ava in high spirits had been routed with very heavy losses. Their great general, Bandoola, had been killed, and fugitives from the army were scattered over the land, bearing with them reports of the extraordinary fighting powers of these white enemies, and of the hopelessness of attempting to resist them. The consequence was that in issuing the order for the new levy, a bounty of twenty pounds, which to the Burmans was a very large sum, was offered to each man who obeyed the call.

The first step on the part of the British general was to send proclamations through the country guaranteeing protection to all, and inviting the population to return to their towns and villages. The troops were employed in erecting, with the assistance of as much native labour as could be procured, comfortable huts outside the town, so that the natives on returning should find their homes unoccupied and untouched. It was not long before this excellent policy had its due effect. As soon as those who first returned sent the news to their friends, the fugitives came out from their hiding-places in the forests in great numbers and returned to the city. Those whose homes were still standing, settled down in them and resumed their ordinary avocations, just as if their native rulers were still in authority, while those whose houses had been burned set to work, with a cheerfulness characteristic of their race, to re-erect their light wooden dwellings.

So favourable were the reports spread through the country of our conduct that in a short time the population of Prome was considerably larger than it had been before the advance of our army. Similar results were speedily manifest throughout the whole district below the town. From the great forest that covered more than half of it, the villagers poured out, driving before them herds of cattle, and in two or three months the country that had appeared a desert became filled with an industrious population. Order was established; the local civil officers were again appointed to their former posts, but their powers of oppression and intimidation were abrogated by the order that no punishment beyond a short term of imprisonment was to be inflicted on any person whatever until the case had been brought before the British authorities, and soon the only fear entertained by the people of the rich district of the lower Irrawaddy was that the British troops would march away and leave them again to the oppression and tyranny of their former masters.

The markets of Prome were abundantly supplied with food of all sorts, and as everything was liberally paid for any number of bullocks were obtainable; for although the Burmese are forbidden by their religion to kill cattle, and therefore keep them only for draught purposes, they had no objection to our killing them, or indeed to eat the meat when they could obtain it. Labour of all kinds was abundant, and great numbers of canoes were constructed for the purpose of bringing up supplies from the villages on the river, and for the advance of the force at the end of the wet season. Until this set in in earnest, small bodies of troops marched through the forests, driving out the bands that infested them and plundered and killed the country people without mercy. The general's aides-de-camp had a busy time of it, being constantly employed in carrying orders to the towns and villages, in hearing complaints, and, in Stanley's case, entering into agreements for the purchase of cattle and grain.

When in Prome he spent a good deal of his spare time with his cousin, who, having bought a horse, frequently obtained leave to accompany him on his excursions on duty. A warm friendship had sprung up between them. Harry was two years older than Stanley, and had been at Eton up to the time that he entered the army. He was, however, in manner no older than his cousin, whose work for the three years previous to the outbreak of the war had rendered him graver and more manly than a life spent among lads of his own age could have done. Meinik always accompanied Stanley wherever he went. He had now, to the latter's quiet amusement, modified his Burmese costume, making it look like that of some of the whites, and indeed he would have passed without notice as one of the Goa-Portuguese mess waiters in his suit of white nankeen. When riding, or on any service away from the headquarters camp, he was dressed in a suit of tough brown *khaki* which he had obtained from one of the traders at Rangoon. The coat differed but little from that of the suit Stanley had handed over to him except that it was somewhat shorter and without the small shoulder cape, and in fact resembled closely the modern regimental tunic. Below he wore knee-breeches of the same material, with *putties* or long bands of cloth, wound round and round the leg, and which possessed many advantages over gaiters. He still clung to the turban, but instead of being white, it was of the same colour as his clothes, and was much larger than the Burmese turban.

"Burmese are great fools," he often said to Stanley. "They think they know a great deal; they know nothing at all. They think they are great fighters; they are no good at fighting, for one Englishman beats ten of them. Their government is no good—it keeps everyone very poor and miserable. You come here; you know nothing of the country, and yet you make everyone comfortable. We ride through the villages; we see every one rejoicing that they are governed by the English, and hoping that the

English will never go away again. What do you think, sir—will you stay here always? You have had much trouble to take the country; a great many people have been ill; a great many died. Now you have got it, why should you go away again?"

"It is quite certain that we shall not give it all up, Meinik. It has been, as you say, a troublesome and very expensive business; and the farther the king obliges us to go up before he makes peace the more he will have to pay, either in money or territory. Of course I cannot say what the terms of peace will be; but I should think that very likely we shall hold the country from the sea up to here, with Aracan and a strip along the sea-coast of Tenasserim."

"That will be good," Meinik said. "I shall never go outside the English land again. There will be plenty to do, and a great trade on the river; every one will be happy and contented. I should be a fool to go back to Upper Burma, where they would chop off my head if they knew that I had been down to Rangoon when the English were there."

CHAPTER XII.

HARRY CARRIED OFF.

EARLY in September Stanley was sent to purchase cattle from some of the villages near the foot of the hills, and at the same time to make inquiries as to the movements of a large band of marauders who had been making raids in that neighbourhood. He had with him four troopers of the body-guard; Harry Brooke accompanied him. Although from the healthier situation of Prome the amount of illness during the wet season did not approach that which had been suffered at Rangoon, a great many men were in hospital, and there were many deaths. Harry had had a sharp attack of fever, and as he had now recovered to a certain extent, the medical officer of his regiment strongly recommended that he should have a change; and he therefore without difficulty obtained his colonel's leave to accompany Stanley, as the ground would be much higher than that on the river, and the mere fact of getting away from a camp where so many deaths took place every day would in itself be of great value.

Stanley's daily journeys were not likely to be long ones, as he had instructions to stop at all villages, and to see how things were going on, and whether the people had any complaints to make of oppression and exaction by their local authorities.

"It is a tremendous pull your being able to speak the language, Stanley," Harry said. "If it hadn't been for that, you would have been stuck at Prome like the rest of us. Instead of that you are always about, and you look as fresh and healthy as if you were at a hill station in India."

"Yes, it has been an immense advantage to me in all ways. Of course I should never have got my staff appointment if it had not been for that. By the way, I have not told you that while you were down with the fever the gazette containing the confirmation of my appointment by the general and the notice of my commission, dated on the day of my appointment, came out. I had quite a lump sum to draw, for although I have been paid as interpreter all along, the paymaster made a difficulty about my pay as a subaltern until I was gazetted regularly; so I have quite a large sum coming to me on my pay and allowances. I don't know how you stand for cash, but if you are short at all I can let you have anything that you want."

"I have got really more than I know what to do with, Stanley. I bought an uncommonly good native horse, as you know, six weeks ago, and I am going to ride him for the first time now, but, really, that is almost the first penny that I have spent since we left Rangoon. There is nothing to buy here except food, and of course that is a mess business. I had an idea that this was a rich country, but so far one has seen nothing in the way of rich dress materials, or shawls, or carpets, or jewelry that one could send home as presents. Why, in India I was always being tempted; but here it is certainly the useful rather than the ornamental that meets the eye.

"I saw some nice things at Ava; but, of course, all the upper classes bolted as we came up the country, and the traders in rich goods did the same. Are you going to take a servant with you, Harry? I don't think that there is any occasion to do so, for Meinik can look after us both well enough."

"Yes, I am thinking of taking my native, the man I hired just after I got here. He is a very good fellow, and made himself very useful while I was ill. I picked up a *tat* for him yesterday for a few rupees. I know that your man would do very well for us both; but, sometimes, when you make a village your head-quarters and ride to visit others from it, I may not feel well enough to go with you, and then he would come in very handy, for he has picked up a good many words of English. Your man is getting on very well that way."

"Yes; he was some time before he began, for, of course, he had no occasion for it; but now that he has taken to what he considers an English costume, and has made up his mind that he will never settle down again under a Burmese government, he has been trying hard to pick up the language. I found that it was rather a nuisance at first, when, instead of telling him what was wanted in his own language, I had to tell him in English, and then translate it for him. However, he does understand a good deal now, and whenever he has nothing else to do he is talking with the soldiers. Of course, from his riding about so much with me, he is pretty well known now; and as he is a good-tempered, merry fellow he makes himself at home with them, and if the campaign lasts another six months I think he will speak very fair English."

"I fancy that you will have to make up your mind that he is a permanency, Stanley; I am sure he intends to follow you wherever you go, whether it is to England, India, or anywhere else."

"I sha'n't be sorry for that, Harry; certainly not as long as I am out here. In the first place he is really a very handy fellow, and ready to make himself useful in any way; then there is no doubt that he is greatly attached to me, and would go through fire and water for me. A man of that sort is invaluable to anyone knocking about as I shall be when the war is over and I take up trading again. His only fault is that he is really too anxious to do things for me. Of course when I am on duty there is nothing much he can do, but if I am sitting in a room he will squat for hours in the corner and watch me; if my cheroot gets low there he is with a fresh one and a light in a moment; if I drop my handkerchief or a pen, there he is with it, before I have time to stoop. Sometimes I have really to invent errands to send him on, so as to give him something to do for me. I own that I have not contemplated what position he would occupy if I go trading, but I quite recognize that he will go with me, and that he would become a portion of my establishment, even if that establishment consisted only of himself. Will you be ready to start at four in the morning? The sun is tremendously hot now on the days between the rain; at any rate it will be much better for you, till you get your strength, to travel in the cool of the morning or in the evening."

"I shall be ready. I will be round here with my servant by that hour. By the way, what shall I bring with me?"

"Nothing at all; I shall take a couple of chickens and some bread and coffee and sugar, and a bottle of brandy for emergencies; but we shall have no difficulty in getting food in the villages. The troopers will only carry their day's rations with them; after that I always act as mess caterer, and charge expenses when I get back here."

Accordingly the next morning they started at four o'clock. Stanley insisted that Harry should ride his second horse for the present, as his own, having been six weeks without exercise, and fed very much better than it had been accustomed to, was in much too high spirits to be pleasant for an invalid. Meinik, therefore, took Harry's, and the latter rode beside his cousin, whose horse had had abundant exercise, and was well content to canter quietly along by the side of his companion. By the end of ten days Harry had picked up some of his strength; they now reached a village which Stanley decided to use as his head-quarters for a few days, while he made excursions to other places within a day's ride. It was a good place for a halt, standing as it did at some height on the hills, where the air was much cooler at night than in the flat country. It was surrounded by a clearing of about a hundred acres in extent, planted with cacao-trees, pepper, and many kinds of vegetables.

"This is delightful!" Harry said, as they sat in front of the hut that had been cleared for them and looked over the plain. "It must be twenty degrees cooler here than it was at Prome. I think I shall do nothing to-morrow, Stanley, but just sit here and enjoy myself. I know it is very lazy, for I am feeling quite myself again; still, after ten days' riding I do think that it will be pleasant to have a day's rest."

"Do, by all means," Stanley said. "I think you had better stay here for the three days that we shall remain. Your man is a very good cook, and there is no lack of food. Those chickens we had just now were excellent, and the people have promised to bring in some game tomorrow. There are plenty of snakes, too, and you lose a good deal, I can assure you, by turning up your nose at them. They are just as good as eels, as Meinik cooks them, stewed with a blade of cinnamon and some hot peppers. I cannot see that they can be a bit more objectionable to eat than eels; indeed, for anything one knows, the eel may have been feasting on a drowned man the day before he was caught, while the snakes only take a meal once a week or so, and then only a small bird of some kind."

"I dare say that you are quite right, Stanley, and I own that the dishes your man turns out look tempting; but I cannot bring myself to try, at any rate as long as I can get anything else to eat. If I knew that it was a case of snake or nothing I would try it, but till then I prefer sticking to birds and beasts."

The next morning Stanley rode off with two of his escort and Meinik, who declined altogether to be left behind.

"No, master," he said, "there is never any saying when you may want me, and what should I ever say to myself if misfortune were to come to you and I were not to be there?"

Stanley had a long day's work. As a rule the villagers had few complaints to make, but at the place he went to on this occasion the head-man had been behaving as in the old times, and Stanley had to listen to a long series of complaints on behalf of the villagers. The case was fully proved both as to extortion and ill-treatment. Stanley at once deprived the man of his office, and called upon the villagers to assemble and elect another in his place.

"If you are not satisfied," he said to the fellow, "you can go to Prome and appeal to the general there; but I warn you that if you do you must give notice to the villagers of your intention, so that they may, if they choose, send two or three of their number to repeat the evidence that they have given me. I have noted this fully down, and I can tell you that the general, when he reads it, will be much more likely to order you a sound flogging than to reinstate you in your office."

It was dusk when Stanley arrived within two miles of the village where he had left Harry. Meinik, who was riding just behind him, brought his horse up alongside.

"Do you see that, sir? There is a light in the sky. It is just over where the village is. I am afraid there is a fire there."

"You are right, Meinik. I hope nothing has gone wrong." He touched his horse with his heel, and rode on at a gallop. He became more and more anxious as he approached the village. No flames could be seen leaping up, but there was a dull glow in the sky. As he rode into the clearing he reined up his horse in dismay. A number of glowing embers alone marked the place where the village had stood, and no figures were to be seen moving about.

"There has been foul play, Meinik. Get ready for action, men," he said to the two troopers, and they dashed forward at a gallop. Two or three little groups of people were sitting in an attitude of deep dejection by the remains of their houses.

"What has happened?" Stanley shouted as he rode up.

"The robbers have been here, and have slain many and burned the village."

"Where is my friend?"

"They have carried him off, my lord; or at least we cannot find his body. His servant and one of the soldiers are lying dead, but of the other soldier and the officer there are no signs."

"This is terrible!" Stanley exclaimed. "Tell me exactly how it happened."

"It was four hours ago, my lord. The robbers came suddenly out from the plantation and fell upon the people. Many they killed at once, but many also have escaped as we did, by running in among the plantations, and so into the forest. We heard the firing of guns for a little time, then everything was silent, and we knew that the robbers were searching the houses. Half an hour later smoke rose in many places, and then flames; then after a time all was quiet. A boy crept up among the bushes, and came back with the news that they had all gone. Then we came out again. Twenty-three of our people had been killed, and eight carried off, at least we cannot find the bodies; the white officer and one of his soldiers have gone also."

"Which way did they go?"

"The tracks show that they went up the hill. Most likely they will have gone to Toungoo if they have gone to any town at all; but indeed we think they have taken the prisoners to get a reward for them."

Stanley had thrown himself off his horse as he rode up, and he stood for some time silently leaning against it. Then he said to Meinik:

"Picket the horses, and then come and have a talk with me." Then he turned to the two troopers: "There is nothing to be done now," he said. "You had better look about and see what you can find in the way of food, and then get a grave dug for your comrade and another for Mr. Brooke's servant."

The two Mahommedan troopers saluted, and led their

horses away. Meinik, after picketing the animals, returned to Stanley, but, seeing that the latter was pacing up and down and evidently not disposed to speak, he went away. There were a good many fowls walking about in a bewildered way near the huts. They had been away as usual searching for food in the plantations and fields when the robber band arrived, and on their return home at dusk had found everything changed. A boy at once caught and killed two of these, plucked them and brought them to Meinik, who, getting some embers from the fires, cut the fowls in two and put them on to roast. A few minutes sufficed to cook them. As soon as they were ready Meinik took them to Stanley.

"You must eat, master," he said. "You have had nothing since we started this morning, and sorrow alone makes a poor supper. You will want to do something, I know, and will need all your strength."

"You are right, Meinik. Yes, give me one of them, and take the other one yourself, and while we eat, we can talk. Of course I must make an effort to rescue my cousin from the hands of this band."

"Yes, master, I knew that you would do that."

"Did you ask how many there were of them, Meinik?"

"Some say forty, some say sixty."

"If we knew where they are now, and could come up to them, we might manage to get them off while the robbers were asleep."

Meinik shook his head. "They are sure to keep a strict guard over a white officer," he said; "but if we rushed in and shouted and fired pistols they might all run away."

"I am afraid not, Meinik. There might be a scare for a minute, but directly they saw that there were only two of us they would turn and kill us. Your people are brave enough; they may feel that they cannot stand against our troops owing to our discipline, but they fight bravely hand-to-hand. However, we don't know exactly which way they have gone, and it would be hopeless to search for them in the forest during the darkness. What should they go to Toungoo for?"

"I have been thinking it over, master, and it seems to me that many of them may belong there or to the villages near. They may not dare return to their homes, because they are afraid that they would be punished for having left the army, and would certainly be sent off again to it. Now they may think that if they go back with a white officer and soldier, and tell some story of having beaten a great many English, they will be rewarded, and may even be able to remain some time in their homes before they are sent off, or they may be ordered to march with their prisoners to Ava, where they would get still more reward. I can see no other reason for their carrying off the officer."

"I think very likely that is so, Meinik. Anyhow we are more likely to rescue my cousin at Toungoo than we should be while on the road. It would be next to impossible to find them among all the hills and trees, and even if we did come upon them at night, and could creep into the midst of them, we might find that my cousin is too severely wounded to travel, for, as there was a fight, it is almost certain he must have been wounded before he was captured. Therefore, I think it is best to make straight for Toungoo. How many miles is it from here, do you think?"

Meinik went over to the natives and asked the question. "About forty-five miles, they say; very bad travelling; all mountains, but ten miles to the north is a road that runs straight there."

"Then we had better follow that, Meinik. In this broken country and forest we should be losing our way continually."

"How will you go, master? On horse or foot?"

"We will go on horseback as far as we can; we are not likely to meet people travelling along the road at present. Another thing is that, if we can get the horses as near the town as possible, they would be very useful, for if Mr. Brooke has been wounded badly he may not be able to walk far. You do not know whether the country near the town is open or whether the forests approach it closely."

The natives were again applied to.

"It is a rich country there, they say, and well cultivated for five or six miles round the town."

"I will go and have a talk with them presently. It will, of course, be necessary for me to disguise myself again."

Meinik nodded. "Yes, you must do that, master."

"Do you think that we can get two or three men to go with us from here?"

"If you will pay them, master, no doubt they will be ready to go. They are well content with the white rulers. They find that they are not oppressed, and everything is paid for, and that the white officers treat them kindly and well. They have lost many things in this affair to-day, and would be glad to earn a little money. How many would you like to have?"

"Four or five, Meinik. I don't exactly know at present what there would be for them to do, but they could help to make fires and keep watch while we are doing something; at any rate, they may be useful. Of, course I shall get the trooper out too if I can. Very likely they will be confined together, and if we rescue one we can of course rescue the other. Now I must do some writing. Get me a torch of some sort and I will do it while you are speaking to the natives."

Stanley always carried a note-book and pen and ink to take down statements and complaints as he rode about. He now sat down and wrote an account of what had taken place during his absence.

"We had no previous news of the existence of the band," he went on, "and the natives themselves had certainly no fear of any attack being imminent. Had I thought that there was the slightest risk I should not have made the village my head-quarters, or have left Mr. Brooke there with only his servant and two troopers. I regret the matter most deeply, and am about to set off to Toungoo with my man. I shall, of course, go in disguise, and shall make every endeavour to free my cousin. I trust, general, that you will grant me leave for this purpose. I am, of course, unable to say how long it may take me; but, however long, I shall persevere until I learn that my cousin is dead or until I am myself killed. I trust that in starting at once, on the assumption that you will grant me leave, I am not committing a breach of duty. But if so, and you feel that you cannot, under the circumstances in which you are placed, grant leave to an officer to be absent on private business, I inclose a formal resignation of my commission, stating why I feel myself constrained, even in the presence of the enemy, to endeavour to rescue my cousin from the band that has carried him off. At any rate, it could not be said that I resigned in order to shirk danger. I sent off, two days ago, by one of the natives here, a report of my proceedings up to that date, and have now the honour to inclose the notes I took of my investigations to-day into the conduct of the head-man of Pilboora, and my reasons for depriving him of his office. I shall leave the two troopers of my escort here, with orders to remain until either I return, or they receive instructions from Prome. I am taking a few of the villagers with me. Should anything occur to me at Toungoo they will bring back the news to the troopers, and I shall leave instructions with them to carry it at once to you. If I find that Mr. Brooke has been sent on to Ava I shall, of course, follow and endeavour to effect his rescue on the road. As it is possible, general, that I may not have another opportunity of thanking you for the many kindnesses that you have shown me, allow me to do so most heartily now."

When Stanley had concluded the letter, and written the paper offering his resignation and giving his reasons for so doing, he called Meinik to him.

"Well, Meinik, have you found men willing to go with us?"

"Yes, master, I have got five men; two of them know

Toungoo well. All are stout fellows. I offered them the terms that you mentioned, fifty ounces of silver to each man if you succeeded by their aid in rescuing the officer. They were delighted at the offer, which would enable them to replace everything that they have lost. I told them, of course, that if it were necessary to fight they would have to do so, and that as many of their countrymen were enlisted as gun-lascars and in other occupations with the English, and are of course exposed to the attacks of their countrymen, they would only be doing what others have been willing to do. They said that they were ready enough to fight. You were the government now, and you were a good government, and they would fight for you; and, besides, as the officer was carried off from their village it was their duty to help to get him back. One of them said, 'These men who attacked us are Burmese soldiers. As they attack us there is no reason why we should not attack them.' So I think, master, that you can count upon them. The Burmese have always been fond of fighting, because fighting means booty; the troops don't want to fight any more, because they get no booty, and a number of them are killed. But now that the villagers have been forced to go to the war against their will, and have been plundered and many killed by Burmese soldiers, they are quite ready to take sides with you. Three of them have had wives or children killed to-day, and that makes them full of fight."

"Well, you had better tell them to cook at once food for two or three days. At four o'clock they are to start through the forest to the road you spoke of. We will set out at the same time on horseback, but we shall have to make a detour, so they will be on the road before we are. Tell them when they get there to stop until we come up."

"Yes, master. It is a good thing that I rode your second horse yesterday instead of Mr. Brooke's animal."

"Yes, he is worth a good deal more than the other, Meinik, and I should certainly have been sorry to lose him."

"One of the men who is going with us says that he knows of the ruins of an old temple eight or nine miles this side of Toungoo, and that this would be a good place for us to leave our horses. It is very very old, one of those built by the people who lived in the land before we came to it, and the Burmans do not like to go near it, so that there would be no fear of our being disturbed there. Even these men do not much like going there, but I told them that no evil spirits would come where white men were."

"It is rather far off, Meinik, but as you say the country is cultivated for some distance round the town, we shall certainly have to leave our horses some six or seven miles away, and two or three miles will not make much difference. We can put on our disguises there. You had better take a couple of boys to look after the horses while we are away."

"They would not sleep there at night," Meinik said doubtfully. "I don't think the men would either, if you were not there."

"That would not matter, Meinik, if, as you say, there is no fear of anyone else going there."

"Certainly, no one else will go there at night, master."

"At any rate if you can get two boys to go we may as well take them. They might go there in the day and feed and water the horses, and sleep some distance away at night."

Meinik found two boys sixteen years old, who said that they would go with them, and at the hour agreed on Stanley and Meinik started on horseback. They descended the hill to the plain at its foot, and, turning to the right, rode for some ten or twelve miles, when they struck into the road, and following this at an easy pace they came in the course of another hour upon the party of villagers sitting by the roadside. The sun was just rising, and they travelled for three hours without meeting anyone; then they drew off into the wood at a point where a small stream crossed the road, and, after eating a meal, and giving a good feed to the horses, lay down to sleep till the heat of the day abated, the natives, who were all armed with spears and swords, keeping watch by turns. At four o'clock they started again, and at ten approached the spot where, in the depth of the wood, lay the temple. The man who knew its position declared, however, that he could not find it at night. Stanley had no doubt that he was really afraid to go there, but as he did not wish to press them against their will, he said carelessly that it made no difference if they halted there or close by the road, and, a fire being speedily lit, they bivouacked round it. Meinik had procured the necessary dyes from a village, and Stanley was again stained, and covered with tattoo marks, as before.

"What am I to do about your hair, master?" he asked. "It will never do for you to go like this."

Stanley had not thought of this point, and for a time was completely at a loss. His own hair was now short and could not possibly be turned up.

"The only thing that I can see," he said after a long pause, "is for you and the men each to cut off a lock of hair from the top of your heads where it will not show. The six locks would be ample; but I don't see how you are to fasten it below the turban."

"There are berries we can get wax from," Meinik said. "We boil them in water, and the wax floats at the top. With that, master, we could fasten the hair in among yours, so that it would look all right."

The men had all laughed at the proposal, but willingly consented to part with a portion of their hair. Meinik therefore proceeded to stain Stanley's close crop black, and the first thing in the morning the boys went out, soon returning with a quantity of berries. Some water was poured over them in an earthenware pot and placed over the fire, and in half an hour a thick scum of oil gathered on the surface. Meinik skimmed it off as fast as it formed, and as it cooled it solidified into a tenacious mass somewhat resembling cobblers' wax. The six locks of hair had already been cut off, and the ends were smeared with the wax and worked in among Stanley's own hair; then a little of the hot wax was rubbed in, and the men all declared that no one would notice anything peculiar in his appearance. The long tresses were curled round at the top of the head and a ring of muslin tied round. The Burmans were immensely amused at the transformation that had been wrought in Stanley's appearance, and followed him through the wood to the temple without any signs of nervousness.

The ruins were extensive. A considerable portion of the building had been hewn out of the face of a precipitous rock in the manner of some Hindoo temples; and it was evident that it had been the work of a people more closely allied to the Indian race than to the Tartar or Chinese people, from whom the Burmese sprung. Uncouth figures were sculptured on the walls. At these the Burmese looked with some awe, but as Stanley laughed and joked over them, they soon recovered their usual demeanour.

"I am a great deal more afraid of tigers than of ghosts," Stanley said, "a deserted place like this is just the sort of spot they would be likely to be in. At any rate, if these caves do not go any further into the hill, and there are no signs of their doing so, it may be hoped that the tigers have their superstitions about it too. At any rate, it will be a good thing to pile a great quantity of firewood at the entrance; and I think one of you had better stay here with the boys. They and the horses would be a great deal safer here, with a fire burning, than they would be in the woods, where a tiger might pounce upon them at any moment. As to this folly about spirits, it is only old women's chatter."

The Burmese talked among themselves, and one of the men finally agreed to stay with the boys. An hour was spent in gathering a pile of brushwood and logs, and the man said that he and the two boys would gather plenty more during the day. They were, at four o'clock, to take the horses down to the river, a mile distant, and let them drink their fill. They had brought with them a large bag of grain, which had been carried by the men, a quantity of plantains, and some fowls. Therefore, the party that were to remain would be well provided. Moreover, in collecting the wood a score of snakes had been killed. Some of these and a chicken had been cooking while they were at work, and as soon as this was eaten they started for the town. When they came within a mile of it Stanley entered a plantation of fruit-trees, and Meinik and the four men went on. They returned in two hours with the news that a party of ten men had arrived in the town on the previous day with two prisoners. One, a coloured man, had been able to walk; the other, a white man, had been carried in on a litter. They had both been lodged in the jail.

By this time the conduct of the English towards the natives at Rangoon and the territory they occupied had had one good effect. Signally as they had been defeated by them, the Burmese had lost their individual hatred of the strangers. They knew that their wounded and prisoners always received kind treatment at their hands; and although the court of Ava remained as arrogant and bigoted as ever, the people in Lower Burma had learned to respect their invaders, and the few prisoners they had taken received much better treatment than those who had been captured at the commencement of the war.

As soon as it was dusk Stanley went with Meinik into the town. It was a place of considerable size, with buildings at least equal to those at Prome. Toungoo had formed part of the kingdom of Pegu before it had been subdued by the Burmese. The peculiar and characteristic facial outline of the latter was here much less strongly marked, and in many cases entirely absent; so Stanley felt that, even in daylight, he would pass without attracting any attention. The prison was surrounded by a strong and high bamboo fence, and in the space inclosed by this were eight or ten dwellings of the usual wooden construction. A dozen armed men were seated by a fire in the yard, and two sentries were carelessly leaning against the gate.

"There should be no difficulty in getting in there with two rope-ladders—one to climb up with, and one to drop on the other side," Stanley said. "You may be sure that most of the guard go to sleep at night. The first thing to ascertain is which house the prisoners are kept in, and in the second place how my cousin is going on. We can do nothing until he is able to walk for a short distance. Let us move round to the other side of the inclosure. It may be that a sentry is posted at their door."

On getting to the other side and looking through the crevices between the bamboos, they could make out two figures squatted by the door of one of the houses, and had no doubt that this was the one in which Harry Brooke was confined.

"Now, Meinik, the first thing is for you to go and buy a rope. When the place gets quite quiet we will make a loop and throw it over the top of the palisade behind that hut, then I will climb up and let myself down inside, and then crawl up to the hut and see what is going on there. If my cousin is alone I will endeavour to speak to him, but of course there may be a guard inside as well as at the door. If he is very ill there will probably be a light."

"Let me go, master!"

"No, Meinik, I would rather go myself. I shall be able to judge how he is if I can catch a sight of him."

CHAPTER XIII.

PREPARING A RESCUE.

STANLEY remained where he was until Meinik returned in half an hour with the rope. Stanley made a loop at one end, and then knotted it at distances of about a foot apart to enable him to climb it more easily. Then they waited until the guard-fire burnt down low, and most of the men went off into a hut a few yards distant, three only remaining talking before the fire. Then Stanley moved round to the other side of the palisade, and, choosing a spot immediately behind the hut where the sentries were posted, threw up the rope. It needed many attempts before the loop caught at the top of one of the bamboos. As soon as it did so, he climbed up. He found that the position was an exceedingly unpleasant one. The bamboos were all so cut that each of them terminated in three spikes, and so impossible was it to cross this that he had to slip down the rope again. On telling Meinik what was the matter, the latter at once took off his garment, and folded it up into a roll two feet long.

"If you lay that on the top, master, you will be able to cross."

This time Stanley had little difficulty. On reaching the top he laid the roll on the bamboo spikes, and was able to raise himself on to it and sit there, while he pulled up the rope and dropped it on the inside. Descending, he at once began to crawl towards the hut. As he had seen before climbing, a light was burning within, and the window was at the back of the house. This was but some twenty yards from the palisade, and when he reached it he stood up and cautiously looked in. The Indian trooper was seated in a chair asleep, without his tunic. One arm was bandaged, and a blood-stained cloth was wrapped round his head. On a bamboo pallet, with a dark rug thrown over it, was another figure. The lamp on the wall gave too feeble a light for Stanley to be able to make out whether the figure lying there was Harry, but he had no doubt that it was so. In a low tone he said, in Hindustani, "Wake up, man!" The soldier moved a little. Stanley repeated the words in a somewhat louder tone, and the trooper sprang to his feet, and looked round in a bewildered way.

"Come to the window," Stanley said; "it is I, your officer."

The man's glance turned to the window; but, surprised at seeing a Burmese peasant, as he supposed, instead of the officer, he stood hesitating.

"Come on," Stanley said. "I am Lieutenant Brooke."

The soldier recognized the voice, drew himself up, made the military salute, and then stepped to the window.

"I have come," Stanley said, "to try and rescue Lieutenant Brooke and yourself. I have some friends without. How is he?"

"He is very ill, sir. He is badly wounded, and is unconscious. Sometimes he lies for hours without moving, sometimes he talks to himself, but as I cannot understand the language I know not what he says; but sometimes he certainly calls upon you. He uses your name often. I do what I can for him, but it is very little. I bathe his forehead with water, and pour it between his lips. Of course he can eat nothing, but I keep the water my rice is boiled in, and when it is cool give it to him to drink. There is some strength in it."

"Then nothing can be done at present," Stanley said. "To-morrow night I will bring some fruit. You can squeeze the juice of some limes into a little water, and give it to him. There is nothing better for fever. As soon as he is well enough for us to get him through the palisades, we will have a litter ready for him, and carry him off; but nothing can be done until then. How are you treated?"

"They give me plenty of rice, sahib, and I am at liberty to go out into the court-yard in the daytime, and now that I know that you are near I shall have no fear. I have been expecting that they would send me to Ava, where, no doubt, they would kill me; but I have thought most that if they were to send me away from here, and there was no one to look after the sahib, he would surely die."

At this moment Stanley felt a hand roughly placed on his shoulder. Turning round, he struck out with all his strength full in a man's face, and he fell like a log.

"If they ask you who was here," he said hastily to the trooper, "say that you know not who it was. A Burmese came and spoke to you, but of course you thought that he was one of the guard."

Then he ran to the rope, climbed up, and as he got over pulled it up, and threw it down to Meinik, as he thought that there might be some difficulty in shaking it off from the bamboo, then he dropped to the ground, bringing down the pad with him.

"Did you kill him, master?" Meinik asked as they hurried away. "I was watching the window and saw you talking to someone inside; then I saw a man suddenly come into the light and put his hand upon you, and saw you turn round, and he fell without a sound being heard."

"There is no fear of his being killed, Meinik. I simply hit him hard, and he went down, I have no doubt, stunned. It is unfortunate, but though they may set extra guards for a time I think they will not believe the man's story; or at any rate will suppose that it was only one of the guard, who, not being able to sleep, wandered round there and looked into the hut from behind. The worst of it is that I am afraid that there is no chance of my being able to take my cousin some limes and other fruit to-morrow night, as I said I would. He is very ill, and quite unconscious."

"That is very bad, master; I will try and take him in some fruit to-morrow. If they won't let me in I will watch outside the gates, and when one of the guard comes out will take him aside, and I have no doubt that for a small bribe he will carry in the fruit and give it to the trooper. I wonder that they put them into that hut with the window at the back."

"I don't suppose they would have done so if my cousin had not been so ill that it was evident that he could not for some time attempt to escape."

They joined the villagers outside the town, and telling them that there was nothing to do that night, returned to the temple. They found the man and the two boys sitting by a great fire, but shivering with terror.

"What is the matter?" Stanley asked.

"The spirits have been making all sorts of noises outside, and there are other noises at the end of the cave, close to the horses."

Stanley took a brand and went over to them. They were both munching their grain quietly.

"Well, you see the horses are not frightened; so you may be sure that whatever were the noises you heard, there was nothing unnatural about them. What were they like?"

The question was not answered, for at that moment a sound like a loud deep sigh was heard overhead. The natives started back, and even Stanley felt for a moment uncomfortable.

"It is only the wind," he said. "There must be some opening above there, and the wind makes a noise in it just as it does in a chimney. We will see all about it in the morning. Now as to the noises outside."

"They were wailing cries," the man said.

"Pooh! they must have been tigers or leopards, or perhaps only wild-cats. No doubt they smelt you and the horses, but were too much afraid of the fire to come any nearer. Why, you must have heard tigers often enough to know their cries."

"I thought myself that they were tigers," the man said rather shamefacedly, "but the boys said they were certain that they were not, and I was not sure myself one way or the other."

Sitting down by the fire, Stanley told the men the exact position of the prisoners, and said that he feared it would be altogether impossible to get Harry out for the present.

"I would give anything to have him here," he said; "but it would be impossible to get him over the palisade."

"We might cut through it, master," Meinik said; "with a sharp saw we could cut a hole big enough in an hour to carry his litter out. The only thing is, we could not get his bed through that window."

"We might get over that by making a narrow litter," Stanley said, "and lifting him from the bed on to it. The difficulty would be, what to do with him when we got him out; as to carrying him any distance in his present state it would be out of the question; besides, the guard are sure to be vigilant for some considerable time. I think that the best plan would be for you all to go back to your village to-morrow, taking the horses with you, and for one of you to come over every other day for orders. Then there would be no occasion for anyone to watch the horses; they certainly will be of no use to us at present, for it will be weeks before my cousin is strong enough to ride. Meinik and I will take up our abode close to the edge of the forest, for that will save us some four or five miles' walk each day. The first thing in the morning you shall go with me and choose a spot, so that you may both know where to find us. Two of you have got axes, and we will make a shelter in a tree, so as to be able to sleep without fear of tigers when we go out there, though I dare say that we shall generally sleep near the town. However, one or other of us will always be at the spot at mid-day on the days when you are to meet us. Now that I think of it, two of you may as well stay at the shelter for the present while the other three and the two boys go home. Then there will be no occasion to take the long journey so often. When we do get my cousin out we shall have to take up our abode for a time either here or in the forest, until he is well enough to bear the journey."

In the morning Stanley closely examined the roof of the cave, but could see no opening to account for the noise that he had heard. He had, however, no doubt that one existed somewhere. He left a man with the two boys in charge of the horses, and went with the others until they approached the edge of the forest. They kept along within the trees for half a mile, so that any fire they might light would be unseen by people travelling along the road. The men considered this precaution needless, as they declared that no one would venture to pass along it after nightfall, partly owing to the fear of tigers, and partly to the vicinity of the temple. A suitable tree was soon fixed on, and the Burmese, now in their element, ascended it by driving in pegs at distances of two feet apart. Once among the high branches they lopped off all small boughs that would be in the way, and then, descending, cut a number of poles and many lengths of tough creeper, and with these they constructed a platform among the higher branches, and on it erected a sort of arbour, amply sufficient to hold four or five people lying down. This arbour would hardly be noticed even by persons searching, as it was to a great extent hidden by the foliage beneath it. Stanley told Meinik that they had better buy some rope for a ladder, and take out the pegs, as these might catch the eye of a passer-by, and cause him to make a close search above.

As soon as the work was finished two of the men went

back to the temple to start at once for home with their companion, the boys, and the horses. Stanley had brought with him his pistols, the two horse blankets, and other things that might be useful, and when these were stored above, he, with Meinik and the two men, went towards the town. He stopped, as before, a short distance outside. Just as it was dusk the men returned carrying the rope that Meinik had bought, and a store of food. With these they were sent to the shelter, and Stanley entered the town, where he met Meinik.

"I have sent in the fruit," the latter said; "I had no difficulty about it. I told the first soldier who came out after I had bought it that I came from the village where the white officer had been captured by the bandits. He had been very kind to us all, and as we knew that he had been carried off badly wounded, I had come over to get some fruit for him, but I found that they would not let me in at the gate. I said I would give an ounce of silver to him if he would hand the things to the prisoner for me. He said at once that he would do so. He had heard that the whites always treated their wounded prisoners very well, and that there would be no difficulty about it, for that there was a window at the back of the hut where he was lying, and he could easily pass things in there without anyone noticing it. If the prisoner was, as I said, a good man, it was only right that he should be helped. I told him that I should look out for him, and might want him to do the same another day. I think that he was an honest fellow, and might have passed the fruit in even without a reward. Still, everyone is glad to earn a little money. He told me that a strange thing had happened last night. One of his comrades had declared that he had found a giant standing at the window where the prisoner was. He put his hand upon him when he was struck down by lightning. No one would have believed his tale at all if it had not been that his nose was broken. The other prisoner had been questioned, but as he did not understand Burmese, they could learn nothing from him. Two guards were in future to be placed at the back of the house as well as in the front."

"That part of the business is bad, Meinik."

"I dare say we shall be able to bribe them, master. You may be sure that most of them are eager to get back to their own villages, and for a few ounces of silver they would be glad enough to help us and then to make their escape and go off to their homes. The man I saw to-day might find one among them ready to do so with him, especially if their homes happened to be on the other side of the hills; and there would then be no chance of their being seized and sent back again by their head-man. The sentry would only have to let us know what night he would arrange for them both to be on guard together behind the hut; then we should be able to manage it well."

"It would be a capital plan that, Meinik, if it could be arranged. Well, it is a great comfort to know that the fruit has got in safely; the limes especially will be a great help to my cousin. Next time you see the man you must try and get him to find out how he is going on."

For a fortnight Stanley remained in the forest. Meinik met the soldier every other day, and sent in fruit, and at the end of the ten days he heard that the prisoner had recovered his senses. It was said that as soon as he was well enough to move he was to be sent to Ava.

"Now you had better begin to sound the man as to his willingness to aid him to escape."

"I have very little doubt about it, master, for I have already learned that his home is on the other side of the hills. He went down with Bandoola, and returned after his defeat with a number of others, travelling up the bank of the Pegu river. If they had not had their military chief with them they would have started straight for home. But they were marched here, and have been kept on duty in the town ever since. He has heard how well off the people are on the other side of the hills under English rule; so I feel sure that he will be glad to escape if he sees a chance of getting off."

"That is good. In the first place, let him know that the other English officer who was at the village with the one they captured, had said that he would be ready to pay well any-one who would aid in his escape. If he says that he would willingly do so if he also could get away, tell him that one man would be of no use, but that if he could get another to join him, so that they could both go on guard together behind the house, it could be managed. But say that, in the first place, I must myself speak to the white officer, and learn exactly how he is, and whether he can endure a journey as far as this tree or the temple—whichever we may decide upon as best. When I have seen him I will send for the other men from the village. I am in no hurry to get him away, for the longer he stays quiet the better. But at any moment the governor may decide that he is sufficiently recovered to be carried, and may send him off to Ava under a strong escort. Therefore, although we will put off moving him as long as possible, we must not run the risk of his being sent away."

Four days later Meinik said that the man had arranged with another to join him, and that both would be on duty behind the hut that evening between nine and midnight. Accordingly at ten o'clock Stanley arrived with Meinik and the two villagers at the palisade. Meinik had insisted upon accompanying him to the hut.

"I believe that the man is to be trusted, master, indeed I am sure he is, but I do not know the second man. He may have pretended to accept the offer only on purpose to betray his comrade, and to obtain honour and reward for preventing the escape of the white man. Therefore, I must be with you in case you are attacked. Our other two men may be useful to give the alarm if a party is sent round to cut us off."

Stanley, who had brought a horse blanket with him to lay on the top of the palisade, was the first to drop into the inclosure. Meinik followed him closely. Nothing had been said to the guard as to the white officer, of whom Meinik had spoken, being himself of the party, and Stanley had purposely left his pistols behind him lest he should be tempted to use them. In case he was attacked he carried a spear and a long Burmese knife. Meinik had begged to be allowed to go forward first, while Stanley remained by the rope. He pointed out that some change might possibly have been made and that other men might have been placed on sentry.

"I know you, master," he said; "if you got there, and found two strangers, and they attacked you, you would fight; then they would give the alarm, and others would come up before you could cross the palisade. I shall steal up; when I am close I shall make a noise like the hiss of a snake. If my men are both there they will repeat the sound. If they are not, and one comes forward to look for and kill the snake, I shall slay him before he has time to utter a sound. If the other runs forward at the sound of his fall I shall kill him also. If no alarm is given you can come forward and speak to your cousin. If there is an alarm you must climb the rope. They will not know which way I have run, and I shall have plenty of time to get over the palisade and pull up the rope; then they will think that the guards have been killed by some of their comrades."

"I hope no such misfortune will happen," Stanley said gravely, "for there would then be no chance whatever of our getting him away. He would probably be moved to some other place, and our one hope would be that we might rescue him on the road, which would be a difficult matter indeed if he were sent, as he certainly would be, under a strong escort. However, your plan is no doubt the best, for if I were killed or captured there would be an end of any chance of his being rescued."

Meinik crawled forward, and in a minute or two Stanley heard a low hissing sound, followed by two others. He walked forward a step or two to meet Meinik as he came back.

"It is all right, master; you can go on fearlessly." Meinik returned with him to the window and posted himself outside, standing in the shadow, while Stanley stepped in through the open casement, which, indeed, was provided only with a shutter, outside. This would ordinarily have been closed; but owing to the illness of the prisoner and the strong desire of the governor that he should live to be sent to Ava, it had been opened to allow a free passage of air. The trooper sprung from his couch as Stanley made a slight sound before attempting to enter, but Stanley said in Hindustani, "Silence! it is I,—Mr. Brooke."

The trooper stared doubtfully at the dark, tattooed, half-naked figure.

"It is I, Runkoor, but I am disguised. I was like this when I spoke to you through the window a fortnight since, but you could not then see my figure. Are you awake, Harry?" he asked in English, as he approached the pallet.

"Yes, I am awake; at least I think so. Is it really you, Stanley?"

"It is I, sure enough, man," Stanley replied, as he pressed the thin hands of the invalid. "Did not Runkoor tell you that I had been here before?"

But Harry had broken down altogether; the surprise and delight was too much for him in his weak state.

"Of course," Stanley went on quietly, "I knew that he could not speak English, but I thought that he might make signs."

"He did make a sign. Each time he gave me fruit, he said 'Sahib Brooke', pointed outside, and waved his arms about, but I could not make head or tail of what he meant. Why he should keep on repeating my name each time he gave me the fruit was a complete puzzle for me; as to the signs that he made it seemed to me that he had gone off his head. I have been too weak to think it over, so I gave up worrying about it, and it never once struck me that it was you who sent me the fruit. What an awful figure you are?"

"Never mind about that, Harry. I have come in to see how strong you are. I have bribed the two guards stationed behind."

"I can just sit up in bed to take my food, Stanley, that is all; I could not walk a step to save my life."

"I did not expect you to walk. What I want to know is whether you are strong enough to be carried a few miles on a litter. I have five men from the village where we were, and they can cut through the palisading behind the hut. I want to give you as long a time as possible, but I am afraid that any day the governor may have you taken out and sent in a litter to Ava, under a strong escort."

"I could bear being carried out, no doubt, but if I could not, I should think it would do me no harm so long as my wounds do not break out afresh. I suppose the worst that could happen to me would be that I should faint before I got to the end of the journey. Are you sure, old man, that this is not a dream?"

"Quite certain; if you were well enough I would give you a sharp pinch. If you are willing to venture I will make my preparations at once. I have to send to the village, but in three days I shall be ready, and the first night after that the men manage to be on guard together behind, we shall be here. It may be a week, it may be more, but at any rate don't worry about it if they take you away suddenly. I shall try to get you out of their hands somehow."

"My dear Stanley," Harry said, with a feeble laugh, "do you know that you are spoiling your chance of an earldom."

"You may take it that if you don't succeed to the title, old fellow, I sha'n't, for if you go under I shall too. Now good-bye; it would be fatal were I to be caught here. Try to get yourself as strong as you can, but don't let them notice that you are doing so."

Without giving Harry time to reply, Stanley pressed his hand and left his bedside. He paused for a minute to inform the trooper of the plans for the escape, and then he got through the window. Meinik joined him at once, and without a word being spoken they crossed the palisade, threw down the rope and blankets, and dropped after them to the ground.

On their way back to their tree Stanley told the two men that the officer was better, and that the next morning at daybreak one of them must start for the village to fetch their three comrades. The boys were also to come back with him, as they were big fellows and carried spears, and might, as Stanley thought, be useful either in a fight or in assisting to carry Harry.

On the following morning after the man had started, Stanley went with Meinik to examine the temple more closely than he had done before. He thought that it would be a far better hiding-place than their hut in the tree. There would certainly be a hot pursuit, and the next day they might be discovered, whether in the temple or in the tree, but in the latter they would be powerless to defend themselves, for the Burmese with their axes would be able to fell it in a few minutes, whereas in the temple a stout defence might be made for a time; moreover, the rock chambers would be far cooler in the middle of the day than the hut.

His chief object in visiting the temple was to find a chamber with a narrow entrance that could be held by half a dozen men against a number of foes; and it was desirable, if possible, to find one so situated that they might, in case of necessity, retreat into another chamber, or into the open air. Meinik was so confident in the white man's power to combat even evil spirits that he approached the temple with Stanley without betraying any nervousness. They had provided themselves with some torches of resinous wood, and Meinik carried a couple of brands from their fire. The chamber they had before been in was apparently the largest in the temple, but there were several other openings in the rock.

"That is the entrance we will try first," Stanley said, pointing to one some ten feet from the ground. "You see there were once some steps leading up to it. No doubt where we are standing there was a temple built against the face of that rock, and probably that doorway led into one of the priests' chambers."

It was necessary to pile three or four blocks of stone on the top of the two steps that alone remained intact, in order to enable them to reach the entrance.

"Let me light the torches before you go in," Meinik said. "There may be snakes."

"That is hardly likely, Meinik. You see the face of the

rock has been chiselled flat, and I don't think any snake could climb up to that entrance."

"Perhaps not, master, but it is best to be ready for them."

They lighted two torches, and passed through the doorway. There was an angry hiss some distance away.

"That is a snake, sure enough, Meinik. I wonder how it got here."

Holding their torches above their heads, they saw that the chamber was some fourteen feet wide and twenty long. In the corner to the left something was lying, and above it a dark object was moving backwards and forwards.

"It is a big boa," Meinik said. "Now, master, do you take the two torches in one hand and have your knife ready in the other. If it coils round you cut through it at once. This is a good place for fighting it, for there is nothing here for it to get its tail round, and a boa cannot squeeze very hard unless he does that."

Stanley, feeling that in a combat of this sort the Burman would be perfectly at home, while he himself knew nothing about it, did as he was told, determining to rush in should it attack his follower.

"You can advance straight towards him, master; I will steal round. He will be watching you, and I may get a cut at him before he notices me."

Stanley moved slowly forward. As he did so the great snake moved its head higher and higher, hissing angrily, with its eyes fixed on the torches. Stanley did not take his gaze from it, but advanced grasping his knife. He knew that the boa's bite was harmless, and that it was only

"THE GREAT SNAKE MOVED HIS HEAD HIGHER AND HIGHER, HISSING ANGRILY."

its embrace that was to be feared. He was within some eight feet of the reptile, when there was a spring. The snake's head disappeared, and in a moment it was writhing, twisting, and lashing its tail so quickly that his eyes could hardly follow its contortions.

"Stand back, master," Meinik shouted. "If its tail strikes you it might do you an injury. It is harmless otherwise. I have cut its head off."

Stanley stepped back a pace or two, and stood gazing in awe at the tremendous writhing of the headless snake.

"It is a monster, Meinik," he said.

"It is a big snake, master. Indeed, I should say that it must be about forty feet long, and it is as thick as my body. It would be more than a match for a tiger."

"Well, I hope there are not many more of them about, Meinik."

"That depends, master; it may have its mate, but it is more likely there will be no other. It would eat any smaller ones of its own kind, of course, but there may be some small poisonous ones about."

As the writhing of the snake ceased, Stanley looked round and saw a narrow doorway in the corner opposite that in which it had been lying.

"Here is a passage, Meinik. Let us see where it goes to."

Meinik had by this time lighted two more torches.

"The more light the better," he said, "when you are looking for snakes;" and, holding them in one hand and his knife in the other, he passed through the doorway, which was about four feet high. Stanley followed him. The apartment was similar to the last, but narrower, and was lighted by an opening not more than a foot square.

"See, Meinik, there is a staircase in the corner facing us."

The steps were very narrow, but in perfect preservation. Without staying to examine the room, Meinik led the way up, examining every step carefully, and holding the knife in readiness to strike. They mounted some forty steps, and then entered a room about ten feet square. Except a window some eighteen inches by three feet, there was no apparent exit from the chamber.

"I should think that there must be some way out of this place, Meinik. Why should they have taken the trouble to cut that long flight of steps through the rock just to reach this miserable little chamber?"

Meinik shook his head. The ways of these ancient builders were beyond him.

"There must be an outlet somewhere, if we could but find it. Besides, we have not found where the snake came in yet."

"He could have come in at the door, master. A small snake could not have climbed up, but that big fellow could rear his head up and come in quite easily; we have found no little snakes at all."

"Well, that may be so, but I still think that there must be some way out from here. Why should men go to the labour of cutting this long stair and excavating this chamber here without any reason whatever? Let us look through the window, Meinik."

It was a passage rather than a window, for the rock face had been left four feet in thickness. Crawling out,

Stanley saw that he was fifty feet above the foot of the cliff; a yard below him was a ledge of rock some two feet wide, it was level, and had deep grooves cut at regular intervals across it. He had no doubt that the roof of the outside temple had started from this point, and that the grooves were made for the ends of massive rafters of teak or stone. At that time the passage to the chamber that he had left was doubtless used for an exit on to the flat roof. Stepping on to the ledge, he called Meinik to him. "Now, Meinik," he said, "we will follow this ledge; there may be some way up from it."

Walking with a good deal of care, Stanley made his way along to a point where the ledge stopped abruptly. Looking down, he saw the remains of a wall of solid masonry, and perceived that he had been correct in his surmise as to the purpose of the ledge. Then they turned and went back to the other end of the ledge. A few feet before they reached this Meinik, who was now leading the way, stopped.

"Here is a passage, master."

The entrance was about the same size as that through which they had stepped out on to the ledge, but instead of going straight in, it started upwards.

"Another flight of steps, Meinik. I am beginning to hope that we shall find some way out at the top. If we can do so, it will make us safe. We could defend those stairs and the entrance for a long time, and when we wanted to get away we could make quietly off without anyone knowing that we had left."

CHAPTER XIV.

IN THE TEMPLE.

THEY went up the flight of steps for a considerable distance; then they found the passage blocked by a number of great stones. Stanley uttered an exclamation of disgust.

"It has fallen in," he said. "No doubt we are near the top of the rock. Either the staircase was roofed in or there was a building erected over the entrance, and either the roof or building, whichever it was, has fallen in. That is very unlucky. When we go down we will climb up the hill and see if we can discover anything about it. With plenty of food and water," he went on, as they descended into the lowest chamber, "one could hold this place for any time."

"Yes, master, one could store away the food, but where should we store the water? We might bring skins in that would last us for a week, perhaps two weeks, but after that?"

"After that we should make our way off somehow, Meinik," Stanley said confidently. "Well, there is no doubt that this is the place to shelter in; they are less likely to find us here than anywhere, and if they do find us, we can defend ourselves stoutly. I should say, too, that if we think it over, we ought to be able to hit upon some plan for making noises that would frighten them. You know how scared the man and the two boys were at that sighing sound in the other chamber. We certainly could make more alarming noises than that."

Meinik nodded. "That we could, master. With some reeds of different sizes I could make noises, some as deep as the roar of a tiger, and others like the singing of a bird."

"Then we will certainly bring some reeds in here with us, Meinik. I don't suppose they will mind in the daytime what sounds they hear; but at night I don't think even their officers would care to move about here if we can but make a few noises they do not understand. Well, for the present we have done our work here, and you had best go off with the Burman to buy food to serve in case of a siege. You had better go to some of the cultivators' houses near the edge of the wood for rice and fruit; if you can get the food there you will be able to make two or three journeys a day instead of one. But before we start back, we will climb round to the top of the hill and see what has happened to shut up the staircase."

It took them a quarter of an hour's climbing through the forest and undergrowth before they reached the upper edge of the rock wall in which the chambers had been excavated. It had evidently, in the first place, been a natural cliff, for when on the ledge, Stanley had noticed that while below that point the rock was as smooth as a built wall, above it was rough, and evidently untouched by the hand of man. Following the edge of the cliff until standing as nearly as they could guess above the entrance to the steps, they walked back among the trees; at a distance of some thirty yards they came upon a ruin. It was built of massive stones, like those which strewed the ground where the temple had stood. A great tree rose on one side, and it was evident that its growth had, in the first place, overthrown the wall at this point; climbers and shrubs had thrust their roots in between the blocks that had been but slightly moved by the growth of the tree, and had in time forced them asunder, and so gradually the whole building had collapsed.

"This tree must be a very old one," Stanley said, looking up at it, "for it is evident that this wall was thrown down a great many years ago."

"Very old, master; it is one of our hardest woods, and such trees live, they say, five or six hundred years. There are some which are known to be even older than that."

"Well, it is clear that the staircase came up here, but we have no means of knowing how far the point we reached is below this. I should say that the stones we saw are the remains of the pavement and roof, for you see these great blocks that formed the walls don't go as far as the middle, where there is a great depression; still, of course, the steps may have come up on one side or the other, and not just in the middle of this little temple; for, no doubt, it was a temple. Now you see the reason for the steps up to that little square room are explained. Probably those three chambers were the apartments of the principal priests, and from them they could either go out on to the roof of the temple, or could, by taking the upper staircase to this point, leave or enter without observation. Now let us be off."

On arriving at their tree-shelter they found that the Burman had got a meal ready, and after partaking of this, Meinik, with the man, started to buy provisions. It was fortunate that Stanley had, before starting from Prome, drawn some twenty pounds' worth of silver from the paymaster. He had expected to be away for three or four weeks, and during that time would have had to buy provisions for himself, Harry, and the four troopers, and might possibly have occasion for money for other matters. He had not paid the men from the village; for he knew that one of these would willingly accompany him to Prome to receive payment for them all. A very small amount of silver sufficed for the purchase of a considerable quantity of food in Burma. Fruit, of which many kinds grew wild in the woods, was extremely cheap, as was rice and grain. Therefore, as yet, with the exception of the small sum expended in Toungoo, his money was virtually untouched.

The two Burmans made three journeys before nightfall, and returned each time with large baskets of fruit, grain, and rice. On the following morning they went into the town and bought six of the largest-sized water-skins, such as are carried for the use of the troops in India, one on each side of a bullock. As soon as they returned with these they started for the temple. At a stream about a hundred yards from the entrance they partially filled one of the skins, and placing a strong bamboo through the straps sewn on it for the purpose, Meinik and the Burmans carried it to the temple, and, with Stanley's assistance, lifted it into the lower chamber. The others were one by one placed beside it, then water was carried in the smaller skins and poured in until they were all as full as they could hold.

"There is water enough to last us for a month, if needs be," Stanley said, as, after securely tying up the mouths, they laid the skins down, side by side. The smaller mussucks were then filled and placed with the large skins, and then, having done a long day's work, they returned to their tree just as the sun was setting. The four men and two boys were already there, they having done the sixty miles from the village without a halt. They had already cooked some rice and some slices of venison, which Meinik had brought with the water-skins from the town that morning, and were now lying smoking their cigars with placid contentment.

For the next six days Meinik went to the town every afternoon. On his return on the last evening he said that the guard had told him that the governor had paid a visit to the prison that day and had seen the white captive, and had decided that he was now well enough to travel, and that in two days' time he was to start for Ava, the court having sent down an urgent order that he should be carried there as soon as he was well enough to bear the fatigue.

"Then to-morrow we must get him out," Stanley said. "Will our two men be on duty?"

"Yes, master, they have not been on since the last night we were there. They will form the second watch, and will go on guard at midnight. I have bought two very sharp saws, and have cut two strong bamboos for the litter."

This was constructed the next day. It was very simple, being formed by sewing a blanket strongly to the two bamboos. Two slighter bamboos, each four feet long, were tied loosely to the main poles. These were to be lashed across as soon as they had got beyond the palisade, so as to keep the poles three feet apart, which, as the blanket was four feet from pole to pole, would allow it to bag comfortably. The cross pieces could not be attached until they were beyond the palisade, for the window was but two feet wide, and it was therefore proposed to make the gap through the palisade the same width only. Late in the evening they entered the town and sat down in a deserted corner until the time came for them to begin their work. At last Meinik said that, by the stars, it was already past midnight, and they then proceeded to the spot where they had before climbed the palisade. Here they at once set to work. The saws were well oiled, and in a very few minutes five bamboos were cut away at the level of the ground and six feet above it; as the stockade was bound together by cross pieces behind, the other portions of the bamboos remained in their places. Meinik and Stanley went first, followed by three of the Burmans, one of whom carried the litter. The other two Burmans with the boys remained on guard at the opening.

All were barefooted, except that Stanley wore a pair of the lightest leather sandals. They went noiselessly up to the window, the guard as before responding to Meinik's hiss. Without a word one after another entered the chamber. The trooper had been sitting at the table, evidently anxiously expecting their arrival. Stanley went up to the bed.

"Are you better, Harry?" he asked in a whisper.

"Better, but still weak."

Everything had been arranged beforehand. The litter was laid down on the ground, with the poles as far apart as possible. Then Stanley made a sign to the trooper to take one end of the rug on which Harry was lying, while he took the other. The Burmans ranged themselves on each side, and the blanket was lifted up with the occupant and the pillow composed of his clothes, and laid quietly on to the blanket of the litter. Then two Burmans went outside while the other four men lifted the poles and carried one end to the window. The Burmans outside held the ends well above their heads, Stanley and the trooper raising their hands similarly. The other Burmans then crawled under it out of the window. As the litter was moved forward through the window, they took the places of Stanley and the trooper at the poles and silently moved on towards the palisade. Stanley and Meinik followed, joined by the two Burmese guards. Not the slightest sound was made as the eight men crossed the short distance to the palisade and passed through the opening, where the others, spear in hand, were awaiting them, ready to rush in and take part in the fray should an alarm be given. Stanley breathed a great sigh of relief as they passed out; a few paces further they halted and the cross pieces were lashed to the poles.

"Thank God that you are out, Harry!" Stanley said, as soon as they did this. "Has it hurt you much?"

"Nothing to speak of," Harry replied; "you managed it marvellously. Am I really outside the place altogether?"

"Yes, fairly out. You will be more comfortable when we have lashed these cross pieces; you will not be lying then at the bottom of a bag, as you are now."

When the work was completed, they proceeded at a rapid pace, for Harry's weight, reduced by fever as he had been, was a trifle to his bearers. The others followed close behind, and in a quarter of an hour they were well beyond the town. Stanley spoke to Harry once or twice but received no answer; so he had no doubt that his cousin had dozed quietly off to sleep. The gentle motion of the litter would be likely to have that effect, especially as Harry had probably been lying awake for the last night or two, listening for the friends who might arrive at any time.

When they reached the confines of the forest the torches, which had been carried by the boys, were all lit, and each carried two, with the exception of the bearers, who had but one each, while all kept close together round the litter. They waved their torches as they went; and although they heard the cries of several tigers in the forest, they had no fear of being attacked, as so many waving lights would deter the most hungry beast from venturing near.

Once in the chamber at the temple the litter was laid down on a pile of reeds and leaves, that had been gathered the day before, together with a great store of brushwood and logs, Harry still sleeping quietly. In a short time a bright fire was blazing, and with this and the light of the torches the chamber assumed quite a cheerful appearance. On the way Stanley had spoken to the two guards, thanked them for their service, and assured them that they would receive the reward promised by Meinik.

"I am the British officer," he said, "who was at the village with my friend, though I was absent when he was carried off. As you see, I am disguised."

Both had shown signs of uneasiness when they approached the temple, but Meinik had assured them that the spirits would not venture to approach a party having a white man with them, and that a night had already been passed in the temple without any harm coming of it. A meal, consisting of slices of venison, was at once prepared, and when this was eaten, and the whole party had lighted cigars, their spirits rose at the success of the enterprise. The soldiers, however, had been disappointed at hearing that there was going to be a stay for some little time there, to enable the wounded man to gain strength.

"We may not stop long," Stanley said; "but, you see, with the litter we could not travel fast, and you may be sure by this time the alarm has been given, for when they came to relieve you at the end of three hours it would be found that you were missing, and then they would at once discover that the captives had gone too. By daybreak the whole garrison will be out. How many are there of them?"

"There are three thousand men in the town," the guard said. "After a party of your soldiers came within a short distance of it two months ago, fifteen hundred men were added to the garrison."

"Well, you see, with three thousand men they could scour all the woods, and if they overtook us we should be unable to make any defence. Here we may hope that they will not discover us, but if they do we can make a desperate resistance, for, as only one man can enter that door at a time, it would be next to impossible for them to force their way in. You have your guns, and I have a brace of pistols, and as all the others have spears, it will be as much as the three thousand men could do to get in through that door. If they did, there is a still narrower door in the corner to defend, and beyond that there is a long, narrow, steep flight of stairs that one man could hold against a host. The first thing in the morning, we will carry our stores to the upper chamber. We have water and rice enough to last us for a month if we are careful, so that, although I hope they won't find us, I shall not be at all afraid of our beating them off if they do so."

As soon as it was daylight the stones that had been added to the steps at the doorway were flung down, and then by their united efforts the two remaining steps were removed. Then they helped each other up, the last man being aided by two of his comrades above.

"There," Stanley said; "if they do come to search for us they are not likely to suspect that we have got a badly wounded man up here. They may search the big chamber that we were in before, and any others there may be on the same level; but this narrow entrance, ten feet above them, is scarcely likely to attract their attention. If it does, as I said, we must fight it out, but it will be a wonderfully hard nut for them to crack."

He then ordered the men to carry all the stores to the upper chamber. Just as they began the work there was a slight movement on the bed. Stanley at once went up to it. Harry was looking round in a bewildered way.

"Well, Harry, how are you feeling? You have had a capital sleep."

"Oh, is it you, Stanley? I was not quite sure but that I was dreaming. Where am I? I must have gone off to sleep directly we started, for I don't remember anything after you spoke to me when they were making the hammock more comfortable."

"You are in a temple some four or five thousand years old, I should say, and this is a rock chamber. The temple itself is in ruins. We are ten miles from Toungoo, and shall wait here till the pursuit for you has slackened. In another week you will be more fit to move than you are at present. I should not like to carry you far as you are now; besides, if we had pushed on, they would have been sure to overtake us, for these fellows can run like hares."

"But why should not they find us here, Stanley?"

"Well, of course, they may do so, but the entrance to this chamber is ten feet above the ground; and another thing is, they have all sorts of superstitions about the place. Nothing would induce them to approach it after nightfall, and even in the daytime they don't like coming near it. Lastly, if they do find us, it will take them all their time to force their way in. I have five men and two young fellows quite capable of fighting; then there are your two guards, Meinik, the trooper, and myself; so you see we muster twelve. We have two guns and a brace of pistols, and spears for us all, and if we cannot defend that narrow passage against any number of Burmans, we shall deserve our fate. Besides, there is another and even narrower door in the corner behind you. They would have to force that, and in the chamber beyond there is a narrow, straight staircase, some forty feet high, which a man with an axe ought to be able to hold against an army. They are taking the stores up there now. We have got provisions and water for a month. When everything is straight there we shall carry you up, and unless they sit down in front of this place and regularly starve us out, we are as safe as if we were in Prome."

"I wish to goodness you had that hideous dye off you, Stanley. I know it is you by your voice, but what with the colour and all that tattooing and your extraordinary hair, I don't know you in the least."

"I am in just the same disguise as that in which I made my way down from Ava," Stanley laughed. "I felt very uncomfortable at first with nothing on but this short petticoat thing, but I have got accustomed to it now, and I am bound to say that it is cool and comfortable. Now, tell me about your wounds."

"They are not very serious, Stanley. I had a lick across the head with a sword,—that was the one that brought me down,—and a slice taken out of my arm from the elbow nearly up to the shoulder; also a spear-wound in the side; but that was a trifle, as it glanced off the ribs. If I had been left as I fell, and somebody had bound up my wounds at once, I should have been all right by this time. The fellows did bandage them up to some extent, but the movement of the litter set them off bleeding again, and I fancy that I lost pretty nearly all the blood in my body. I think that it was pure weakness rather than fever that kept me unconscious so long, for I gathered from the pantomime of the trooper that I must have been nearly a fortnight unconscious."

"Yes; you were certainly so when I came the first time, Harry; but I think, perhaps, on the whole, it is lucky that you were. You would probably have had a great deal more fever if you had not been so very weak; and if you had escaped that and had gone on well, you might have been sent off to Ava before I could get all the arrangements made for your escape."

"Tell me all about it," Harry said; "it seems to me wonderful how you managed it."

Stanley told him the whole story. By the time that he had finished the stores had all been taken upstairs, and the fire most carefully extinguished, as the smoke would at once have betrayed them. The cross pieces of the litter had been taken off to allow Harry to be carried in through the door, and he was now lifted. Two of the men took off their cloths and wrapped the materials of the bed into these, carrying them up at once. As soon as they had gone on, Harry was slowly and carefully taken to the upper chamber and laid down again on the bed. Stanley took his place beside him, and the rest of the party went down to the lower room having received the strictest orders not to show themselves near the entrance, and not to smoke until well assured that their pursuers must have passed on ahead. The bamboos of the litter were converted into a rough ladder, and on this Meinik took his post at the little window in the second of the lower rooms. Owing to the immense thickness of the rock wall he did not get an extensive view, but he could see the path by which anyone coming up through the forest would approach the temple.

It was now about half-past seven, and by this time the pursuers might be at hand; in ten minutes, indeed, distant shouts could be heard, and Stanley at once went down and joined the men below. He placed himself in the line of the doorway; as the wall here was four feet thick, the room was in semi-darkness, and, standing well back, he was certain that his figure could not be perceived by anyone standing in the glare of sunshine outside. The sounds grew louder and louder, and in a minute or two an officer, followed by some twenty men, emerged from the trees. All paused when they saw the temple. The men would have drawn back at once, but the officer shouted to them to advance, although showing small inclination to do so himself. They were still standing irresolute when a superior officer on horseback, followed by some fifty footmen, came up the path.

He shouted orders for them to search the temple, and as the fear of him was even greater than their dread of the spirits, the whole of the men made their way over the fallen stones and up to the face of the rock. They first entered the chamber where the horses had been stabled. The officer who had first arrived went in with his men, and, coming out, reported to his senior that there had been a fire made and that some horses had also been there, but that three weeks or a month must have passed since then.

"Are you sure of that?"

"Quite certain, my lord. It is extraordinary that anyone should have dared to enter there, still less to stable horses, when, as everyone knows, the temple is haunted by evil spirits."

"I care nothing for spirits," the officer said; "it is men we are in search of. Go and look into any other chambers there may be."

At this moment a deep mournful sound was heard; louder and louder it rose, and then gradually died away.

The soldiers stood as if paralysed; even the high official, who had been obliged to leave his horse and make his way across the fallen blocks on foot, stepped back a pace with an expression of awe. He soon recovered himself, and shouted angrily to the men to go on. But again the dirge-like noise rose louder and louder. It swelled, and then as gradually died away; but this time with a quavering modulation. The men looked up and round, some gazed at the upper part of the rock, some straight ahead, while others turned round and faced the forest.

"Search!" the officer shouted furiously. "Evil spirits or no evil spirits, not a man shall stir from here until the place is searched."

Then rose a shrill, vibrating sound, as if of eerie laughter. Not even the officer's authority or the fear of punishment could restrain the soldiers. With cries of alarm they rushed across the ruins and plunged into the forest, followed, at a rate which he tried in vain to make dignified, by the officer, who, as soon as he reached his horse, leapt upon it and galloped away. The Burmese keenly appreciate a joke, and as soon as the troops had fled, the villagers and guards inside the temple threw themselves down on the ground and roared with laughter.

Stanley at once made his way into the upper room.

"Splendidly done, Meinik! It was like the note of an organ. Although I knew what you were going to do, I felt almost startled myself when that deep note rose. No wonder they were frightened."

"Well, at any rate, master, we are safe for the present."

"For the present, no doubt, Meinik; but I question if we

sha'n't hear of them again. That officer was a determined-looking fellow, and though he was scared, too, he stuck to it like a man."

"That is the governor of the town, master. I saw him carried through the streets in his chair. Everyone was bending to the ground as he passed. He was a famous general at one time, and they say that he is likely to command a part of the army again when fighting begins."

"Well, I think that we shall hear of them again, Meinik. I don't suppose that he really thought that we were here, for certainly no Burman would take up his abode in this place even to save his life. They will push on the chase through the woods all day, and by that time they will feel sure that they would have overtaken us had we gone straight on. Then I should not be at all surprised if he tries here again."

"Perhaps he will, master. Like enough he will chop off the heads of some of the men that ran away, and pick out some of his best troops for the search. Still, I hope he won't think of it."

Stanley shook his head.

"I hope so too, Meinik. There is one thing about which I feel certain—if he does find us here, he will stay here, or at any rate leave some troops here until he gets us. He would know that he would get into trouble at Ava for letting the prisoners escape, and it would be all-important for him to recapture them. Now we are up here, Meinik, we will go and have a look at that upper staircase again. If we are besieged that is our only hope of safety."

They again went along the ledge and up the staircase.

Stanley examined the stones that blocked the passage for some time, and at last exclaimed:

"There, Meinik, look along by the side of this stone; I can see a ray of light. Yes, and some leaves. I don't think they are more than thirty feet above us."

Meinik applied his eye to the crevice. "I see them, master. Yes, I don't think those leaves are more than that distance away."

"That is what I came to look for," Stanley said. "It was evident that this rubbish could only be the stones of the roof and pavement over the depression in the middle of the ruin, and that these could not block up this staircase very far. The question is, will it be possible to clear them away? Evidently it will be frightfully dangerous work. One might manage to get one stone out at a time in safety. But at any moment the loosening of one stone might bring a number of others down with a run, and anyone on this narrow staircase would be swept away like a straw."

Meinik agreed as to the danger.

"Well, we need not think it over now, Meinik, but if we are really besieged, it is by this way that we must escape, if at all. We must hope that we sha'n't be beset, but if we are we must try here. I would rather be killed at once by the fall of a stone on my head than tortured to death."

Meinik nodded, and they descended the stairs, put out the torches that they had used there, and returned along the ledge to the chamber where Harry was lying.

"So Meinik scared them away," the latter said as Stanley sat down beside him. "I could not think what he was going to do when he came up here with that long reed as thick as my leg. He showed it to me, and I saw that it had a sort of mouthpiece fixed into it, and he made signs that he was going to blow down it. When he did it was tremendous, and as it got louder and louder, I put my hands to my ears; everything seemed to quiver. The other row—that diabolical laughing noise—he made with a smaller one; it was frightful; but the big note was more like a trombone, only twenty times louder. Well, do you think that we have done with them?"

"I hope so, Harry. At any rate you can be assured that they will never fight their way up here, and long before our provisions are finished I have no doubt that I shall be able to hit on some plan of escape."

The day passed quietly, the woods were as silent as usual. The Burmans were all in high spirits at the success of Meinik's horn. When it became dark they hung a blanket before the entrance, placed one of the lads on watch just outside it, and then lighted a fire. Stanley took a couple of torches and went up to Harry, taking the precaution to hang a cloth before the window.

"I have not said much about thanking you, old fellow," Harry said, "but you must know how I feel."

"You had better say nothing about it, Harry; I have only done what you would have done had you been in my place; had you been in charge of that party, and I had been carried off, I know you would have done all in your power to rescue me. You might not have succeeded quite so well, because you do not know their language, but I know that you would have tried. After all, I have not run anything like so much risk as I did when I rescued Meinik from the leopard. And he, of course, was an absolute stranger to me. Besides, you are not rescued yet, and we won't holloa until we are out of the wood."

"It is very cool and pleasant here," Harry said, after lying without speaking for a few minutes. "It was dreadfully hot in that hut in the middle of the day, and I used to feel that I lost almost as much strength in the day as I picked up at night. I am wonderfully better this evening. Of course, that long sleep had something to do with it, and the pleasure of being free and with you had still more, but certainly the coolness, and the air blowing through that opening, have counted for something."

"Well, we shall feed you up as long as you are here, Harry, and I hope in a fortnight to see you pretty firm on your legs again, and then if there is nothing to prevent it we will carry you off triumphantly."

Meinik here came in with two bowls of broth, for they had bought a few earthenware utensils on one of the visits to Toungoo.

"That is first-rate!" Harry said, as he finished his first one. "What is it made of?"

"I never ask questions," Stanley replied, who tried, successfully, to keep down a smile. "Meinik is a capital cook, and turns out all sorts of nice little dishes. Here comes his step again. What have you there, Meinik?" he asked, as the Burman entered with two plates.

"A slice of mutton done on sticks over the fire, master, and some rice with it."

"That is first-rate!" Harry said heartily, when he had

finished. "They did not give me meat in prison. I suppose they thought that I was not strong enough for it."

"They eat very little meat themselves, Harry. Now I fancy your dinner is done, except some fruit. We have got plenty of that."

There were, however, some fried bananas, and Harry declared that he had feasted like a king. "If this goes on, Stanley, I will wager that I shall be about in a week, and shall be offering to run a race with you in a fortnight."

"You will be a good deal longer than that before you are fit to walk any distance. Still, with a good appetite,—which you are sure to have after your illness,—plenty of food, and the cool air in these caves, I do expect that you will pick up fast."

The next day passed quietly.

"I shall be glad when to-morrow is over," Stanley said to Meinik the last thing before going up to Harry's cell. "To-day I expect they are all marching back again, and if they pay us another visit it will be early to-morrow morning. Be sure that two men are on watch. They can relieve each other every hour, and I shall come down myself occasionally to see that all is right, but I don't think that even the governor could get his men to come near this place after dark."

"We will keep good watch, master, but I have no fear of their coming."

CHAPTER XV.

THE ATTACK.

STANLEY got up several times during the night, and went below to the watchers, as he felt sure they would be nervous, for though they had now, to a large extent, got over their superstitious fears, they would still be timid at night. They reported that everything was still, round the temple, but that they had heard distant sounds in the woods; and on the first of these occasions he had, after returning to the room above, gone out on to the ledge, and from that height could see the reflection in the sky of a number of fires extending in a semicircle, at a distance of a mile or so from the temple. From this he felt convinced that the governor was determined to have a thorough search made in the morning. As soon as it was daylight the sound of the blowing of horns and the beating of drums was heard in the forest, and half an hour later a large body of men poured out from the trees, headed by the governor himself.

"Now," he shouted, "this place is to be searched in every hole and corner. As to the evil spirits, there is no fear of them either by day or night. Did you ever hear of their attacking a large body of men? They may strangle a single traveller who ventures into their haunts, but no one ever heard of a Burmese army being attacked by them. Now, every man has to do his duty, and the first who wavers, his head is to be struck off at once. Forward!"

The troops rushed impetuously across the ruins, penetrated into the various chambers in the rock, and in a few minutes all these were reported to be empty.

"There are chambers higher up," the governor said. "We will search them, and—look at that door up there, it must lead to somewhere. Bring stones, and make a stair up to it."

It was evident now that there was no longer any hope of concealment, and Stanley stepped to the entrance. "My lord-governor," he shouted, "there is a strong force here, and all your army could not gain an entrance. We do not wish to take the lives of brave men, but if we are attacked we must defend ourselves, and I pray you to withdraw with them and not to throw away life."

This address from an apparent peasant excited the wrath of the governor, who shouted: "Shoot him, men!"

But before the order could be obeyed Stanley had stepped back into the chamber, where he had already ordered the men to stand out of the line of the door. A number of muskets were fired, and several bullets struck the back wall of the chamber. The firing continued, and Stanley said: "Keep where you are, men, until they have finished, then approach the door, for directly they begin the attack the men behind must stop firing. They will be some minutes yet." He ran quickly up to Harry's room.

"They are attacking us," Harry exclaimed; "oh, how I wish I could come down and help!"

"They can never get in, Harry. British soldiers might do it, but not these fellows. They can only enter two abreast, and with a dozen spear-points facing them what can they do? I thought that I would just come up and tell you it was all right. It will take them five minutes, at least, to pile up stones level with the doorway."

Stanley again joined those below. Meinik, the trooper, and one of the Burmese were to form the first line; the four other Burmese were to stand behind, with their spears, between the men in front; the two guards with their muskets, and the boys, were to act as a reserve. Stanley had armed himself with one of the axes, and was to stand by the side of the entrance, so that if the spearmen were pressed back, and any of the assailants succeeded in passing the entrance, he would strike them down. Presently there was a silence outside.

"Keep well back," he said. "They have laid their stones, and we shall have a rush directly, but they will most likely pour in a volley first."

The pause lasted for a minute or two. Then a drum was beaten, and a hundred muskets were fired. A rain of bullets flew into the cave.

"Now," Stanley shouted, "form up!"

A wild yell was raised by the Burmese. Now they knew that they were fighting human foes, their courage returned and there was a rush of men up the pile of stones to the entrance, but in vain they tried to force their way into the chamber. Those in front fell pierced by the spears, and while the defenders could see their figures against the light, the assailants, coming out from the sunshine, could see nothing in the chamber, which was now darkened by their filling up the entrance. Not once was it necessary for Stanley to strike. The Burmans' spears did their work thoroughly, and in two or three minutes the entrance was

"IN VAIN THE BURMESE TRIED TO FORCE THEIR WAY INTO THE CHAMBER."

nigh choked up with dead bodies, adding to the difficulty of the assailants. Pressed on by those behind, the foremost fell over these obstacles, and were instantly pierced by the spears, until it was no longer possible to get through the outer entrance, much less make their way into the chamber. Again and again the attack was repeated and as often repulsed.

Before advancing, the Burmese each time endeavoured to clear the passage by drawing out the bodies of their comrades, but the two guards now posted themselves in front, and shot man after man who made the attempt. At last the Burmese drew off, but not till some fifty or sixty had been killed. The governor was seen gesticulating furiously to a party of officers, and presently a final attack was made, led by several officers of rank. This was as unsuccessful as the others; the bodies, indeed, of the killed now forming a well-nigh impassable barrier, and after several of the officers and many of the bravest men had fallen, the remainder withdrew suddenly. The governor appeared to recognize that the task was an impossible one, and two or three hundred men were at once set to work felling trees, and by nightfall a high stockade had been erected round the open ground in front of the temple.

"They are going to try to starve us out," Stanley said. "There is no more chance of fighting to-night."

As soon as the stockade was finished musketeers took their place behind it and opened a dropping fire at the entrance, while the wood-cutters continued to fell trees.

"We must get rid of these dead bodies if we can," Stanley said, "or the place will be uninhabitable in a day or two. Get those two bamboos we had for the litter, Meinik; we will push the bodies out, one by one, beginning with those on the top of the heap. We can keep down behind the shelter of the pile till we have got most of them out; after that we must take our chance of a shot."

It took them some hours' work, but at last the passage was cleared, and the bodies all thrown outside. The fire was lighted in the next room, and Stanley, bidding two men listen attentively for any movement, went up again to Harry, to whom he had paid a flying visit as soon as the Burmese drew off.

"We cannot risk having a light here, Harry," he said. "I don't want them to have any idea that this chamber, which is nearly fifty feet above the entrance, is in any way connected with the rooms below. If such an idea struck them they might lower men from above by ropes, and so take us in the rear."

"Did you say that we are regularly shut up in front by that stockade?"

"Yes; there is certainly no getting out that way. Behind, you know, it is a sheer wall of rock, and the only possibility that I can see, is that we may clear a staircase, which runs up through the rock, from a ledge on the level of this room, to the ruins of a building above. At present the upper part is entirely choked up with blocks of stone and rubbish, and it will be a very awkward job to get through it; but so far, it seems to me, it is that or nothing."

"What are they going on chopping down trees for?"

"I believe their general is doing it to bring large numbers

of his troops close up to the stockade; partly perhaps to keep up the spirits of the front line by their company, partly to render impossible any attempt on our part to make our way out by a sudden rush. Of course, they don't know what our strength is; but they have had so sharp a lesson to-day that they will take every precaution in future. Well, what is it, Meinik?"

"We have been talking together, master, and we think that if we were to call out that they might take the bodies away without any interference by us they would do so. Several officers of rank have fallen there, and it is our custom always to carry off the dead when it is possible."

"It would be worth trying the experiment anyhow, Meinik. But we must all stand to arms while they are doing it, as they might make a sudden rush. However, we would risk that, for those bodies have been worrying me very much, and I would give anything to have them taken away. I will go down with you."

Meinik accordingly went down to the entrance and shouted out: "Peace, peace! I am ordered by the English officer to say that he would wish those who have fought so bravely to be honoured after death, and that no shot shall be fired and no interference made with those who come to carry away the dead."

There was silence for two or three minutes, and then a voice called back: "It is well; for two hours there shall be peace between us."

"I have no doubt the governor is as glad to do this as we are. It is considered a disgrace if the dead are not carried off the ground to burial; and if he sends despatches to Ava he will be glad to be able to put in that the brave men who fell have all been buried with due honours. Besides, Meinik, it would not be encouraging to his troops for them to have that pile of dead bodies before them; and, indeed, would be enough to cause a pestilence in a few days."

The men were formed up again round the entrance. The Burmese did their work silently. Occasionally a slight movement was heard, but no one could have imagined that a hundred men were busy outside. A number of them carried torches, and all worked steadily and in good order under the direction of two or three officers. One of the posts of the stockade had been pulled up, and through this the bodies were carried. It was less than two hours before a horn sounded, and there was a loud call of: "The peace is over; all is done."

Beyond the stockade great fires blazed among the trees. The work of chopping down the forest continued, and by the morning the ground had been cleared for a distance of thirty or forty yards from the paling. Then the Burmese raised another stockade forty feet behind the first, so that, if by carelessness or treachery the besieged should manage to pass through the first line, there would yet be another in front of them.

"I expect, master," Meinik said, as standing well back he watched the men at work, "the general is building this second line, not because he thinks that there is a chance of our getting through the first, but to keep the men at work so as to prevent them from thinking anything about the spirits. Now that they have passed one night there they will have got somewhat over their fear, and of course every day that passes without ill befalling them they will think less and less about the evil ones."

"Do you believe in them, Meinik?"

Meinik hesitated. "Everyone knows, master, that evil spirits guard the treasures of the people that lived in the land long, long ago. No one can doubt that people who have rashly sought the treasures have been found dead with staring eyes and swollen bodies; but as at present they must know well that neither we nor those outside are searching for treasure, they may not interfere."

"Then you think that there are treasures buried here somewhere?"

"I cannot say, master; everyone says so. The story has been handed down that this was once the greatest of the temples of the old people, and that when they were defeated by tribes from the east—I know not whether it was us or some people before us—the priests from all the other temples came here. The remains of their army came here too and fought outside the temple until all were killed. When the conquerors entered they found the priests all lying in regular lines on the pavements. All were dead. One story is that they had stabbed themselves; another, that they had taken poison. At any rate, no treasures were found, although it was known that the riches of the temple were great, and that all the other priests that had come here had brought the treasures from their temples with them. That was the beginning of the destruction of the place, for the pavement was torn up, and the walls in some places levelled, and the images of the gods broken up in search for the treasures. The work of the guardian spirits had already begun. They say that all who took part in the search died of a terrible pestilence that broke out. Since that time the place has been accursed. Once or twice kings have sent bodies of troops to search, and they say that some could never find the temple, but wandered about the forest for days searching in vain for it; others found so thick a darkness, like the blackest of smoke, filling the forest, that even the bravest dare not enter. I say not that those things were so; I only say that these are the stories that have come down to us."

"Well, Meinik, we are not going to search for the treasure, and it is evident that the spirits bear us no ill-will; indeed I feel obliged to them, for it is likely enough that the soldiers will put down their misfortune to their influence, and that even the governor may feel that it would be useless to try to get them to renew the assault. This evening we will go up and have another look at the stairs and see how we can best set to work to clear them. There is no great hurry about it, but the sooner we set to work the better."

All day long a dropping fire was maintained on the entrance by the troops behind the first stockade; but as, with the exception of three men kept always on watch, the defenders were stationed in the next chamber, the bullets pattered harmlessly against the wall. During the night the accumulated dust of ages had been swept up from the floor, and this had been strewn three inches deep in the passage between the outer air and the chamber, so as to cover the blood that had been shed there. As soon as it was quite dark, Stanley, Meinik, and three of the villagers went out on to the ledge in front of the upper opening, made their way along it to the entrance of the stairs and mounted. They carried with them two or three glowing brands from the fire in one of the earthenware cooking pots, which was covered with a cloth to prevent the slightest glow being noticed by the enemy. The men, by Stanley's order, brought with them the bamboos of the litter, the saw they had used at the stockade, a hatchet, and some blocks of firewood. When they got to the point where the steps were choked up, they lighted the two torches, the men who brought up the rear of the party holding up a rug to prevent any reflection from the torches being seen outside. When Stanley and Meinik had again examined the obstacle, the latter retired, and the Burmans one by one came up and looked at it.

"What do you think of it?" Stanley asked them.

"It would be dangerous to touch it, my lord," one of them said. "If only one stone moved out from its place it would be death to us all. They are firm now, quite firm, but if two or three were disturbed the whole might come down at once."

"I quite see that," Stanley said. "Can any of you suggest a plan by which we could get out without much risk of setting them in motion?"

The Burmese were silent.

"I will tell you my scheme then. I propose to cut the bamboos into lengths that will just reach across the passage. It is the lower stones that one is most afraid of. So long as these remain fixed there is no fear of any general movement, but if they went, the whole mass might come down. This passage is less than three feet wide, and the bamboos are twelve feet long, so that each would make four the width of the passage. I propose to drive them tightly in and fix them firmly with wedges. They must be put in so that they will actually touch the stones, so as to prevent their making the slightest downward movement. If they began to slide, no doubt they would carry away the bamboos, but if these were fixed firmly by wedges they ought to be sufficient to prevent any movement from taking place, especially as there would be enough of them almost to touch each other, extending from this lowest step on which the rocks rest, some five feet upwards, that is, to within some two feet of the roof, which would be sufficient for us to crawl through, and the bamboos would serve as a ladder. Then I propose that we should work our way along the top, passing the small stones and rubbish backwards, after filling up all the cracks and crevices below us.

"I see, of course, that we should meet with many obstacles. Great stones may be sticking up, perhaps jammed against the roof, these would have to be broken off or chipped in pieces. No doubt the work will take time; but at any rate there is plenty of food for three weeks, and working by turns night and day we ought to be able to burrow our way out. As we get on we may not find the stones so tightly pressed together as they are here. At any rate, as we saw the light above us only some thirty feet up, there ought not to be above twenty feet of closely-packed stuff to get through. No doubt the work will be dangerous as well as hard; but as we know that if we do not succeed all our lives are forfeited, we can face the danger. Every one of us will take his share in turn; I shall do so myself, and shall direct the work in general. What do you think of the plan?"

"I think that it is possible, master," Meinik said. "At any rate we must try it, since it is the only way that offers us any chance of life."

The Burmese all agreed, and they at once set to work. The bamboos were first cut into lengths, and then, by means of the axe and wedges, were jammed so firmly from side to side, that it would have required great force to dislodge them. These supports were somewhat irregularly placed, as it was necessary that they should absolutely touch the stones. As they proceeded with the work, the spaces behind the bamboos were filled tightly up with rubble, so as to solidify the whole.

When the last support was in its place, Stanley said: "Now, Meinik, do you with these three work to-night, four others will take your place before dawn. Mind, at first I don't want you to attempt to move any fixed stones, but simply to clear away all small stones and rubble; you can stow a good deal behind the two upper bamboos, the rest you must put on the stairs. I will see to-night what we can manage in the way of tools for chipping away the big stones that cannot be moved. You had better relieve each other very often; the three who are not at work should sit down on the ledge outside, so that any stone accidentally dislodged will not fall on anyone. Every ten minutes one will come up to take the place of the man at work. Be sure that each as he passes up or down replaces the blanket carefully."

They had, indeed, before beginning to saw up the bamboos fastened the blanket to one of the cross pieces of the stretcher, and cutting this to the width of the passage, had jammed it close up to the roof, so that the curtain hanging down effectually shut off the light. Stanley then descended the steps and rejoined Harry below. Before going down further, Stanley, who had during the day informed Harry of his plan, told him of the start that they had made.

"Of course it all depends upon what stones you meet with," Harry said. "If you come to a big solid block I don't see how you are going to get through it."

"We have the hatchets and can whittle it away, and perhaps we can make some chisels from the ramrods of your guards' guns. A lot can be done with patience and plenty of hands."

Stanley then went down below and explained to the others the plan proposed. The news gave them great satisfaction; for although Meinik had told them there was a staircase above blocked with stones, it had seemed so impossible to him to clear it that he had placed no stress upon the fact, and the preparations made by the enemy to cut off any possible retreat had greatly depressed them. Stanley took one of the iron ramrods, and raking some of the embers from the fire, placed it in them about a foot from one end; then he directed the others to fan the embers until they raised them almost to white heat. Taking the ramrod out, he laid the edge of one of their knives upon it, and striking its back with a stone, soon cut through the glowing rod. He repeated the operation, and had then three short rods of equal length. He now heated one end of each, and laying it on an axe on the ground, hammered it into chisel shape with the back of a light hatchet, repeating this several times until it had the required shape and sharpness, then he plunged this into a pot of water.

He did the same with the other two, and had now three chisels with which he hoped to be able to chip away the stones. The other ramrod he left intact, except that he sharpened one end, then going up to Harry's room he lay down and slept for some hours, putting the two boys on watch and bidding the trooper look after them. The two Burmans, with one of the guards, were to go to work with him. Several times he woke; the last time, on looking out, he thought that there was a faint light in the sky, and going down called up the three men, and bidding them bring up the two heavy axes, a light hatchet, and the three short chisels, he led them up the steps to the working party.

"How have you got on, Meinik?"

"We have cleared four feet, master, but there is a big stone sticking up now, and we can do nothing with it."

"We will have a try, and do you all go down at once. Take off your cloth, one of you, and fill it with this rubbish on the steps. Do it as quickly as you can, the day will be breaking in a few minutes."

Stanley now climbed up and investigated the passage. The bottom was level, every crack and crevice between the stones being filled up with rubbish. The obstacle Meinik had spoken of evidently formed part of a flat slab. It reached within an inch of the roof, and at one side touched the rock wall; at the other there was an interval of some four or five inches, and the earth and rubbish had already been scraped out from behind it. Putting his hand in he found that the block was some four inches in thickness. He thought that if he could but get a fair blow at it with the back of one of the heavy axes he might break it off, but this was impossible. The total width of the passage did not exceed three feet, and as the men had, as they went, worked down somewhat, there was now about thirty inches between the bed of earth and rubbish on which he was lying and the roof. Taking the handle of the axe in both hands he used the head as a battering-ram, but without any success. He then called up the slightest of the three men, and told him to crawl in beside him, and with their united strength they pounded the stone for some time. Finding that nothing could be done this way, Stanley sent the man back again, and then taking one of the three chisels and a small hatchet, he proceeded to mark a line along the bottom of the stone, and then for ten minutes worked away on it with the chisel and hammer. Then he called up one of the others, and showed him what he was to do. All day they worked by turns, and though progress was very slow, by nightfall the groove was half an inch deep.

Stanley and the strongest Burman then went in together, and lying on their backs again tried the effect of the heavy axe, but still without success. Then Stanley told the man to get down and take out the wedge at the top of the axe, and to cut away the wood below the head, so that the latter would slip down four or five inches, then to take off the head of the other heavy axe and put it on above it, and replace the wedge. In a few minutes the man rejoined him.

"We must strike it as near the roof as we can," Stanley said. Both grasped the handle firmly. "We will sway it backwards and forwards three times, and the third time strike. One, two, three—hooray!"

As the two-headed axe, driven with their united force, struck the stone, there was a sharp crack.

"That has done it," Stanley said, turning over. There was a dark line along the groove, and the top of the stone inclined back two inches from the perpendicular, being kept in its place by the rubbish behind it. Stanley put his hand into the hole, and got his fingers behind the stone, while the Burmese put the chisel into the crack and used it as a lever. In two or three minutes the stone was moved out of its position, taken out of the hole, and laid down on the steps. Half an hour later Meinik came up with a trooper, another guard, and one of the boys, and was delighted to find that the obstacle, which had seemed to him fatal to their hopes, had been removed. Stanley showed how they had carried out the work, and then with his party went down into the rock chambers.

"It was pretty tiring work, Harry," he said, "though we were only at it about a quarter of an hour at a time. My wrists and arms and shoulders are aching as if I had been beaten with sticks. To-morrow I will take up a good supply of fire-wood. The chisels got blunted before we had worked an hour, and we should get on a deal faster if we could sharpen them frequently."

"Is the stone hard?"

"No; it is a sort of marble, I think. We had the under-part of the slab on our side, and I did not think of looking when we took it down. Anyhow, it was not very hard, and with a good strong chisel and a short, heavy hammer I am sure we could have done it in an hour. Anyhow, it is a comfort that nothing came down on top of us. I examined the pile carefully, and there had not been the slightest movement among the lower stones; so that part of the difficulty seems to have been got over. Now, I must go down and get something to eat, and then I will go in for a good sleep. You are feeling all right, I hope?"

"Could not be doing better, Stanley. I have eaten three solid meals to-day, and have been sitting up on the edge of my bed for some time. I tried standing, but it was no go; still, I do think that in a day or two I shall manage it."

For six days the work continued. One party watched, another slept, and the third worked, by turns. Some of the stones gave much greater trouble than the first they had met with, but having the fire close by proved a great assistance, as the chisels could be frequently sharpened. The men became more accustomed to the work, and the steady progress they made greatly excited their hopes. At the end of the week but one stone barred the way. This, however, was much the most formidable that they had encountered. It seemed to have been a pillar or a huge gate-post, and was square, measuring some twenty inches on each face. The obstacle was all the more formidable, as the upper end was inclined towards them, greatly increasing the difficulty in using the chisel. Beyond this, as far as they could see, there was merely a mass of smaller stones. The party who had been working upon this block were much disheartened when Stanley went up to relieve them. Owing to the inclination of the stone, their chisels could get but little bite, and though they had been working for six hours at it, they had scarcely made any impression; indeed at only one point had they so far broken the face that the chisel would cut. Meinik had come down two hours before to report to Stanley the nature of the obstacle, and when he went up he took with him the second ramrod, which had not hitherto been used.

He saw at once that, as Meinik had told him, it would be impossible to get through this block by the same means as before, for as the groove deepened the labour would become greater and greater, and from the inclination of the stone they would in time arrive at a point where the axe could no longer be used to strike the chisel. The point at which the slight indentation had been made was nearly at the corner of the stone. This was gradually enlarged by hammering upon it with the head of the axe, and after an hour's work the surface had been so far pounded that the chisel could get a flat hold upon it. Then Stanley and one of the Burmans lay down and placed the cutting end of the long ramrod against it, and the others by turns struck the end with the back of a light hatchet, those holding the rod turning it slightly after each blow. Every half-hour the edge of the chisel was resharpened, and by the time the next party relieved them, a hole of half an inch in diameter and two inches deep had been drilled in the stone. Stanley remained with the new-comers for half an hour, instructing them in the work, and then went below.

"Well, Stanley, what are you going to do with this monstrous stone Meinik tells me of?"

"There is only one thing to do with it, Harry; that is, to blast it. The block is so inclined that one can do nothing with the chisels, and we are now drilling a hole. I don't know that I shall succeed, but at any rate I am going to have a try. If it fails, I must hit on some other way. The provisions are holding out all right, and Meinik calculates that, with a little stinginess, we could manage for another three weeks. We have drilled the hole in two inches today, and as we get more accustomed to the work I dare say we could do three inches in each shift. The block is twenty inches through on the straight, and may be two feet on the line that we follow, so that in four days we shall be nearly through it. In three weeks we shall have made five holes, which will weaken it so that we may be able to break it off. However, I hope we shall find one hole sufficient. I shall make it fifteen inches deep, and then charge it with the contents of a dozen cartridges. I think that ought to do it."

In two days and a half the hole was of the required depth. Harry had progressed so rapidly that he was able that morning to walk across his room.

"We must try the shot at once," Stanley said, "because if it fails we must go on working; if it succeeds we can, if we like, wait for another week before we make off. By that time you will be strong enough to be got through that low passage, and walk for a little distance, when we can cut some poles and rig up that hammock again. Do you know anything about mining, for I know nothing? I only had an idea how to drill the hole from seeing some engineers at work at Agra years ago, but I am sure I don't know how they fired the shot or prepared it."

"I can tell you a little about it, Stanley, for I have been down a coal-mine once or twice, and watched the men doing it. They first of all put in the charge, then they put in a wooden rod just the thickness of the fuse they use, then they dropped in a little dry dust round it, which they pressed down very carefully with a small wooden rod; then they damped some dust, and hammered that down hard. After putting in about half an inch of this, they used dust slightly moistened, beating it down as before. When it was quite full they pulled out the centre stick, and put the fuse into the hole that it left."

"We have not got any fuse," Stanley said; "but I think that if we take a narrow strip of cloth, moisten it, and rub gunpowder into it, let it dry, and then roll it up, it would be all right. Then we could lay a train of damp powder to it, set the end alight, and bolt."

"I should think that that would do," Harry agreed; "but you would have to bolt very sharp, for if it went off before you got to the bottom of the steps it might be very awkward."

"I don't think the effect of the shock will be as great as that, Harry. It may crack the stone, but I should hardly think it would send anything flying out of the hole."

CHAPTER XVI.

REJOINING.

EVERY day since the siege had begun the defenders had fired an occasional shot at the stockade, not with any idea of doing any damage, but in order that the assailants should know that they were still in the cavern. That evening, when the hole had got to the proper depth, Stanley, having prepared his fuse, went up with twenty cartridges in his pocket, accompanied by Meinik. The hole was charged and tamped and the fuse inserted; this took a considerable time. The fuse had been cut so that an inch of it projected outside the hole. The other eight cartridges were then broken up, and the powder moistened, and a train some two feet long laid from the fuse towards the entrance of the hole. Then a piece of rag was wrapped round one end of the ramrod, and this, again, was tied to a long rod that had the night before been cut by one of the boys, who had slipped out noiselessly from the entrance. The rag had been moistened and rubbed with gunpowder.

"Now, Meinik," Stanley said, "everything is ready. This rod is sixteen feet long, so that, lying down, my feet will be just at the edge of the hole, and I shall be able to drop down as soon as I have lighted the train, and bolt. I shall fix a torch a foot or so from the train, then I shall only have to lift the rod to it, light the rag, set fire to the train, and then slide down and bolt Now, you must go down first."

"No, master," Meinik said firmly; "I will light the train. I do not think that there is any danger, but whether there is or not I shall undertake it. If I am killed it does not matter, while if you were killed all would be lost, for if the explosion did not burst the stone, I am sure that we should never be able to get through it without you to direct us. No, master, if you stay, I stay, and that would only lessen our chances of running down the steps in time."

Stanley argued, and even ordered, but Meinik was obstinate, and seeing that the faithful Burman was not to be moved, he reluctantly left the matter in his hands, and went downstairs. He moved a short distance along the ledge and waited. The time seemed an age to him, so that he gave an exclamation of delight when Meinik suddenly came into sight, and took his place beside him.

"I have lit the train, master. The powder fizzed up, but did not seem to burn very fast."

It was indeed another two minutes before a deep muffled roar was heard. There was no further noise, but they heard shouts from the Burmans behind the stockades.

"They will be wondering what the sound is," Stanley said, "but they will not be able to tell from what direction it came, for I expect they were pretty nearly all sound asleep. Now let us go up and see the result."

They made their way up the steps, which were now in entire darkness. The curtain still hung in its place some ten feet below the obstacle. They lit a torch from the embers in the pan, and then Stanley climbed up into the passage and hastily crawled along. He gave a cry of satisfaction as he approached the end. The explosion had been completely successful—the end of the block lay on the ground; whether the whole of it had been blown off or not he could not see, but he felt sure that the greater portion must have split off. It was evident that it would take a considerable amount of time, and would require the strength of several men to get the block out. They therefore descended at once to gladden the hearts of those below, with the news that the way out was now available to them whenever they chose to leave.

Harry manifested no surprise whatever at the news. "I made sure that you would succeed, Stanley. After getting me off as you did, and making your own escape before, it seems to me that you have got hold of the 'open sesame' of Ali Baba, and have only to use the cabalistic words to walk in and out wherever you want to go."

"I don't feel by any means so certain of my own powers as you seem to be, Harry, and I can assure you I was very doubtful whether that shot would succeed. I hoped at any rate that it would blow a good bit of the stone out, and in that case we could have got the chisels to work again. It was the slanting position of the block that beat us. However, thank goodness, the work is done now, and you have only to get a bit stronger, and we will be off."

"I am quite ready to start now, Stanley; I think it is absurd waiting any longer, for there is never any saying what might take place. That Burmese general, who seems to be an obstinate beggar, might take it into his head to place a guard on the top of the hill, and then all your labour will have been thrown away."

"That is true enough, Harry; and as I really don't think that travelling now would be likely to do you any serious harm I will decide on to-morrow. At any rate, I will take some men up at once and get that stone out."

The task was a difficult one. The block of stone was so nearly the size of the passage that they could not get a rope round behind it, and after trying for two hours in vain they determined that the only course was to push it before them. They soon found, however, that this was impossible, and that a part at least of the stone was remaining in its place. Finally, they succeeded in pushing a loop in the rope over the top of the block, and then by main force eight of them pulled it out of the hole and lowered it on to the top step. By the time that they had done this dawn was approaching, and they therefore returned at once to the chambers below.

The men were all much pleased when Stanley told them that they would leave that night. Confident as they felt that the Burmese could not force their way in, a new feeling of nervousness seized them, now that the way was open, lest some unforeseen circumstances might occur to prevent their going. The rice that remained was made up into three or four packages; the meat had long before been finished. Stanley had a discussion with Meinik as to how Harry had best be taken through the passage. He could, they agreed, walk along the ledge with one before and one behind to steady him, and could then be carried up the steps in a blanket by four men. He must, of course, be lifted into the passage and dragged through it to the end; after that it would be easy enough. Six men could carry him in a blanket until far enough away for them to chop poles without the sound of the axes being heard by the Burmese. From the time they began their work, every pains had been taken to deaden sounds. The blanket hung across the passage had acted as a muffler to some extent, but a piece of cloth had always been tied over the hammer heads of the axes to prevent the sharp clinking sounds of the blows on the chisels or stone being heard.

As soon as it was dark enough for them to pass along the ledge Meinik went with Stanley to examine the ground. Fortunately the portion of stone that remained above the level and prevented the rock from being rolled back was but small, and they were able to break it up in half an hour with the axes. Then, making their way along without difficulty for another four feet, they found themselves standing upright in the depression in the centre of the ruin. Mounting six more steps, they were among the bushes that covered the site of the temple. They now carefully cleared away every fragment of stone from the floor of the passage, and returning, Stanley gave orders for the start to be made. Two or three shots were fired from the lower entrance to show the enemy that they were there and on the watch, and then all went up to Harry's room. He had been dressed for the first time and was ready for the start. Two of the strongest of the Burmans went on first.

"Now, Harry, you are to put your hands on my shoulders. Meinik will follow close behind you, and will keep his arms round you in case you need help. Of course we shall go along very slowly."

"I don't think that all these precautions are necessary,"

Harry said. "I am sure that I can walk that distance easily enough. Why, you say the stair is only about forty feet."

"I dare say you could, Harry; but we don't want to run any risks. Your head is not very strong at present, and you might turn giddy, or you might stumble. So at present you will have just to do as you are told. Let us start."

Harry did not find it as easy as he had expected getting out through the lower opening, and he was by no means sorry to have the support of Stanley and Meinik as he proceeded along the ledge. They moved very carefully and slowly, and all were greatly relieved when he sat down on a blanket laid on the steps.

"Now lie back, Harry; we shall have no difficulty in getting you up here."

Two Burmans took the upper end of the blanket, Stanley and Meinik the lower, and they were soon at the top of the steps.

"You are not very heavy now, Harry, but you are a good deal heavier than you were when we brought you in below. Now the next is the most difficult part of the work—once we get you through this passage it will be plain sailing. You see, you will have to be dragged. The place is only two feet high, so that it would be impossible to lift you at all. We have made the floor as smooth as we can, but I am afraid that there are a good many projecting corners that will try you a good deal."

"It cannot be helped, Stanley. Fire away as soon as you like."

The rest of the party were now all gathered on the steps below, and Meinik and Stanley, getting up first into the hole, received Harry as the others lifted him, and with the aid of two of the Burmans laid him on his blanket in the passage.

"Now," Stanley said to the two men who took the other end of the blanket, "keep it as tight as you can, and when I say 'lift' we will all lift together and move him forward a few inches. Do not hurry over it—we have plenty of time before us."

They were packed so closely that they had each but one arm available. Little by little they moved him along, gaining some six inches each time; then all had to move so as to place themselves for the next effort. However, in five or six minutes they had him through, and carried him up into the open air. The rest of the party at once joined them, and, with three of the natives on each side of the blanket, they were soon beyond the circle of ruins, and making at a brisk pace through the forest. After going for a quarter of a mile they stopped, cut some poles for the hammock, and in a short time were on their way again, having placed in it one of the bags of rice as a pillow for Harry.

They travelled for some hours, and then halted to cook some rice. All had slept a good deal during the day, so that after resting for an hour they proceeded on their way again. They had no fear whatever of pursuit, and the only danger that they could incur was from meeting with a band similar to that which had carried Harry off. When they rigged up the hammock, they had cut wood for torches to protect themselves from tigers; these were thrown away as soon as daylight broke. At mid-day they halted again for another hour, and then, continuing their journey, arrived at the village before nightfall. They were received with great joy, the villagers setting up a shout of welcome, the friends of the men and boys being specially exuberant in their joy, for they had become extremely anxious at their long absence. The two troopers were still there, and these saluted Stanley with less than the usual stiff formality of the Mohammedan soldier. He himself laughed.

"I don't look much like a British officer at present," he said in their language. "Well, has everything been quiet here?"

"Yes, sahib; a sowar brought us orders from the general to remain here, and to send at once if we heard any news of you. We sent off one of the villagers when the man came back to fetch the others, and said that you had good hopes of getting Lieutenant Brooke sahib out of the hands of the Burmese."

"I will write a note," Stanley said. "Get your horse saddled at once. Directly we have made Mr. Brooke comfortable, I will give you the letter."

During the time that Stanley had been absent the houses had been re-erected, and the village had assumed its general appearance. A hut was at once handed over to them, and Harry laid on a bamboo pallet. He had slept most of the way down.

"You see I was quite right, Stanley. I told you that the journey would be nothing."

"Fortunately it has turned out so. Meinik has already

killed a chicken, and will make it into broth for you. It will be a change for you after your diet of rice. The cooking was excellent for the first three or four days, but it fell off sadly. That was one of the reasons why I gave way to your wish to start at once. You have done wonderfully well, but a constant diet of rice is not quite the thing for building up a sick man.

"Now I am going to write a few lines to the general to say that you have got safely down, but will need at least another week before you are able to sit on a horse. Of course you can be carried on; but I think that the air here is a great deal more healthy and bracing than it is at Prome, and the longer you stay here the better."

Stanley's note was a short one; it merely said that he had succeeded in getting his cousin and the trooper who was carried off at the same time, from the hands of the Burmese, but that Harry was still very weak, and that if he himself could be spared he would stay with him at the village for another week or ten days, at the end of which time he would ride by easy stages to Prome. Three days later the trooper returned with a note from the general.

"*I congratulate you most heartily on having rescued your cousin,*" he wrote. "*By all means stay where you are until he is quite strong again; this place is not at all healthy at present. We shall not be moving forward for another three weeks.*"

Stanley remained at the village for another fortnight, and at the end of that time Harry had so far recovered that he was quite capable of making a short day's journey on horseback. Two of the men who had aided in the rescue had gone to Prome with an order from Stanley on the staff paymaster, for the rewards that had been promised to the villagers and the two Burmese soldiers. They returned with the money, and the men were all highly delighted at the result of the expedition.

Stanley retained the services of the two soldiers as long as he remained in the village. He had no fear whatever of the same band returning that had before visited the village, and he learned that no others had been heard of in the neighbourhood; but at the same time he thought it as well that a man should be on guard night and day at each end of the village. The peasants agreed to watch at one end, while the two Burmese soldiers and the troopers took charge of the other end. The bulk of the villagers were engaged in forming a strong stockade round it to defend themselves in case of further attack, and Stanley promised to send them down twenty muskets and a supply of ammunition as soon as he got to Prome. There was real regret on the part of the Burmese when the time came for the party to start. It had been something altogether new to them to have officials among them who paid for everything. These Englishmen had treated them kindly, and were pleased and contented with everything. The money that the five men and two boys had earned had enriched the village, and had enabled them to more than replace their losses by the recent raid, and if Stanley had accepted all the presents of fruit, fowls, and eggs they would have given him, he would have needed a couple of extra horses to convey them. A strong pony had been purchased for Meinik, and after taking a hearty leave of the villagers the party rode off.

"I wish we had such a good cook as your man is, Stanley," Harry said as they journeyed along at a walk. "I never tasted better soup than he serves up. I must really get him to teach our mess cook how to make it."

"Do you know what it is, Harry?"

"I have not the least idea; it might be anything. I think that it tasted to me more like stewed eels than anything else."

"You are not very far out. It is made of the creatures you turned up your nose at—snakes."

"Nonsense, Stanley!"

"It is, I can assure you. I would not tell you before because it might have set you against it. That soup you had in the cave was made from snake-flesh. The recesses in parts of the caves swarmed with them, and the men laid in quite a store of them before we were besieged. Unfortunately they would not keep well even in these cool chambers, so we had to fall back on rice. You liked it so much that, though there was no occasion to have gone on with snake soup after we got to the village, I continued to give it to you, for it is very nourishing."

"Well, I am glad you did not tell me at the time, but I must own that it was excellent, and I think that in future I shall have no objection to snake in that form."

"They are just as good in other ways," Stanley replied. "The Burmans are no fools, and I consider that snake and lizards are very much better eating than their mutton, which is tasteless stuff at the best."

"We shall have to have a big settlement when we get back, Stanley. Of course all those men you paid and the guards you bribed are entirely my account, to say nothing of my share of the general expenditure."

"The general expenses are practically nothing, Harry. I invited you to come with me, and of course you were my guest. As to the other matter, that also is my business. I would not say so if I had not plenty of funds, but what with my pay as interpreter, and the year of back pay that I got when the *Gazette* came out, I have plenty out of my income to pay for it without breaking in upon the amount I told you I had got for those rubies."

"I should pay you, Stanley, if you were rolling in money. Not that I should mind taking money from you if I wanted it, but my expenses since I landed here have not been anything approaching my pay and allowances; and I have besides, as I told you, an income of £500 a year of my own. You have risked your life for me, and I am not going to let you pay the piper as well."

"All right, if it pleases you, Harry. I am delighted at having been able to save you, and just at present money does not seem an important matter one way or the other, so if it really would be a satisfaction to you to pay I will certainly not deprive you of it."

Although they only travelled ten miles the first day, Harry acknowledged that he was as tired as a dog when he dismounted, and was so stiff the next morning that he had to be helped on to his horse. However, this gradually wore off, and on the evening of the fourth day, they arrived at Prome. Leaving Harry at his regimental camp, Stanley rode to the head-quarters, and there dismounted. Meinik had led the second horse after Harry dismounted, and now took them both across to the lines with the air of a man who has only been away a few hours. Stanley at once went up to the general.

"Welcome back, lad!" Sir Archibald said, "you have been longer away than we expected when you started. I am glad, indeed, that you succeeded in rescuing your cousin; and we are all burning to hear about it. I wrote that note to you in a hurry, for I was on the point of going on a round of inspection of the camp when your sowar arrived. I intended to question him concerning you on my return, for I had no idea that after making such a long journey he would start back at once, but I found that he had ridden straight off directly the note was handed to him. You must dine with me to-day, and tell me all the story. I see from the colour of your skin that you have been in disguise again."

"Yes, sir; there were materials for dyeing the skin in the village, but nothing that availed to take it off. It is gradually going, and as I shall be now able to get some strong alkali from the doctor, I hope I shall be presentable by tomorrow."

"They are honourable marks," the general said with a smile. "I don't think any of us would mind being so coloured for a bit if we had done such good work as you have; but I won't detain you now, for dinner will be ready in half an hour."

Stanley hurried to his room, took a bath, donned his mess uniform, and was ready by the time the bugle sounded. Three or four of the staff were, as usual, members of the party. After the meal was over, he was requested to narrate his adventures at full length. The story was necessarily a long one, and when he concluded all joined the general in hearty commendation for the manner in which he had carried out the adventure.

"Your last story was a stirring one, Mr. Brooke," the general said; "but this is even more so. When I received your first note I thought it next door to madness for you to try to get your cousin, badly wounded as you knew him to be, from the hands of the Burmese. It is not an easy thing to get any man out of prison, but when the man was unable to help himself it seemed well-nigh impossible; and I was greatly afraid that, instead of saving his life, you would lose your own. Of course, the fact that you had successfully traversed the country before, was strongly in your favour; but then you were unencumbered, and the two things were, therefore, not to be compared with each other. I shall, of course, put you in orders to-morrow as having performed a singularly gallant action in rescuing Lieutenant Brooke of the 47th and a sowar, from their captivity by the Burmese in a prison at Toungoo. You have arrived just in time, for after endeavouring to fool us for the past three months by negotiations never meant to come to anything, the enemy are now advancing in great force, and are within a few miles of the town. So we are likely to have hot work of it, for, from all accounts, they have got nearly as large an army together as Bandoola had. I don't know whether they have learned anything from his misfortunes, but I am bound to say that the court does not seem to have taken the lesson in the slightest degree to heart, and their arrogance is just as insufferable as it was before a shot was fired."

Stanley learnt that there had already been one fight. The enemy were advancing in three columns; their right, consisting of 15,000 men, commanded by Sudda Woon, had crossed the Irrawaddy and was marching down the other bank with the apparent object of recrossing below Prome and cutting the British line of communication; the centre, from 25,000 to 30,000 strong, commanded by the Kee Wongee, was coming down the left bank of the river, accompanied by a great fleet of war-boats; the left division, 15,000 strong, led by an old and experienced general, Maha Nemiow, was moving parallel with the others, about ten miles distant from the centre, but separated from it by a thick and impenetrable forest; a reserve of 10,000 men, commanded by the king's half-brother, occupied a strongly fortified post at Melloon. In addition to these, a large force was gathered near Pegu, and threatened an attack upon Rangoon. On the 10th of November, a fortnight before Stanley's return, two brigades of native infantry, under Colonel M'Dowall, had marched out to dislodge Maha Nemiow, whose division threatened to turn the British right and to move round to its rear.

The force was divided into three columns, one moving directly towards the enemy's position, the others marching by circuitous routes, so arranged as to arrive at the point of attack at the same time, were to attack in flank and rear, while the main body assailed the enemy in front. The Burmese had, however, obtained information from spies of the intended movement, and advancing boldly met the British columns half-way, skirmishing with them hotly in the woods and threatening an attack by large bodies of horse. The centre drove the Burmese before them and reached their stockaded position. Colonel M'Dowall, while reconnoitring it, was killed by a ball from a musket; and as the two flanking columns did not arrive as expected, the force was compelled to fall back. The retreat was conducted in good order, but the loss was heavy, as the Burmese pressed hotly upon them for several miles.

Since this unfortunate affair the enemy had steadily advanced. Maha Nemiow had moved directly upon Prome, advancing slowly, and constantly stockading himself. The centre had also advanced, and was now fortifying some heights above the river five miles away, within sight of Prome. Sudda Woon was intrenching himself on the opposite bank. All these divisions were working day and night, advancing steadily but slowly and erecting formidable lines of intrenchments as they went; and it seemed to be the intention of the Burmese general to proceed in that manner until the whole of his troops were gathered within a very short distance of the town, and then to rush upon it from all sides.

In the morning Stanley went to the lines of the 47th. Harry had of course told his story on his arrival, and the tale had circulated generally through the regiment, and as he rode in, the men ran out from their huts and cheered him heartily. No less warm a greeting did he receive from the officers, in spite of his protest that there had really been no great difficulty or danger in the affair.

"What I specially admire," one of the officers said, laughing, "is that any man should have run all this risk on purpose to prevent himself from coming into an earldom.

You had only to leave the matter alone, and there you were—heir to title and estates."

"I should have been haunted by Harry's ghost," Stanley laughed. "It would have been as bad as Banquo and Macbeth; he would have sat at my table and stood at the head of my bed. No, no; that would have been a much more serious affair to face, than a party of Burmese. The title and estates would have been too dear at the price."

"Well, you behaved like a brick, anyhow," the colonel said, "and there is not a man in the regiment who would not have been proud indeed if he had accomplished such a feat. Half my subalterns were talking at dinner last night of learning the language, so that if the chance fell in their way they might emulate your doings."

"It is rather a tough language to master," Stanley replied. "It gave me more trouble than the four or five Indian languages I speak. I am afraid the campaign will be over a long time before any of your officers learn to talk Burmese well enough to pass as natives."

After the failure of the expedition of the 10th no further effort had been made against the enemy. Indeed, the troops had been withdrawn from their outlying positions, and there had even been a feint made of embarking stores, as if with the intention of retiring down the river, in hopes of tempting the Burmese to make an attack.

The season had now come when operations could again be carried on, and the general was anxious to strike a decisive blow at the enemy, and then to set forward on the march towards Ava. As to the result of the fight, no one entertained the slightest doubt, although the disparity in numbers was very great, for while the Burmese commander had nearly 70,000 men at his disposal, Sir Archibald Campbell had no more than 6000, of whom about one-half were British. It was determined that the main attack should be made on the division of Maha Nemiow.

This was now some six or seven miles away, and beyond the fact that it was very strongly intrenched in the jungle, no information whatever could be gained; for the most vigilant watch was kept up by them, and all efforts to pass native spies into their lines failed. But it was known that among his division were 8000 Shans from Upper Burma; and as these men had not hitherto come in contact with us, it was expected that they would fight with more courage and resolution than those who had become acquainted with our power. A large number of princes and nobles were with the force; and great reliance was placed by the Burmese upon three young ladies of high rank who were believed by them to be endowed with supernatural gifts, and to have the power of rendering the missiles of the English innocuous. These young women, dressed in warlike costume, constantly rode among the troops, animating them by their presence, and exhorting them to deeds of courage. The English had received vague rumours of the doings of these Burmese Joans of Arc, and thought it probable that the enemy would fight better than usual.

On November 30th arrangements were made for attacking the enemy on the following morning. The flotilla were to open a furious cannonade upon their works on both sides of the river; a body of native infantry were to drive in the advance posts of the centre, while the main force was to attack their left in two columns, one moving directly against it, while the other was to attack on the right flank, thus preventing the enemy from retreating in the direction of the centre. Four regiments of native infantry were left in Prome.

General Cotton commanded the main attack, and soon after the column moved out from the camp a tremendous cannonade showed that the flotilla was engaged with the Burmese on both sides of the river. The column, which was composed of the 41st and 89th Regiments, with two battalions of native infantry, proceeded some distance before becoming engaged with the enemy's outposts, as the Burmese had been deceived by the cannonade and believed that the attack was entirely upon the centre; the troops, therefore, reached their main position around two native villages without serious opposition. As they issued from the jungle into the cleared space in front of the stockade they rapidly formed up under a tremendous fire and rushed forward to the attack. The old Burmese general, who was too infirm to walk, could be seen carried from point to point in a litter cheering on his men, while the three Amazons exposed themselves fearlessly to the fire. The ladder parties, however, rushed forward unchecked, and, in spite of the opposition of the enemy, scaled the stockade at one point and won a footing on the rampart of earth behind it.

Others pressed after them, and soon a destructive fire was opened upon the crowded mass pent up between the outer stockade and the next. The Burmese method of forming stockade behind stockade was useful against a foe of no greater dash and energy than themselves, but was absolutely

"THE OLD BURMESE GENERAL WAS CARRIED FROM POINT TO POINT IN A LITTER."

fatal when opposed to English troops, who gave them no time to fall back through the narrow openings in the palings. These were soon blocked by the dying and dead. Some of the Shans, led by their chiefs, fought with desperate courage, but were unable to stand the advance of the British, whose steady volleys, poured in at distances of a few yards, swept them away. Wounded horses rushing wildly about in the throng added to the terrible confusion. Groups of men endeavoured to cut a way through the stockades behind, others strove to climb over. Maha Nemiow was killed while bravely exhorting his men to stand their ground, and one of the heroic Amazons was shot. As soon as the troops reached the spot where she fell and saw that she was a woman, she was carried into a cottage, and there died a few hours afterwards.

Stockade after stockade was carried until the whole position fell into our hands. In the meantime the other column, commanded by General Campbell himself, and consisting of the 13th, 38th, 47th, and 87th Regiments and the 38th Madras Infantry, had moved down on the other side of the Nawine river and taken up a position to command the ford there, by which the fugitives from the stockade must cross on their way to join the centre. As the crowd of frightened men issued from the jungle and poured across the ford the artillery opened upon them with shrapnel and completed their discomfiture. All thought of joining the centre was abandoned, and, re-entering the jungle, they scattered, and the greater portion of them started for their homes, intent only on avoiding another contest with their foes. Another of the Burmese heroines was killed at the ford. Three hundred men had been killed at the storming of the stockade, but a far greater loss took place in the retreat, very few of the Shans ever regaining their country, the greater portion perishing from starvation in the great forests through which they travelled in order to escape the Burmese authorities, who would have forced them to rejoin the army.

CHAPTER XVII.

THE PRIDE OF BURMA HUMBLED.

AS soon as the victory was completed the troops piled arms, and were allowed two hours' rest. Then they marched back to the point where General Campbell's division had forded the Nawine river in the morning. From this point a path led towards the enemy's centre; this it was determined to attack at daybreak on the following morning before the news of the defeat of its left could reach it. The day had been a long and fatiguing one, and it was late before the troops all reached their halting-place. A meal was served out, and then all lay down to rest. A messenger was sent to Prome to announce the success that had been gained, and to request the commander of the flotilla to open fire in the morning as soon as the foe was seen to issue from the jungle in front of the Wongee's main position at Napadee.

Long before daylight the troops were in motion. General Campbell's division led the way along the narrow track leading towards the river, while General Cotton, who followed, was ordered to break off at any path which led towards the Burmese division, to make his way through the forest, and to attack the stockades directly he reached them. The main division would attack as soon as they heard his guns.

After a two hours' march the first division came out on open ground by the river side, signalled their arrival to the flotilla, and formed up in front of the stockaded heights of Napadee. The position was an extremely strong one. The enemy occupied three ranges of hills rising one behind the other, and each commanding the one in front of it. One flank of these hills was protected by the river, the other by the almost impenetrable forest. The hills were all covered with stockades; and as they moved forward, the troops were exposed to so heavy a fire from an enemy intrenched at the edge of the jungle on the right, that before they could advance further, it was necessary to first drive them from this position. Six companies of the 87th were sent back into the forest, and making their way through this, came down in the rear of the stockades, speedily cleared them of their defenders, and compelled the advanced force of the enemy to join their main body.

The troops then moved forward to the foot of the first hill, where two strong redoubts had been erected by the enemy. The fleet opened fire, but the column was halted for a time awaiting the sound of firing that should tell them that General Cotton's column was engaged. No sound, however, was heard, for this force had been unable to make its way through the dense forest, and General Campbell at last gave the order for the attack. It was commenced by the 47th and 38th Native Infantry under Colonel Elvington, who pushed through the jungle and forest until they reached some of the flanking outworks on the hill. These they attacked with such dash and determination that they speedily obtained possession of them, and thus produced a favourable diversion for the main attack. This, consisting of the 13th, 38th, and 87th Regiments, advanced steadily without returning a shot to the incessant fire from the enemy's various intrenchments, captured the two redoubts at the bottom of the hill, and then pressed upwards, carrying position after position at the point of the bayonet, till they arrived at the summit of the first hill.

The Burmese fugitives, as they fled to the next line of defence, shook the courage of the troops there, and the British pushing forward hotly on the rear of the flying crowd, carried work after work, until in the course of an hour the whole position, nearly three miles in extent, was entirely in their possession. Between forty and fifty guns were captured, and the enemy's loss in killed and wounded was very great, while by desertion alone the Wongee lost a third of his army. While the attack had been going on, the flotilla had passed the works protecting the river face of the hills, and had captured all the boats and stores filled with supplies for the use of the Burmese army.

Thus two of the three Burmese divisions had now been completely routed, and there remained only that of Sudda Woon on the other side of the river. The troops were allowed two days' rest, and on the morning of the fifth a force advanced on board the flotilla. Their passage across the river was covered by the fire of a rocket-brigade and a mortar-battery, which had on the previous night been established on an island, and they landed at some distance above the enemy's stockades. They then marched round and attacked these in flank and rear, while the batteries and boats of the flotilla cannonaded them in front.

The enemy's troops were already disheartened by the defeat they had seen inflicted upon the Wongee's army, and after a feeble resistance fled to a second line of stockades in the jungle to their rear. The troops, however, pressed so hotly upon them that they were unable to make any effectual opposition here. Numbers fell while endeavouring to pass through the narrow entrances of the work, and the rest fled in terror into the woods.

These extensive operations had been carried out with the loss of six officers and some seventy or eighty men only.

It was known that the enemy had very strongly fortified several positions in and around Meaday, and it was determined to push forward at once on the long march of three hundred miles to Ava, before the enemy could rally from their defeat and gather for the defence of these positions. On the 9th the first division, under General Campbell himself, started from Prome. The roads were extremely bad, and they were able to move but slowly. Their course was first directed inland, as it was intended to turn the enemy's position at Meaday, by following a road several miles from the river and thus forcing them to fall back as we advanced. On the next day the force reached the spot where Colonel M'Dowall had been killed in the unsuccessful attack upon Maha Nemiow, and it then turned north and followed the road parallel to the river.

On the 12th tremendous rains for some hours converted the road into a morass, and although the march was but five miles long, the greater portion of the column failed to reach its destination. This, however, was not the worst. Cholera broke out at once, and carried off a large number of victims—two of the British regiments being rendered almost unfit for service by its ravages. On the 14th the division encamped on dry ground, on a ridge of wooded hills, and waited for a couple of days to allow the baggage train to come up. The change greatly benefited the health of the troops, and amusement was afforded by the partridges, jungle-fowl, and deer which abounded in the neighbourhood of the camp. Up to this point no single native had been seen, the villages were all destroyed, and the country was completely deserted. On the 16th a strong Burmese fortification was taken, it being unoccupied save by a small picket, which retired on our advance. This had evidently been erected for the purpose of preventing the river fortifications from being turned, and its abandonment proved that the object of the land march had been gained, and that the enemy had abandoned the positions they had with so much care prepared for the defence of the river.

On the 18th they joined General Cotton's column, and the next day entered Meaday. Here a terrible spectacle was met with. The town and the ground within the stockades was strewn with dead and dying, some from wounds, others from cholera—for the ravages of this plague had been as great among the Burmese as in the British force. A number of men were found crucified on gibbets, doubtless as a punishment for attempting to desert. The air was pestilent, and the force was glad indeed to march on the next morning from the locality. They gained something, but not much, from the change. For the next fifty miles dead bodies were met with at very short intervals, and each day before camping many corpses had to be removed before the tents could be fixed. It was now known that the Burmese army, in its retreat, had been concentrated at Melloon, where the reserve of 10,000 men had been posted. On the 27th the division encamped within four miles of that town. They had now marched a hundred and forty miles from Prome without meeting a single inhabitant of the country or being enabled to obtain any cattle whatever for the supply of the troops, so effectually had the enemy wasted the country as they retired.

Melloon stood on the opposite bank of the Irrawaddy, and letters had arrived from that town, saying that a commissioner had arrived from Ava with full powers from the king to conclude a treaty of peace. Colonel Adair and Stanley accordingly were sent off the next morning to Melloon to arrange for an immediate meeting for the commissioners. However, they could come to no arrangement, the Burmese leaders insisting that so important a business could only be carried on when a favourable day arrived, and that no time could at present be stated. Seeing that the principal object of the Burmese was to gain time, The colonel informed them, through Stanley, that as no arrangements had been made, the troops would recommence their advance as soon as he returned to the camp, and accordingly the next morning the division moved forward to a town immediately opposite Melloon. That place stood on the face of a sloping hill, and as the Irrawaddy was here but 600 yards broad, a good view was obtained of the fortifications. The principal stockade was in the form of a square, about a mile on each face, mounting a considerable number of guns, especially on the side facing the river, and a succession of stockades extended for a mile farther along the banks. The great work was crowded with men.

In front of the town lay a large fleet of war-boats, and larger craft with stores. A short time after the troops reached the spot, a great noise of gongs, drums, and other warlike instruments arose on the other side, and crowds of boatmen were seen running down to the vessels. These were soon manned, and oars got out, and they began to row up the river. As, owing to the intricacy of the channel, the steam-boat and flotilla had not yet arrived, a few shots were fired at the boats by the field-guns. This had the desired effect, many of the boatmen jumping overboard, leaving their craft to drift down the river, while the great bulk hastily turned their vessels about, and anchored in their former position. As soon as the steamer with the flotilla came up, two war-boats pushed off from shore, saluted the steamer, and rowed alongside of her, until she and the flotilla were safely anchored above the town. This was so evidently a mark of a real desire for the suspension of hostilities that the two officers were again sent across the river. A truce was agreed upon, and an arrangement made for the meeting of the negotiators upon the following day.

Four meetings were held between the two commissioners

and those appointed by the British general, the meetings taking place on boats moored in the centre of the river. At length the treaty was accepted and signed by the Burmese, and fifteen days' truce allowed for the ratification of the treaty by the king. As the end of that period approached, the Burmese protested that they had not yet received an answer, and asked for further time, which was refused, unless on the condition that Melloon was evacuated, and the Burmese army fell back until the ratification of the treaty reached them. As had been for some time strongly suspected, the negotiations were simply a device to arrest our advance, and the treaty was afterwards found in the Burmese camp, it never having been forwarded to Ava. At midnight, on the eighteenth, when the armistice came to a conclusion, the troops began throwing up earthworks, the heavy guns were landed from the flotilla, and at ten o'clock the next morning twenty-eight guns were in position ready to open fire.

In spite of remonstrances that had been made, the Burmese had, night after night during the armistice, continued to work surreptitiously at their intrenchments. It was hoped for a moment that when they saw the speed with which our batteries had been thrown up and armed they would offer no further resistance. As, however, they were evidently preparing for action our guns opened fire at eleven o'clock. This was kept up for two hours. While it was going on, the troops intended for the assault were embarked in boats some distance up the river so as to ensure their not being carried by the force of the stream across the face of the Burmese works and exposed to the concentrated fire of the enemy. They were divided into four brigades, the first of which, consisting of the 13th and 38th Regiments under Lieutenant-colonel Sale, were to land below the stockade, and to attack its south-western angle, while the other three brigades were to land above it, to carry some outworks there, and to attack the northern face.

A strong northerly wind and the violent current prevented the assaults being made simultaneously. The first brigade was carried too far across, and as it passed the stockade was exposed to the fire of the guns and musketry of the river defences, while the three other brigades were unable for some time to reach their intended landing-places. Colonel Sale was among those wounded by the Burmese fire, but directly the first brigade reached the shore they formed up under the partial cover of a shelving bank, and, led by Lieutenant-colonel Frith, moved forward to the assault in admirable order. When within a short distance, there was a forward rush, in spite of the storm of shot, the ladder-party gained the foot of the stockade, and placing the ladders, climbed up, and leapt down among the surging crowd of the enemy. Others followed, and soon a firm footing was obtained in the works. Then the men of the two regiments, whose total strength did not exceed five hundred, advanced steadily, drove before them some 10,000 armed men, and expelled them from the works that the Burmese had deemed impregnable.

While this was going on the other three brigades had landed above the stockade, and now falling upon the enemy as they poured out from their works, completed their defeat.

All the stockades were carried, and the whole of the artillery and stores fell into our possession.

Four days later the army again began its advance. They were met by four Englishmen who had been taken prisoners, and an American, who had also been held in confinement. These had been sent to assure the English general that the king was in earnest in his desire for peace. It was but too evident, however, that no confidence could be placed in Burmese negotiations, and it was, moreover, known that another army was being assembled in the greatest haste to bar the advance. On the 14th of February the British reached Pakang-Yay, having passed Sembeughewn on the opposite shore. This was the point where the road from Aracan reached the Irrawaddy, and it had been arranged that the force that had been operating in Aracan should, if possible, effect a junction with Sir Archibald Campbell here.

A message brought down by a native was, however, received, stating that the force had suffered very severely from fever and cholera, and that the natural obstacles were found to be too great to be overcome by troops debilitated by disease, that the attempt had therefore been abandoned. Fortunately the English general was well able to do without this addition to his strength. He had already proved that his command was perfectly capable of defeating any Burmese force that could be brought against him, and an addition would only have increased the difficulty of transport. On the 9th of March the British force, which, owing to the necessity for leaving strong bodies to hold Melloon and other points that had been captured, now mustered less than 2000 fighting men, advanced to attack the enemy, whose numbers were estimated at 16,000. The new commander of the Burmese adopted other tactics than his predecessors. His stockaded position was in front of the town of Pagahn, but he occupied the jungle in great force and attacked our advance-guard five miles from the town.

As the enemy occupied the hills on both sides of the main road, Sir A. Campbell divided his force and led half of it through the jungle on the right, while General Cotton led the other half through the woods on the left. The Burmese fought with considerable obstinacy. General Campbell and his staff, with thirty-eight troopers and fifty men of the 13th, were somewhat in advance of the column, when the enemy closed in on both flanks and even got in their rear. These were, however, dispersed by the rest of the 13th, and, driving back the Burmese on the flanks, the advance was continued. Presently, however, as the British issued from the jungle, a mass of the enemy's horse charged down, drove back the skirmishers, and for a time the position of the general and his staff was one of great peril.

His little body of troopers, however, dashed boldly at the assailants and held them in check until the guns that had followed the staff were brought forward from the jungle; then the troopers divided and rode right and left, and the guns, opening fire, checked the assailants until the infantry came up. The Burmese army was now seen drawn up in the form of a semicircle in the open. The two British columns were united and together moved forward to attack the centre of the crescent, disregarding the fire from its wings. When within charging distance, they went forward with a rush, and, cheering lustily, fell upon the Burmese, and broke their centre, thus isolating the two wings. The Burmese at once retreated with the greatest haste to the stockaded position in their rear. As usual the narrow entrances to the stockades caused great delay, and the British were upon them before they were in any way prepared to resist the assault. Heralding their advance by sweeping volleys they fell upon the Burmese with the bayonet and drove them out of their works. The enemy made an attempt to rally behind the walls and in the pagodas of the town, but the effort was vain; they were driven out with great slaughter, hundreds were drowned in endeavouring to swim the river, and the army was finally dispersed in all directions.

The effect of this victory was at once apparent. The country people who had, on the advance of the British force from Prome, been cleared out from the villages along the whole line of route, being now freed from the restraint of their troops, came flocking back in great numbers, some by the roads and some in boats; and it was evident that they regarded the struggle as definitely terminated. There was, indeed, no possibility of further resistance, as the armies of Burma, raised with immense difficulty and by heavy bounties and the promises of great reward, were hopelessly scattered, and Ava lay open to the British advance. In other directions their position was equally desperate. Aracan had been wholly rescued from their grasp. A British force in Pegu had marched up the river Sitang, and after the repulse of a party of a hundred and fifty men imprudently sent to attack Sitang itself, captured the place after a sharp fight, and, receiving reinforcements from Rangoon, continued their way up the river and captured Toungoo; while the northern force had driven the Burmese out of Manipur, and had reached the river Ningti by the 2nd of February, and were in a position to advance direct upon Ava.

After a halt of two days, General Campbell advanced on the 12th of February; Mr. Price, the American who had been sent down after the capture of Melloon, went forward to Ava with the treaty that had been drawn up before the capture of that place; and the king had no longer any hesitation in complying with its terms, and was, indeed, delighted to find that the recent victory of the invaders had not increased their demands. He at once sent down to accept them, but as no official ratification was sent, the march continued, while Mr. Price again returned to Ava. When the force was within four days' march of the capital the latter returned with the Burmese commissioners and other high functionaries with the ratified treaty, and the first instalment of the money that was to be paid.

It was a disappointment to the army that after their long march and many sufferings they were not to be allowed to enter the enemy's capital in triumph. Undoubtedly, however, the course taken was the wisest. Ava was regarded as a sacred city, and it was to save it from the humiliation of being occupied by the invaders that the king had brought himself to accept the terms of the treaty. Had the English general insisted upon entering the capital and signing the treaty there, he would have found no one to meet him, the population would have been driven out, the king and court would have retired farther up the country, and the war might have continued for an indefinite time.

Already its cost had been enormous, exceeding £5,000,000 sterling. During the first eleven months after landing at Rangoon, nearly half of the Europeans died, and from the time they advanced from that town with fresh reinforcements from India, to the arrival near Ava, a similarly heavy loss was sustained. Four per cent of the number engaged was killed in action. The climate of Aracan was still more deadly, as three-fourths of the white troops employed there died, and very few of the survivors were ever fit for service afterwards. The sepoys suffered less in Aracan, losing only ten per cent of their number, though nearly half the force were in hospital for some time.

According to agreement, the Burmese, as soon as peace was concluded, sent down a large number of boats for the conveyance of the troops down the river. As they descended it, the garrisons left at Melloon and other places were withdrawn. One of the native regiments with some elephants and guns left the force at Sembeughewn, and marched thence to Aracan, for the purpose of investigating the country and proving whether it was practicable for the passage of troops in case another advance upon Ava should ever be necessary. They found the road unexpectedly good, and met with no resistance whatever, except in the passage of some passes over the mountains.

At Melloon, Stanley was very glad to meet his cousin again, for the 47th had been left in garrison there. Harry had been down again with a sharp attack of fever, but was now recovering.

"So it is all over, Stanley, and your chances of an earldom have nearly slipped through your fingers."

"I am glad, indeed, that it is so," Stanley laughed, "in the first place, because I could only have succeeded to it at your death; and in the second place, because I have no ambition whatever for a title. I am not nineteen yet, and should greatly prefer to make my own way, than to find myself with nothing whatever to do, except to spend money as it dropped into my lap. Now that everything is settled, and that Aracan has become English, and we have the seaports on the Tenasserim coast, trade will increase tremendously. You may be sure that the Burmese will be only too glad to flock into our provinces, and to live under a fair rule, to escape the tyranny of their own officials, and my uncle is just the man to take advantage of the new openings. I don't say that I want to live out here all my life. At any rate I hope by the time that I am thirty to be able to come home for a year's holiday, and it is just possible that by then we may have grown into such a big firm that we may establish head-quarters in London, instead of getting all our goods from Calcutta.

"There is certain to be a very big trade here in teak alone. The price in Pegu is a great deal below that in India, and if we had a house in London, we should avoid having to pay commissions, and perhaps get better prices for our wood. Of course, my uncle may by that time think of retiring himself, and in that case I might have to stay somewhat longer out here, but I know that he likes the climate, and I have heard him say that, as he has very few acquaintances in England, he thinks that he should prefer a life in Calcutta to one in London."

"I should not wonder if I go home very shortly," Harry

said; "my last letter told me that my uncle was in failing health, and that he would like to have me at home with him. If the next letter confirms that, I am afraid I shall have either to resign my commission or exchange into a regiment at home. Of course, at his death I should have to leave the army anyhow. It would be ridiculous for a subaltern to be an earl; besides, there are things one would have to do. I suppose there are estates to be looked after, and all sorts of nuisances. Anyhow I shall always be glad I have had my share in this expedition; I have learned what campaigning is, and I must say that under such circumstances as we have gone through, it is not quite so pleasurable as I had expected. Half one's friends are dead or invalided home, and one never knows when one wakes in the morning whether one may not be down with cholera before night. The fighting is all well enough, but, after all, that takes up but a very small portion of one's time, and marching, and I may say, living generally in this hot, sweltering climate, with its six months of rain, is not enviable work. However, I have gone through one regular campaign, and that as severe a one as British troops have ever performed, and, above all, old man, I have met you, and we have come to be great friends, and I have learned what one fellow will do for another."

"I am sure I am very glad to have gone through it, too. I have been fortunate indeed in never having been laid up for a single day, and there is no doubt that having served on the staff will be of great advantage to me even as a trader. I own that I should like to have retired a captain. Of course, promotion has been tremendously fast owing to the death vacancies, but I have still two lieutenants over me."

"You are sure to get the step, Stanley. You have been in general orders twice, besides that notice you got for my rescue; also, the doctors say that a number of the men who have been sent down to the coast are not likely to live many weeks, and as five of your seniors have been invalided, you may get your step, in the natural course of things, at any moment. If I were you I should ask for three months' leave before rejoining your regiment. There will be no difficulty about that after you have been upwards of two years in constant work, and the general will certainly not refuse. Before the end of that time you will have seen your uncle and talked matters over. Then, if you choose to resign your commission, you can, of course, do so; but as you are pretty sure to get your step by death before the end of the three months, and as the general's despatches strongly recommend your services, you may get your brevet majority before your resignation reaches England. A man who has been mentioned two or three times in despatches, and is specially recommended for honours, is sure to get his brevet majority directly he gets his company."

On reaching Rangoon, Stanley learned that two of the invalids had died either on the way down or before they could be put on board a ship, and that one of the majors, who had been sent to India for change four months before, had also succumbed, so that he had already obtained his company—a promotion which would have been at any other time extraordinary, but which in a campaign where half those engaged were carried off was nothing remarkable.

Being still on the head-quarters staff, he embarked with Sir Archibald Campbell.

"You still hold firm to your determination to leave the service, Captain Brooke," the general said, in the course of the passage to Calcutta.

"Yes, sir; I am sure that it is best for me."

"I think it is, Brooke. Of course, you have been exceptionally fortunate in getting such rapid promotion. Still, a good business is a great deal better than soldiering. I wrote very strongly in your favour when I sent off my despatches the day we came down to the coast, and you are certain of your brevet. Still, it is just as well that the news of your resignation should not get home before the *Gazette* comes out with your name in it. I think the best thing that I can do is to give you leave for a time as soon as we get to Calcutta. I am sure that you deserve a rest, for your work has been terribly heavy."

"Thank you, sir; that was just the favour that I was going to ask you. I shall find out as soon as I get there where my uncle is, and join him. My own mind is quite made up, but he has certainly a right to be consulted before I take any final step."

"Quite right. I feel no doubt that his opinion will agree with yours, and I think that you are showing a good deal more wisdom than most fellows would do, to give up the service when you have distinguished yourself and have a much better chance than falls to the lot of one man in a hundred. Still, there can be no real doubt that a man in a good business out here can retire early and go home with a fortune, while in the army you are liable at any time, after you get to the rank of colonel, to be laid on the shelf for years. Besides, you will be your own master, which is more than anyone in the army can say. You can go home when you like either for a stay or for a permanency, and you are not liable to have to run the risk of another campaign such as this has been."

"If one was sure of campaigns, I don't think that I could possibly bring myself to leave the service, but it is the probability of being kept for three or four years at a time, doing nothing, at Calcutta or Madras that decided me."

The general nodded. "You are quite right, Brooke; on active service a soldier's life is, indeed, a stirring one, but there is nothing more dull and monotonous than garrison life in peace time."

Accordingly as soon as they landed in Calcutta, Stanley was put in orders for absence on leave for three months. He learned from his uncle's agent that they had heard from him only a few days before at Chittagong, and that he was then on the point of leaving for Aracan, whither he had ordered a large consignment of goods to be forwarded to him by the next ship. Three days later, Stanley started to join him, leaving his address at Aracan with Sir Archibald Campbell, in case there should be need to recall him before the three months' leave expired. The vessel in which he was sailing carried the consignment of goods to his uncle, and he had therefore no fear of finding that the latter had left Aracan before his arrival. Meinik was still with him. He had left the army after the last battle had been fought, and had travelled to the spot where he had buried his money before embarking with Stanley in the canoe, and, after an absence of three days, rejoined the force. On the way down to Rangoon, Stanley had a long talk with him as to his future plans.

"I have only one plan, master, and that is to stay with you as long as I live."

"But you will have plenty to live comfortably upon now, Meinik. For, after all that you have done for me, of course I shall arrange for you to have a sum that will keep you in comfort."

Meinik shook his head.

"Burma is a bad country, master. After living with the English, I would not go back to live under the king's officers in any case; any money that I had would be squeezed out of me before long. No, master, I will go with you, unless you drive me from you; if you do, I will go to Chittagong, and live there; but I do not think that you will do that."

"Certainly not, Meinik. As long as you are willing to remain with me I shall be very glad indeed to have you; but if at any time you wish to marry and settle down on land of your own, I shall give you five hundred pounds, which is only a small portion of the sum those rubies, which you got your band to give me, brought me in."

"I daresay I shall marry," Meinik said, "but that will make no difference. As long as I live, I shall stay with you."

Meinik had been astounded at Calcutta, which presented a strong contrast, indeed, to the city which, as a Burman, he had regarded as the most important place in the world.

"The Burmese are fools, master; they should have sent two or three men here before they made up their minds to go to war. If they had been truly told what Calcutta was like, they would never have ventured to make war with the English."

CHAPTER XVIII.

IN BUSINESS AGAIN.

WHEN the vessel arrived at the mouth of the Aracan river, a canoe was seen coming out from Akyab, a town situated at the entrance to the principal of the several channels by which the river makes its way through a number of sand-banks and islands into the sea. As it approached, Stanley recognized his uncle sitting in the stern.

"Well, uncle, how are you?" he called out as the boat approached the side.

"What, is it you, Stanley? I am glad indeed to see you. I have watched the papers anxiously to see if your name appeared among those who have been killed or have died; not seeing it I hoped that you were all right. Of course we heard from the Madras regiment that came across from Sembeughewn that it was all over, and that all the troops would be shipped off as soon as they went down to Rangoon, but I have not seen any papers lately, and so have not had a chance of learning any news of you. I fancied, though, that you would be back at Calcutta by this time, and thought that I might get a letter from you by this ship."

IN BUSINESS AGAIN.

By this time he was on deck, and after a hearty shaking of hands Stanley asked what he was doing here.

"I did not expect to see you until we got to Aracan."

"I have been up there, lad. It is a decaying old place, and the stream is in many places shallow, so that it would be very difficult to take up a ship of any size. I foresee, therefore, that this is going to be the chief port of the province; timber will be floated down here, and rice brought down in native boats, so I shall make my head-quarters here as far as this district is concerned, and put Johnson in charge. I doubt whether for a time we shall do as much trade as we shall higher up the coast, but everyone expects a great Burmese immigration, and a large trade is likely to spring up in time. I have not quite determined on my next move, and it is not improbable that I shall go down in this ship and establish myself for a time at Martaban and open a trade in Tenasserim. If I decide on that, I shall only get on shore a portion of my goods and take the rest on with me there. Now what are you going to do, Stanley?"

"Just what you think best, uncle. I should have thought that, as I speak the language, it would be better for me to go on to Martaban, and for you to work Chittagong and the district up to Assam."

"Then you are going to stay with me, lad!" his uncle exclaimed in a tone of much satisfaction. "I was afraid that you would have got so fond of soldiering that you would have thrown this over altogether."

"Not a bit of it, uncle. I am on three months' leave at present, and at the end of that time I shall resign. You know

"The Burmese are fools, master; they should have sent two or three men here before they made up their minds to go to war. If they had been truly told what Calcutta was like, they would never have ventured to make war with the English."

CHAPTER XVIII.

IN BUSINESS AGAIN.

WHEN the vessel arrived at the mouth of the Aracan river, a canoe was seen coming out from Akyah, a town situated at the entrance to the principal of the several channels by which the river makes its way through a number of sand-banks and islands into the sea. As it approached, Stanley recognized his uncle sitting in the stern.

"Well, uncle, how are you?" he called out as the boat approached the side.

"What, is it you, Stanley? I am glad indeed to see you. I have watched the papers anxiously to see if your name appeared among those who have been killed or have died; not seeing it I hoped that you were all right. Of course we heard from the Madras regiment that came across from Sembeughewn that it was all over, and that all the troops would be shipped off as soon as they went down to Rangoon, but I have not seen any papers lately, and so have not had a chance of learning any news of you. I fancied, though, that you would be back at Calcutta by this time, and thought that I might get a letter from you by this ship."

By this time he was on deck, and after a hearty shaking of hands Stanley asked what he was doing here.

"I did not expect to see you until we got to Aracan."

"I have been up there, lad. It is a decaying old place, and the stream is in many places shallow, so that it would be very difficult to take up a ship of any size. I foresee, therefore, that this is going to be the chief port of the province; timber will be floated down here, and rice brought down in native boats, so I shall make my head-quarters here as far as this district is concerned, and put Johnson in charge. I doubt whether for a time we shall do as much trade as we shall higher up the coast, but everyone expects a great Burmese immigration, and a large trade is likely to spring up in time. I have not quite determined on my next move, and it is not improbable that I shall go down in this ship and establish myself for a time at Martaban and open a trade in Tenasserim. If I decide on that, I shall only get on shore a portion of my goods and take the rest on with me there. Now what are you going to do, Stanley?"

"Just what you think best, uncle. I should have thought that, as I speak the language, it would be better for me to go on to Martaban, and for you to work Chittagong and the district up to Assam."

"Then you are going to stay with me, lad!" his uncle exclaimed in a tone of much satisfaction. "I was afraid that you would have got so fond of soldiering that you would have thrown this over altogether."

"Not a bit of it, uncle. I am on three months' leave at present, and at the end of that time I shall resign. You know

I am a captain now, that is to say, that I have got my rank by death vacancies, though until the gazette comes out from England, I can hardly be said to be a pucka captain; and, what is more, the general himself assured me that after being mentioned in despatches two or three times, and at his strong commendation of my services, I was sure of the brevet rank of major."

His uncle took off his hat gravely.

"I must apologize to you," he said, "for addressing you as 'lad'. I had no idea that you were a full-grown captain, still less that you might soon be a major."

"I don't care a snap for the titles, uncle," Stanley said laughing, "except that it may be an advantage to me in places where there are garrisons, and indeed generally where there are white officials."

"A very great advantage, Stanley. Well, lad, I have been coining money since I saw you at Rangoon. I have been sending a consignment of bullocks down there every week, and have done almost as much with the Manipur force; I have also got the contract regularly now for the supply of the troops at Calcutta. Other trade has of course been at a stand-still. Now that everything has quieted down, there will be a perfect rush, and I have been sorely troubled in my mind whether it would be best to stay up here and take advantage of it, or to be one of the first to open trade at these new ports. Of course, if you are ready to take Martaban that will decide me, and I shall take passage in the first ship going up to Chittagong. My own boat and the dhow are both there, and I shall at once work up all the rivers, and set things going again. I have a capital fellow, a native, who is carrying on the cattle business for me, and at Chittagong I shall try and get hold of three or four more trustworthy fellows to take charge of depôts. I see a big future before us, and that before long. I did well with those gems of yours—they fetched £3500, which I used, besides what you handed over to me, for there was no buying up the cattle without cash, and as I generally have to wait two months after they are shipped before I get paid, ready money was invaluable, and indeed I could not have gone into the thing on anything like the same scale if it had not been for your money. The Calcutta people would have helped me to a certain point, but they would never have ventured upon such advances as I required. Your £5000 has doubled itself since I met you at Rangoon. I calculate that our stores at the different depôts are worth £4000, so that at the present moment the firm of Pearson and Brooke have at their command a capital of £14,000."

A portion of the cargo was landed at Akyah. Stanley went down with the rest to Martaban, and his uncle sailed for Chittagong. A few months later a store was opened at Rangoon. Parsee store-keepers were sent from Calcutta by Tom Pearson, and these were placed in control of the stores there and at Martaban, Stanley being in charge of these two stations and Akyah, and having a native craft of his own, and a boat for river work similar to that of his uncle.

A year later he received a letter from Harry, saying that his uncle had died a month after his return to England, and that he was now established as one of the pillars of the state.

"As I went through London on my arrival," he said, "I looked up your mother at the address you gave me at Dulwich. I found her very well and very comfortable. She was full of your praises, and as I was equally so, your ears ought to have tingled while we were together. Of course they wanted to hear all about you, and most of it was new to them, for you had said nothing of your adventure with that leopard, and only a few lines about the rescue of your humble servant, though you had told them that I stood in your way of the earldom. Your mother said that she was prouder of you than if you were an earl, only that she would have liked to have you at home. I told her that you and your uncle were shaking the pagoda tree, and that you would come home as yellow as a guinea and as rich as a nabob in the course of a few years.

"Your sisters are older than I expected to find them. Of course you always spoke of them as when you saw them last. They are both growing into very pretty girls, the elder especially. I made your mother promise to bring them down to stay with me for a bit, when I came into the title, which I knew could not be long, for I had called that morning on my uncle's solicitors, and they told me that he was not expected to live many weeks. As it is only a month since he died, I suppose I ought not to have visitors just yet; but in a few weeks I shall go up to town and bring them down with me. I cannot help thinking that it is a little selfish; for when they see this place they would not be human if they did not feel that it would have been yours if it had not been for your getting me out of the hands of those Burmese. I see that you are gazetted captain this week. I suppose, long before this, you have settled down to your old work of going up sluggish streams, and trying to stir up the equally sluggish native to a sense of the advantages of British goods. At present I am quite content to do nothing particular, to ride and drive about, return calls, and so on; but I expect, before very long, I shall get restless, and want to be doing something. However, there is the Continent open to one, and decent hotels to stop at. No fevers there, and no Burmese brigands."

A month later he had a letter from his mother which had been written before that of Harry, but had been sent to Calcutta and thence to Akyah, and had there lain until his return, two months later, from a boat journey up to Pegu. She said how kind it was of his cousin to come in to give them news of him the very day he arrived in London.

"Of course we were delighted with all that he told us about you, but it made us anxious to think of your running into so many dangers. We like him very much; we could not help laughing because he seemed quite concerned that you should not have the peerage instead of him. He seems likely to come into it soon, for he tells us that the earl is very ill. He says that we must come down and pay him a visit as soon as he is master there; but I don't know whether that can be. Of course it would be a nice change, and I believe that it is a very fine place. I said that it would seem strange our going there, when there are no ladies, and that bachelors did not generally entertain; but he said that, in the first place, he should have his sisters there, who were about the same age as my girls, and that as we were his nearest relations, and you were at present his heir, it would be quite the right and proper thing for us to come down. He seemed quite in earnest about it, and I should not be surprised if we go."

Three months later, Stanley heard that the visit had been paid, and that they had stayed a fortnight there.

"It feels quite funny settling down here again after being in that big house with all those servants and grandeur; not that there is any grandeur about Harry. He insists, being relations, that we shall call him by his Christian name. Everything was delightful; every afternoon we used to go drives, and of a morning he generally rode with the girls. He had a very pretty gentle horse for Agnes, and a grey pony, a beauty, for Kate. I have a strong suspicion that he had bought them both on purpose. I should not be surprised—but no, I won't say anything about it."

Stanley puzzled over this sentence, which was followed by: "His sisters are very nice girls."

"It is evidently something about Harry," he said to himself; "possibly she has taken the idea into her head that he may fall in love with Agnes. That, certainly, would be a very nice thing, but I don't suppose it is anything more than an idea of mother's."

However, four months later he received a letter from Harry announcing his engagement.

"I told your mother that she must let me write by the mail before she did, as it was only right that I should have the pleasure of telling you the news myself. It is splendid.

old man; upon my word I don't know which I ought to feel,—most grateful to you for saving my life, or for getting me to know your sister. It seems to me a regular dispensation of Providence. You did everything you could to prevent yourself from coming into a title, and now your sister is going to take it and me. It is quite right that we should come to be brothers-in-law, for we are quite like brothers already. We are to be married in the spring. How I wish you could be with us! Your absence will be the only thing wanting to make everything perfect. I do hope you don't mean to stay grilling out there many years. It seems to me monstrous that I should be having estates and a big income, and all that sort of thing, when I have done nothing to deserve it, and that you should be toiling in that beastly climate. If I thought that there was the least chance of your rushing home when you get this letter, I declare that I would put off the marriage for a month or so, so that you should be here in time; but as I feel sure that you won't do anything of the sort, it will be of no use for me to make such a noble sacrifice."

Stanley had received the news that he was gazetted brevet-major a month after he was promoted to the rank of captain, and two months before his name appeared as having retired from the army. He derived, as he expected, much benefit from his connection with the army, in his position at his three receiving ports, as it placed him on a very pleasant footing with the military and civil officials; and it rendered his occasional visits to Calcutta and Madras exceedingly pleasant, for in both towns he found many officers whose acquaintance he had made during the expedition. He was always made an honorary member of the messes and clubs during his stays there.

The business grew rapidly; the work of the earlier years had so well paved the way for larger operations, that they were able to more than hold their own against other traders who, after the troubles were at an end, sought to establish themselves at various points on the western coast of the peninsula, and, after six more years of hard and continuous work, the business became to be a very large and important one.

"I think it more than probable," Stanley wrote to his mother, "that before very long I shall be returning home. My uncle spoke about it the last time that I saw him, and said that we were outgrowing Calcutta, and ought to establish ourselves in London. 'We can hold on a bit longer,' he said, 'but we must come to that sooner or later, and when it does you must be the one to go to England and take charge. I may go home before that for a few months, but I have no wish or desire to stop there. We have now got a good staff, and I shall probably fix myself permanently at Calcutta.'"

Two years later Tom Pearson, on his return from England, brought back a wife with him, and established himself at Calcutta. Stanley joined him there three weeks after his return. They had a long talk together that evening.

"I see, Stanley," his uncle said, "that things have gone on improving since I have been away, and that our turn-over last year was £150,000, and the profits close upon £15,000. I think now that it is high time we opened a place in London. We have almost a monopoly of the teak trade in Burma, and it would be much more advantageous for us to make our purchases in England instead of here. We should save in carriage and in transhipment, besides the profits that the people here make out of their sales to us. I have made a great many inquiries at home, as to the prices for cash in Manchester and Birmingham, and find that we should get goods there some fifteen per cent cheaper than we pay at Calcutta, even after putting on the freights; so you see it is an important matter. Besides there would be a better choice of goods, and you know exactly the sort of thing that we require, and the quantities that we can get rid of, and would be able therefore to send consignments each month without waiting for advices from me, and so we should get the things just as readily as we do now from here. I will give you the names of some of the firms that I have visited and with whom I have already paved the way for opening extensive transactions.

"During the eighteen months that I have been away, you have learned all about the banking business, and will find no more difficulty in managing in London than here. Your brother-in-law Netherley went with me to the Bank of England, and introduced me to one of the directors. I told him that we intended to open a house in London, and that as soon as we did so, we should open an account with them by paying in £30,000, and that we should of course require some facilities, but probably not to a large extent, as our payments for teak there would fairly balance our exports from England, and that I reckoned our trade to be, as a minimum, £50,000 each way. The matter was made extremely easy by Netherley saying, to my astonishment: 'You can let them draw what they like, Mr. Townshend, for I will give my personal guarantee up to £50,000.' I remonstrated, but he would not hear anything said. 'Ridiculous,' he exclaimed, hotly; 'Stanley is my brother-in-law; he risked his life for me, and you don't suppose that I should mind risking £50,000 for him. Not,' he went on, turning to the director, 'that there is any risk in the matter; I know all about the business they do in India, and that there is not a shadow of risk in it. I know that my guarantee will be a mere form, but as it may put them on a better footing with you to begin with, I shall be very pleased to do it.'

"Of course, we know that there will be no risk in it, the greater portion of our business is a ready-money one; and although of late we have been dealing more with native local firms instead of selling direct from our own stores, the amounts are never large, and so far we have never lost a penny. Of course, I shall let you know by every mail how things are going on at all our depôts, and you will then be able to form an estimate as to the amount of goods you will have to despatch to each, sending them direct, of course, if there happens to be a ship going. But all these things, of course, we shall go into at length before you start for England."

"Did you go down to Harry's place?"

"Yes, I stopped there a week. Your sister seems perfectly happy, and plays the part of queen of the county admirably. The four youngsters are jolly little things.

As to your mother, you will find very little change in her. I really don't think that she looks a day older than when we saw her off at Calcutta, something like ten years ago. Of course then she was cut up with her loss, but quiet and comfort have agreed with her, and the climate is a good deal less trying than it is out here. At any rate, I should not take her for a day over forty, and she is something like five years older than that."

Three months later Stanley sailed for England. There was the same argument between him and Meinik that there had been when Stanley first left Rangoon, but this time it terminated differently.

"You would be out of your element in England, Meinik. Of course my life there will be very different from what it is here. I shall go away from home to business every morning, and not get back until perhaps seven o'clock in the evening. As a consequence there would be nothing for you to do for me, and we should see very little of each other. You know I should like to have you with me, and would do all that I could to make you comfortable, but I am sure that you would not like the life. Here you have always been on the move, and there is always something for you to do and think of. I have spoken to my uncle about you, and he will be glad to appoint you to the position of purchaser for our house of teak and other native products in these provinces. Besides being buyer, you would go up the country and see to the felling and getting the timber down to the coast, as you have often done before. He knows how absolutely I trust you, and how much you have done for me, and he said that he should be very glad to have you in charge of the buying side of the work here. Besides, you know you have now a wife and children, and even if you could make yourself comfortable in England, they would never be able to do so, and the bitter cold that we sometimes have in winter would try them terribly and might even carry them all off."

To these arguments Meinik had reluctantly yielded. He was somewhat proud of the position that he occupied as one of some authority in the establishment of the principal merchants on the coast. He was fond of his wife and little children, and felt that to be established among strangers of different habits and race would be very terrible for them. Stanley bought him a nice house at Rangoon, and as his rate of pay, which had been gradually increased, was now sufficient to cause him to rank high among the native population, he himself came to feel that he had done wisely in accepting Stanley's advice.

The voyage to England was an uneventful one, and to Stanley, after the active life he had had for ten years, the five months spent at sea seemed almost interminable.

"I should not have known you in the least," his mother said after the first joyful greetings were over. "How much you have gone through since we parted at Calcutta."

"I had a pretty rough time of it for two years, mother, during the war, but with that exception my life has been a very pleasant one, and I have had nothing whatever to grumble about. This is a pretty house that you have chosen, mother, and the garden is charming. How I have longed sometimes for the sight of an English garden. Of course I have never seen one before, but I have heard you talk of them, and thought how delightful the green grass must be. Of course we had flowers in Burma, plenty of them and shrubs, but it was not green like this. It is charming."

"Yes, it is a pretty house, Stanley. We moved in here five years ago, thanks to you, dear boy, and it has been a very quiet happy time. We have a good many friends now among our neighbours, and have quite as much society as I care for. I suppose you have not yet decided whether you will live here with us," she said a little anxiously, "or set up an establishment of your own."

"Of course I shall stay here, mother. I never thought of anything else. I see that you have some stables. I shall get a couple of horses and drive into town in the mornings. I have got out of the way of walking altogether. And where is Kate?"

"You will see her presently. She will be here to dinner with Agnes and Harry. I sent her off because I wanted to have you all to myself for the first hour. The others came up to town three days ago on purpose to be here when you arrived. Of course we heard when your ship called at Plymouth. We had been looking for her, for your last letter told us the name of the vessel that you were coming by, so I wrote to them and they came up at once. They wanted us to go and dine with them, but I would not hear of it. I was sure that you would much rather dine quietly here than in state in Portman Square with three or four footmen behind our chairs."

"Ever so much better, mother. I suppose I shall hardly

know Agnes, but Harry cannot have altered much; besides, I have seen him four years later than her."

Harry's greeting was of the heartiest kind; Stanley's sisters felt at first a little strange with this brother of whom they had but a faint remembrance.

"It does not seem to me, Harry, that your dignities have tamed you down much."

"No, indeed," Harry laughed. "I find it sometimes very difficult to act up to my position. I never quite feel that I am an earl except on the rare occasions when I go to the House of Lords, which I only do when my vote is wanted on an important division. The gloom of that place is enough to sober anyone. I can assure you that when I heard of the fire I felt absolutely pleased. Of course, they will build another one, perhaps grander than the last and as gloomy; but, thank goodness, it must be years before it can be finished, and until then we shall have to put up with temporary premises. Your chances of an earldom are getting more and more remote, Stanley. There are three boys barring the way already. I had proposed to myself not to marry, in which case you or a son of yours would have followed me, but your sister overpersuaded me."

Agnes tossed her head as she said:

"At any rate, Harry, if you made that resolution, it was not worth much, as you gave it up at the first opportunity. I was the first girl you met when you arrived in England, and I doubt whether you had seen another before we came down to stay at Netherley. I had not been there two days before you began to make love to me."

"The temptation would excuse anything, my dear,"

Harry laughed; "besides, you see, I saw at once that it was but fair and right to Stanley, that if he could not get the peerage himself, he might some day have the satisfaction of being uncle to an earl. And so you are home for good, old fellow."

"Yes, and just at present I feel very much at sea as to how to get to work, as Tom Pearson arranged nothing except as to the banking account, everything else he has left to me. I know nothing of London, and have no idea of the situation where I should look for offices."

'I will put you up to all that, Stanley. I don't know anything about it myself, as you may suppose, but if you will go with me to my solicitors to-morrow, they will be able to tell you. But I do know that Leadenhall Street is the centre of the Indian trade, and it's somewhere about there that you will have to fix yourself. Of course, when you have taken a place you will have to get hold of some clerks. If you put an advertisement in the paper you will get any number of applicants, or possibly my men may, through their connection with merchants, be able to hear of some to suit you; anyhow, I am sure that you will find no difficulty."

Thanks to Harry's introductions, Stanley was established in a handsome suite of offices with three clerks, with much greater ease than he had anticipated. Being thoroughly versed in business, he was not long before he was at home in his new life.

Three years after his return, he married Harry's youngest sister. The firm flourished greatly and became one of the leading houses in the Eastern trade. At the age of sixty

Stanley retired from business with a large fortune. He could do this comfortably, as his eldest son and a nephew had become active partners in the firm. He still lives at the age of eighty-six in a noble mansion near Staines, and retains all the faculties even at advanced age.

THE END.

PRINTED BY BLACKIE AND SON, LIMITED, GLASGOW.

BLACKIE & SON'S
BOOKS FOR YOUNG PEOPLE.

BY G. A. HENTY.

In crown 8vo, cloth elegant, olivine edges.

The Tiger of Mysore: A Story of the War with Tippoo Saib. By G. A. HENTY. With 12 Illustrations by W. H. MARGETSON, and a Map. 6s.

"Mr. Henty not only concocts a thrilling tale, he weaves fact and fiction together with so skilful a hand that the reader cannot help acquiring a just and clear view of that fierce and terrible struggle which gave to us our Indian Empire."—*Athenæum.*

A Knight of the White Cross: A Tale of the Siege of Rhodes. By G. A. HENTY. With 12 full-page Illustrations by RALPH PEACOCK. 6s.

"Mr. Henty is a giant among boys' writers, and his books are sufficiently popular to be sure of a welcome anywhere. . . . In stirring interest, this is quite up to the level of Mr. Henty's former historical tales."—*Saturday Review.*

When London Burned: A Story of Restoration Times and the Great Fire. By G. A. HENTY. With 12 page Illustrations by J. FINNEMORE. 6s.

"No boy needs to have any story of Henty's recommended to him, and parents who do not know and buy him for their boys should be ashamed of themselves. Those to whom he is yet unknown could not make a better beginning than with *When London Burned.*"—*British Weekly.*

Beric the Briton: A Story of the Roman Invasion. By G. A. HENTY. Illustrated by W. PARKINSON. 6s.

"We are not aware that anyone has given us quite so vigorous a picture of Britain in the days of the Roman conquest. Mr. Henty has done his utmost to make an impressive picture of the haughty Roman character, with its indomitable courage, sternness, and discipline. *Beric* is good all through."—*Spectator.*

By Pike and Dyke: A Tale of the Rise of the Dutch Republic. By G. A. HENTY. With 10 page Illustrations by MAYNARD BROWN, and 4 Maps. 6s.

"The mission of Ned to deliver letters from William the Silent to his adherents at Brussels, the fight of the *Good Venture* with the Spanish man-of-war, the battle on the ice at Amsterdam, the siege of Haarlem, are all told with a vividness and skill which are worthy of Mr. Henty at his best."—*Academy.*

BY G. A. HENTY.

"Among writers of stories of adventure for boys Mr. Henty stands in the very first rank."—*Academy*.

In crown 8vo, cloth elegant, olivine edges.

The Lion of St. Mark: A Tale of Venice in the Fourteenth Century. By G. A. HENTY. With 10 page Illustrations by GORDON BROWNE. 6s.

"Every boy should read *The Lion of St. Mark*. Mr. Henty has never produced any story more delightful, more wholesome, or more vivacious. From first to last it will be read with keen enjoyment."—*The Saturday Review*.

By England's Aid: The Freeing of the Netherlands (1585-1604). By G. A. HENTY. With 10 page Illustrations by ALFRED PEARSE, and 4 Maps. 6s.

"The story is told with great animation, and the historical material is most effectively combined with a most excellent plot."—*Saturday Review*.

With Wolfe in Canada: or, The Winning of a Continent. By G. A. HENTY. Illustrated with 12 page Pictures by GORDON BROWNE. 6s.

"A model of what a boys' story-book should be. Mr. Henty has a great power of infusing into the dead facts of history new life, and as no pains are spared by him to ensure accuracy in historic details, his books supply useful aids to study as well as amusement."—*School Guardian*.

Bonnie Prince Charlie: A Tale of Fontenoy and Culloden. By G. A. HENTY. Illustrated with 12 page Pictures by GORDON BROWNE. 6s.

"Ronald, the hero, is very like the hero of *Quentin Durward*. The lad's journey across France with his faithful attendant Malcolm, and his hairbreadth escapes from the machinations of his father's enemies make up as good a narrative of the kind as we have ever read. For freshness of treatment and variety of incident, Mr. Henty has here surpassed himself."—*Spectator*.

For the Temple: A Tale of the Fall of Jerusalem. By G. A. HENTY. With 10 page Illustrations by S. J. SOLOMON, and a Coloured Map. 6s.

"Mr. Henty's graphic prose pictures of the hopeless Jewish resistance to Roman sway adds another leaf to his record of the famous wars of the world. The book is one of Mr. Henty's cleverest efforts."—*Graphic*.

True to the Old Flag: A Tale of the American War of Independence. By G. A. HENTY. With 12 page Illustrations by GORDON BROWNE. 6s.

"Does justice to the pluck and determination of the British soldiers. The son of an American loyalist, who remains true to our flag, falls among the hostile red-skins in that very Huron country which has been endeared to us by the exploits of Hawkeye and Chingachgook."—*The Times*.

"Mr. Henty undoubtedly possesses the secret of writing eminently successful historical tales; and those older than the lads whom the author addresses in his preface may read the story with pleasure."—*Academy*.

Specimen Illustration from "THE TIGER OF MYSORE".

"DICK TOOK STEADY AIM, AND FIRED AT THE TIGER."

BY G. A. HENTY.

"Mr. Henty is one of our most successful writers of historical tales."—*Scotsman.*

In crown 8vo, cloth elegant, olivine edges.

The Lion of the North: A Tale of Gustavus Adolphus and the Wars of Religion. By G. A. HENTY. With 12 page Pictures by J. SCHÖNBERG. 6s.

"A praiseworthy attempt to interest British youth in the great deeds of the Scotch Brigade in the wars of Gustavus Adolphus. Mackay, Hepburn, and Munro live again in Mr. Henty's pages, as those deserve to live whose disciplined bands formed really the germ of the modern British army."—*Athenæum.*

The Young Carthaginian: A Story of the Times of Hannibal. By G. A. HENTY. With 12 page Illustrations by C. J. STANILAND, R.I. 6s.

"The effect of an interesting story, well constructed and vividly told, is enhanced by the picturesque quality of the scenic background. From first to last nothing stays the interest of the narrative. It bears us along as on a stream whose current varies in direction, but never loses its force."—*Saturday Review.*

Redskin and Cow-boy: A Tale of the Western Plains. By G. A. HENTY. Illustrated by ALFRED PEARSE. 6s.

"It has a good plot; it abounds in action; the scenes are equally spirited and realistic, and we can only say we have read it with much pleasure from first to last. The pictures of life on a cattle ranche are most graphically painted, as are the manners of the reckless but jovial cow-boys."—*Times.*

With Clive in India: or, The Beginnings of an Empire. By G. A. HENTY. Illustrated by GORDON BROWNE. 6s.

"Among writers of stories of adventure for boys Mr. Henty stands in the very first rank. Those who know something about India will be the most ready to thank Mr. Henty for giving them this instructive volume to place in the hands of their children."—*Academy.*

In Greek Waters: A Story of the Grecian War of Independence (1821–1827). By G. A. HENTY. With 12 page Illustrations by W. S. STACEY, and a Map. 6s.

"There are adventures of all kinds for the hero and his friends, whose pluck and ingenuity in extricating themselves from awkward fixes are always equal to the occasion. It is an excellent story, and if the proportion of history is smaller than usual, the whole result leaves nothing to be desired."—*Journal of Education.*

The Dash for Khartoum: A Tale of the Nile Expedition. By G. A. HENTY. With 10 page Illustrations by J. SCHÖNBERG and J. NASH, and 4 Plans. 6s.

"It is literally true that the narrative never flags a moment; for the incidents which fall to be recorded after the dash for Khartoum has been made and failed are quite as interesting as those which precede it."—*Academy.*

BY G. A. HENTY.

"Mr. Henty is the king of story-tellers for boys."—*Sword and Trowel.*

In crown 8vo, cloth elegant, olivine edges.

Reduced Illustration from "*A Knight of the White Cross*".

St. Bartholomew's Eve: A Tale of the Huguenot Wars.
By G. A. HENTY. Illustrated by H. J. DRAPER. 6s.

"What would boys do without Mr. Henty? Ever fresh and vigorous, his books have at once the solidity of history and the charm of romance. *St. Bartholomew's Eve* is in his best style, and the interest never flags. The book is all that could possibly be wished from a boy's point of view."—*Journal of Education.*

In Freedom's Cause: A Story of Wallace and Bruce.
By G. A. HENTY. Illustrated by GORDON BROWNE. 6s.

"His tale of the days of Wallace and Bruce is full of stirring action, and will commend itself to boys."—*Athenæum.*

By Right of Conquest: or, With Cortez in Mexico.
By G. A. HENTY. With 10 page Illustrations by W. S. STACEY. 6s.

"*By Right of Conquest* is the nearest approach to a perfectly successful historical tale that Mr. Henty has yet published."—*Academy.*

BY G. A. HENTY.

"Mr. Henty is one of the best of story-tellers for young people."—*Spectator.*

In crown 8vo, cloth elegant, olivine edges.

Reduced Illustration from "Wulf the Saxon".

Wulf the Saxon: A Story of the Norman Conquest. By G. A. HENTY. Illustrated by RALPH PEACOCK. 6s.

"*Wulf the Saxon* is second to none of Mr. Henty's historical tales, and we may safely say that a boy may learn from it more genuine history than he will from many a tedious tome. The points of the Saxon character are hit off very happily, and the life of the period is ably reconstructed."—*The Spectator.*

Through the Sikh War: A Tale of the Conquest of the Punjaub. By G. A. HENTY. With 12 page Illustrations by HAL HURST, and a Map. 6s.

"The picture of the Punjaub during its last few years of independence, the description of the battles on the Sutlej, and the portraiture generally of native character, seem admirably true. . . . On the whole, we have never read a more vivid and faithful narrative of military adventure in India."—*The Academy.*

BY G. A. HENTY.

"No more interesting boys' books are written than Mr. Henty's stories."—
Daily Chronicle.

In crown 8vo, cloth elegant, olivine edges.

Through the Fray: A Story of the Luddite Riots. By G. A. HENTY. With 12 page Illustrations by H. M. PAGET. 6s.

"Mr. Henty inspires a love and admiration for straightforwardness, truth, and courage. This is one of the best of the many good books Mr. Henty has produced, and deserves to be classed with his *Facing Death*."—*Standard.*

Captain Bayley's Heir: A Tale of the Gold Fields of California. By G. A. HENTY. Illustrated by H. M. PAGET. 6s.

"A Westminster boy who makes his way in the world by hard work, good temper, and unfailing courage. The descriptions given of life are just what a healthy intelligent lad should delight in."—*St. James's Gazette.*

With Lee in Virginia: A Story of the American Civil War. By G. A. HENTY. With 10 page Illustrations by GORDON BROWNE, and 6 Maps. 6s.

"The story is a capital one and full of variety, and presents us with many picturesque scenes of Southern life. Young Wingfield, who is conscientious, spirited, and 'hard as nails', would have been a man after the very heart of Stonewall Jackson."—*Times.*

Under Drake's Flag: A Tale of the Spanish Main. By G. A. HENTY. Illustrated by GORDON BROWNE. 6s.

"There is not a dull chapter, nor, indeed, a dull page in the book; but the author has so carefully worked up his subject that the exciting deeds of his heroes are never incongruous or absurd."—*Observer.*

Through Russian Snows: A Story of Napoleon's Retreat from Moscow. By G. A. HENTY. With 8 Illustrations by W. H. OVEREND, and a Map. 5s.

"Julian, the hero of the story, early excites our admiration, and is altogether a fine character such as boys will delight in, whilst the story of the campaign is very graphically told. . . . Will, we think, prove one of the most popular boys' books this season."—*St. James's Gazette.*

In the Heart of the Rockies: A Story of Adventure in Colorado. By G. A. HENTY. Illustrated by G. C. HINDLEY. 5s.

"Few Christmas books will be more to the taste of the ingenuous boy than *In the Heart of the Rockies*."—*Athenæum.*

"Mr. Henty is seen here at his best as an artist in lightning fiction."—*Academy.*

One of the 28th: A Tale of Waterloo. By G. A. HENTY. With 8 page Illustrations by W. H. OVEREND, and 2 Maps. 5s.

"Written with Homeric vigour and heroic inspiration. It is graphic, picturesque, and dramatically effective . . . shows us Mr. Henty at his best and brightest. The adventures will hold a boy of a winter's night enthralled as he rushes through them with breathless interest 'from cover to cover'."—*Observer.*

BY G. A. HENTY.

"Ask for Henty, and see that you get him."—*Punch.*

In crown 8vo, cloth elegant, olivine edges.

The Cat of Bubastes: A Story of Ancient Egypt. By G. A. HENTY. Illustrated by J. R. WEGUELIN. 5s.

"The story, from the critical moment of the killing of the sacred cat to the perilous exodus into Asia with which it closes, is very skilfully constructed and full of exciting adventures. It is admirably illustrated."—*Saturday Review.*

Maori and Settler: A Story of the New Zealand War. By G. A. HENTY. With 8 page Illustrations by ALFRED PEARSE. 5s.

"It is a book which all young people, but especially boys, will read with avidity."—*Athenæum.*

"A first-rate book for boys, brimful of adventure, of humorous and interesting conversation, and of vivid pictures of colonial life."—*Schoolmaster.*

St. George for England: A Tale of Cressy and Poitiers. By G. A. HENTY. Illustrated by GORDON BROWNE. 5s.

"A story of very great interest for boys. In his own forcible style the author has endeavoured to show that determination and enthusiasm can accomplish marvellous results; and that courage is generally accompanied by magnanimity and gentleness."—*Pall Mall Gazette.*

The Bravest of the Brave: With Peterborough in Spain. By G. A. HENTY. With 8 full-page Pictures by H. M. PAGET. 5s.

"Mr. Henty never loses sight of the moral purpose of his work—to enforce the doctrine of courage and truth, mercy and lovingkindness, as indispensable to the making of an English gentleman. British lads will read *The Bravest of the Brave* with pleasure and profit; of that we are quite sure."—*Daily Telegraph.*

For Name and Fame: or, Through Afghan Passes. By G. A. HENTY. Illustrated by GORDON BROWNE. 5s.

"Not only a rousing story, replete with all the varied forms of excitement of a campaign, but, what is still more useful, an account of a territory and its inhabitants which must for a long time possess a supreme interest for Englishmen, as being the key to our Indian Empire."—*Glasgow Herald.*

A Jacobite Exile: Being the Adventures of a Young Englishman in the Service of Charles XII. of Sweden. By G. A. HENTY. With 8 page Illustrations by PAUL HARDY, and a Map. 5s.

"Incident succeeds incident, and adventure is piled upon adventure, and at the end the reader, be he boy or man, will have experienced breathless enjoyment in a romantic story that must have taught him much at its close."—*Army and Navy Gazette.*

Held Fast for England: A Tale of the Siege of Gibraltar. By G. A. HENTY. Illustrated by GORDON BROWNE. 5s.

"Among them we would place first in interest and wholesome educational value the story of the siege of Gibraltar. . . There is no cessation of exciting incident throughout the story."—*Athenæum.*

Specimen Illustration from "THROUGH RUSSIAN SNOWS".

"I AM THE COUNTESS STEPHANIE WORONSKI. I AM GLAD TO SEE YOU."

BY G. A. HENTY.

"Mr. Henty's books are always alive with moving incident."—*Review of Reviews.*

In crown 8vo, cloth elegant.

Condemned as a Nihilist: A Story of Escape from Siberia. By G. A. HENTY. Illustrated by WALTER PAGET. 5s.

"The best of this year's Henty. His narrative is more interesting than many of the tales with which the public is familiar, of escape from Siberia. Despite their superior claim to authenticity these tales are without doubt no less fictitious than Mr. Henty's, and he beats them hollow in the matter of sensations."—*National Observer.*

Orange and Green: A Tale of the Boyne and Limerick. By G. A. HENTY. Illustrated by GORDON BROWNE. 5s.

"The narrative is free from the vice of prejudice, and ripples with life as vivacious as if what is being described were really passing before the eye. . . . Should be in the hands of every young student of Irish history."—*Belfast News.*

In the Reign of Terror: The Adventures of a Westminster Boy. By G. A. HENTY. Illustrated by J. SCHÖNBERG. 5s.

"Harry Sandwith, the Westminster boy, may fairly be said to beat Mr. Henty's record. His adventures will delight boys by the audacity and peril they depict. The story is one of Mr. Henty's best."—*Saturday Review.*

By Sheer Pluck: A Tale of the Ashanti War. By G. A. HENTY. With 8 full-page Pictures by GORDON BROWNE. 5s.

"Morally, the book is everything that could be desired, setting before the boys a bright and bracing ideal of the English gentleman."—*Christian Leader.*

The Dragon and the Raven: or, The Days of King Alfred. By G. A. HENTY. With 8 page Illustrations by C. J. STANILAND, R.I. 5s.

"A story that may justly be styled remarkable. Boys, in reading it, will be surprised to find how Alfred persevered, through years of bloodshed and times of peace, to rescue his people from the thraldom of the Danes. We hope the book will soon be widely known in all our schools."—*Schoolmaster.*

A Final Reckoning: A Tale of Bush Life in Australia. By G. A. HENTY. Illustrated by W. B. WOLLEN. 5s.

"All boys will read this story with eager and unflagging interest. The episodes are in Mr. Henty's very best vein—graphic, exciting, realistic; and, as in all Mr. Henty's books, the tendency is to the formation of an honourable, manly, and even heroic character."—*Birmingham Post.*

Facing Death: or, The Hero of the Vaughan Pit. A Tale of the Coal Mines. By G. A. HENTY. With 8 page Pictures by GORDON BROWNE. 5s.

"If any father, godfather, clergyman, or schoolmaster is on the look-out for a good book to give as a present to a boy who is worth his salt, this is the book we would recommend."—*Standard.*

A Chapter of Adventures: or, Through the Bombardment of Alexandria. By G. A. HENTY. With 6 page Illustrations by W. H. OVEREND. 3s. 6d.

"Jack Robson and his two companions have their fill of excitement, and their chapter of adventures is so brisk and entertaining we could have wished it longer than it is."—*Saturday Review.*

BY KIRK MUNROE.

In crown 8vo, cloth elegant, olivine edges.

At War with Pontiac: or, The Totem of the Bear. By KIRK MUNROE. Illustrated by J. FINNEMORE. 5s.

"Is in the best manner of Cooper. There is a character who is the parallel of Hawkeye, as the Chingachgooks and Uncas have likewise their counterparts."—*The Times.*

The White Conquerors of Mexico: A Tale of Toltec and Aztec. By KIRK MUNROE. Illustrated by W. S. STACEY. 5s.

"Mr. Munroe gives most vivid pictures of the religious and civil polity of the Aztecs, and of everyday life, as he imagines it, in the streets and market-places of the magnificent capital of Montezuma."—*The Times.*

Reduced Illustration from "At War with Pontiac".

Crown 8vo, cloth elegant.

Two Thousand Years Ago: or, The Adventures of a Roman Boy. By Professor A. J. CHURCH. With 12 page Illustrations by ADRIEN MARIE. 6s.

"Adventures well worth the telling. The book is extremely entertaining as well as useful, and there is a wonderful freshness in the Roman scenes and characters."—*The Times.*

The Clever Miss Follett. By J. K. H. DENNY. With 12 page Illustrations by GERTRUDE D. HAMMOND. 6s.

"Just the book to give to girls, who will delight both in the letterpress and the illustrations. Miss Hammond has never done better work.'—*Review of Reviews.*

The Heiress of Courtleroy. By ANNE BEALE. With 8 page Illustrations by T. C. H. CASTLE. 5s.

"We can speak highly of the grace with which Miss Beale relates how the young 'Heiress of Courtleroy' had such good influence over her uncle as to win him from his intensely selfish ways."—*Guardian.*

BY GEORGE MANVILLE FENN.

"Mr. Fenn stands in the foremost rank of writers in this department."—*Daily News*.

In crown 8vo, cloth elegant.

Dick o' the Fens: A Romance of the Great East Swamp. By G. MANVILLE FENN. Illustrated by FRANK DADD. 6s.

"We conscientiously believe that boys will find it capital reading. It is full of incident and mystery, and the mystery is kept up to the last moment. It is rich in effective local colouring; and it has a historical interest."—*Times*.

Devon Boys: A Tale of the North Shore. By G. MANVILLE FENN. With 12 page Illustrations by GORDON BROWNE. 6s.

"An admirable story, as remarkable for the individuality of its young heroes as for the excellent descriptions of coast scenery and life in North Devon. It is one of the best books we have seen this season."—*Athenæum*.

The Golden Magnet: A Tale of the Land of the Incas. By G. MANVILLE FENN. Illustrated by GORDON BROWNE. 6s.

"There could be no more welcome present for a boy. There is not a dull page in the book, and many will be read with breathless interest. 'The Golden Magnet' is, of course, the same one that attracted Raleigh and the heroes of *Westward Ho!*"—*Journal of Education*.

In the King's Name: or, The Cruise of the *Kestrel*. By G. MANVILLE FENN. Illustrated by GORDON BROWNE. 6s.

"The best of all Mr. Fenn's productions in this field. It has the great quality of always 'moving on', adventure following adventure in constant succession."—*Daily News*.

Nat the Naturalist: A Boy's Adventures in the Eastern Seas. By G. MANVILLE FENN. With 8 page Pictures. 5s.

"This sort of book encourages independence of character, develops resource, and teaches a boy to keep his eyes open."—*Saturday Review*.

Bunyip Land: The Story of a Wild Journey in New Guinea. By G. MANVILLE FENN. Illustrated by GORDON BROWNE. 4s.

"Mr. Fenn deserves the thanks of everybody for *Bunyip Land*, and we may venture to promise that a quiet week may be reckoned on whilst the youngsters have such fascinating literature provided for their evenings' amusement."—*Spectator*.

Quicksilver: or, A Boy with no Skid to his Wheel. By GEORGE MANVILLE FENN. With 6 page Illustrations by FRANK DADD. New edition, 3s. 6d.

"*Quicksilver* is little short of an inspiration. In it that prince of story writers for boys—George Manville Fenn—has surpassed himself. It is an ideal book for a boy's library."—*Practical Teacher*.

Brownsmith's Boy: A Romance in a Garden. By G. MANVILLE FENN. With 6 page Illustrations. 3s. 6d.

"Mr. Fenn's books are among the best, if not altogether the best, of the stories for boys. Mr. Fenn is at his best in *Brownsmith's Boy*."—*Pictorial World*.

*** For other Books by G. MANVILLE FENN, see page 22.

BY GEORGE MAC DONALD.

In crown 8vo, cloth elegant.

A Rough Shaking. By GEORGE MAC DONALD. With 12 page Illustrations by W. PARKINSON. 6s.

"One of the very best books for boys that has been written. It is full of material peculiarly well adapted for the young, containing in a marked degree the elements of all that is necessary to make up a perfect boys' book."—*Teachers' Aid.*

At the Back of the North Wind. By GEORGE MAC-DONALD. With 75 Illustrations by ARTHUR HUGHES. 5s.

"The story is thoroughly original, full of fancy and pathos. . . . We stand with one foot in fairyland and one on common earth."—*The Times.*

Ranald Bannerman's Boyhood. By GEO. MAC DONALD. With 36 Illustrations by ARTHUR HUGHES. 5s.

"The sympathy with boy-nature in *Ranald Bannerman's Boyhood* is perfect. It is a beautiful picture of childhood, teaching by its impressions and suggestions all noble things."—*British Quarterly Review.*

The Princess and the Goblin. By GEORGE MAC DONALD. With 32 Illustrations. 3s. 6d.

"Little of what is written for children has the lightness of touch and play of fancy which are characteristic of George Mac Donald's fairy tales. Mr. Arthur Hughes's illustrations are all that illustrations should be."—*Manchester Guardian.*

The Princess and Curdie. By GEORGE MAC DONALD. With 8 page Illustrations. 3s. 6d.

"There is the finest and rarest genius in this brilliant story. Upgrown people would do wisely occasionally to lay aside their newspapers and magazines to spend an hour with Curdie and the Princess."—*Sheffield Independent.*

BY HARRY COLLINGWOOD.

The Pirate Island: A Story of the South Pacific. By HARRY COLLINGWOOD. With 8 page Pictures by C. J. STANILAND and J. R. WELLS. 5s.

"A capital story of the sea; indeed in our opinion the author is superior in some respects as a marine novelist to the better-known Mr. Clark Russell."—*The Times.*

The Log of the "Flying Fish": A Story of Aerial and Submarine Adventure. By HARRY COLLINGWOOD. With 6 page Illustrations by GORDON BROWNE. 3s. 6d.

"The *Flying Fish* actually surpasses all Jules Verne's creations: with incredible speed she flies through the air, skims over the surface of the water, and darts along the ocean bed. We strongly recommend our school-boy friends to possess themselves of her log."—*Athenæum.*

⁂ For other Books by Harry Collingwood, see pages 22 and 23.

BY ROBERT LEIGHTON.

In crown 8vo, cloth elegant, olivine edges.

Olaf the Glorious. By ROBERT LEIGHTON. With 8 page Illustrations by RALPH PEACOCK, and a Map. 5s.

"Is as good as anything of the kind we have met with. Mr. Leighton more than holds his own with Rider Haggard and Baring-Gould."—*The Times.*

"Among the books best liked by boys of the sturdy English type few will take a higher place than *Olaf the Glorious*. . . ."—*National Observer.*

The Wreck of "The Golden Fleece": The Story of a North Sea Fisher-boy. By ROBERT LEIGHTON. With 8 page Illustrations by F. BRANGWYN. 5s.

"This story should add considerably to Mr. Leighton's high reputation. Excellent in every respect, it contains every variety of incident. The plot is very cleverly devised, and the types of the North Sea sailors are capital."—*The Times.*

The Pilots of Pomona: A Story of the Orkney Islands. By ROBERT LEIGHTON. Illustrated by JOHN LEIGHTON. 5s.

"A story which is quite as good in its way as *Treasure Island*, and is full of adventure of a stirring yet most natural kind. Although it is primarily a boys' book, it is a real godsend to the elderly reader."—*Glasgow Evening Times.*

The Thirsty Sword: A Story of the Norse Invasion of Scotland (1262-63). By ROBERT LEIGHTON. With 8 page Illustrations by A. PEARSE. 5s.

"This is one of the most fascinating stories for boys that it has ever been our pleasure to read. From first to last the interest never flags. Boys will worship Kenric, who is a hero in every sense of the word."—*Schoolmaster.*

BY ROSA MULHOLLAND.

Banshee Castle. By ROSA MULHOLLAND. With 12 page Illustrations by JOHN H. BACON. 6s.

"One of the most fascinating of Miss Rosa Mulholland's many fascinating stories. . . . The charm of the tale lies in the telling of it. The three heroines are admirably drawn characters."—*Athenæum.*

Giannetta: A Girl's Story of Herself. By ROSA MULHOLLAND. With 8 page Illustrations by LOCKHART BOGLE. 5s.

"Giannetta is a true heroine—warm-hearted, self-sacrificing, and, as all good women nowadays are, largely touched with the enthusiasm of humanity. One of the most attractive gift-books of the season."—*The Academy.*

A Fair Claimant: Being a Story for Girls. By FRANCES ARMSTRONG. Illustrated by GERTRUDE D. HAMMOND. 5s.

"As a gift-book for big girls it is among the best new books of the kind. The story is interesting and natural, from first to last."—*Westminster Gazette.*

Specimen Illustration from "A FAIR CLAIMANT".

"OLIVE LEAPT INTO HER MOTHER'S ARMS."

TWELFTH EDITION OF THE UNIVERSE.

The Universe: or, The Infinitely Great and the Infinitely Little. A Sketch of Contrasts in Creation, and Marvels revealed and explained by Natural Science. By F. A. POUCHET, M.D. With 272 Engravings on wood, of which 55 are full-page size, and 4 Coloured Illustrations. Twelfth Edition, medium 8vo, cloth elegant, gilt edges, 7s. 6d.; also morocco antique, 16s.

"Dr. Pouchet's wonderful work on *The Universe*, than which there is no book better calculated to encourage the study of nature."—*Pall Mall Gazette.*

"We know no better book of the kind for a schoolroom library."—*Bookman.*

BY G. NORWAY.

In crown 8vo, cloth elegant.

A Prisoner of War: A Story of the Time of Napoleon Bonaparte. By G. NORWAY. With 6 page Illustrations by ROBT. BARNES, A.R.W.S. 3s. 6d.

"More hairbreadth escapes from death by starvation, by ice, by fighting, &c., were never before surmounted. . . . It is a fine yarn."—*The Guardian.*

A True Cornish Maid. By G. NORWAY. With 6 page Illustrations by J. FINNEMORE. 3s. 6d.

"There is some excellent reading. . . . Mrs. Norway brings before the eyes of her readers the good Cornish folk, their speech, their manners, and their ways. *A True Cornish Maid* deserves to be popular."—*Athenæum.*

*** For other Books by G. NORWAY see p. 23.

Young Travellers' Tales. By ASCOTT R. HOPE. With 6 Illustrations by H. J. DRAPER. 3s. 6d.

"Possess a high value for instruction as well as for entertainment. His quiet, level humour bubbles up on every page."—*Daily Chronicle.*

The Seven Wise Scholars. By ASCOTT R. HOPE. With nearly 100 Illustrations by GORDON BROWNE. 5s.

"As full of fun as a volume of *Punch*; with illustrations, more laughter-provoking than most we have seen since Leech died."—*Sheffield Independent.*

Stories of Old Renown: Tales of Knights and Heroes. By ASCOTT R. HOPE. With 100 Illustrations by GORDON BROWNE. 3s. 6d.

"A really fascinating book worthy of its telling title. There is, we venture to say, not a dull page in the book, not a story which will not bear a second reading."—*Guardian.*

Under False Colours: A Story from Two Girls' Lives. By SARAH DOUDNEY. Illustrated by G. G. KILBURNE. 4s.

"Sarah Doudney has no superior as a writer of high-toned stories—pure in style and original in conception; but we have seen nothing from her pen equal in dramatic energy to this book."—*Christian Leader.*

BY DR. GORDON STABLES.

In crown 8vo, cloth elegant.

For Life and Liberty: A Story of Battle by Land and Sea. By Dr. GORDON STABLES, R.N. With 8 Illustrations by SYDNEY PAGET, and a Map. 5s.

"The story is lively and spirited, with abundance of blockade-running, hard fighting, narrow escapes, and introductions to some of the most distinguished generals on both sides."—*The Times.*

To Greenland and the Pole. By GORDON STABLES, M.D. With 8 page Illustrations by G. C. HINDLEY, and a Map. 5s.

"His Arctic explorers have the verisimilitude of life. It is one of the books of the season, and one of the best Mr. Stables has ever written."—*Truth.*

Westward with Columbus. By GORDON STABLES, M.D. With 8 page Illustrations by A. PEARSE. 5s.

Reduced Illustration from "To Greenland".

"We must place *Westward with Columbus* among those books that all boys ought to read."—*The Spectator.*

'Twixt School and College: A Tale of Self-reliance. By GORDON STABLES, C.M., M.D., R.N. Illustrated by W. PARKINSON. 5s.

"One of the best of a prolific writer's books for boys, being full of practical instructions as to keeping pets, and inculcates in a way which a little recalls Miss Edgeworth's 'Frank' the virtue of self-reliance."—*Athenæum.*

With the Sea Kings: A Story of the Days of Lord Nelson. By F. H. WINDER. Illustrated by W. S. STACEY. 4s.

"Just the book to put into a boy's hands. Every chapter contains boardings, cuttings out, fighting pirates, escapes of thrilling audacity, and captures by corsairs, sufficient to turn the quietest boy's head. The story culminates in a vigorous account of the battle of Trafalgar. Happy boys!"—*The Academy.*

[11]

BY HUGH ST. LEGER.

In crown 8vo, cloth elegant.

Hallowe'en Ahoy! or, Lost on the Crozet Islands. By HUGH ST. LEGER. With 6 Illustrations by H. J. DRAPER. 4s.

"One of the best stories of seafaring life and adventure which have appeared this season. It contains a capital 'fo'c's'le' ghost and a thrilling shipwreck. No boy who begins it but will wish to join the *Britannia* long before he finishes these delightful pages."—*Academy.*

Sou'wester and Sword. By HUGH ST. LEGER. With 6 page Illustrations by HAL HURST. 4s.

"As racy a tale of life at sea and war adventure as we have met with for some time. . . . Altogether the sort of book that boys will revel in."—*Athenæum.*

BY ALICE CORKRAN.

Meg's Friend. By ALICE CORKRAN. With 6 page Illustrations by ROBERT FOWLER. 3s. 6d.

"One of Miss Corkran's charming books for girls, narrated in that simple and picturesque style which marks the authoress as one of the first amongst writers for young people."—*The Spectator.*

Margery Merton's Girlhood. By ALICE CORKRAN. With 6 page Pictures by GORDON BROWNE. 3s. 6d.

"Another book for girls we can warmly commend. There is a delightful piquancy in the experiences and trials of a young English girl who studies painting in Paris."—*Saturday Review.*

Down the Snow Stairs: or, From Good-night to Good-morning. By ALICE CORKRAN. With 60 Illustrations by GORDON BROWNE. 3s. 6d.

"A gem of the first water, bearing upon every page the mark of genius. It is indeed a Little Pilgrim's Progress."—*Christian Leader.*

Grettir the Outlaw: A Story of Iceland. By S. BARING-GOULD. With 6 page Illustrations by M. ZENO DIEMER, and a Coloured Map. 4s.

"Is the boys' book of its year. That is, of course, as much as to say that it will do for men grown as well as juniors. It is told in simple, straightforward English, as all stories should be, and it has a freshness, a freedom, a sense of sun and wind and the open air, which make it irresistable."—*National Observer.*

Gold, Gold, in Cariboo: A Story of Adventure in British Columbia. By CLIVE PHILLIPPS-WOLLEY. With 6 page Illustrations by G. C. HINDLEY. 3s. 6d.

"It would be difficult to say too much in favour of *Gold, Gold, in Cariboo.* We have seldom read a more exciting tale of wild mining adventure in a singularly inaccessible country. There is a capital plot, and the interest is sustained to the last page."—*The Times.*

BY EDGAR PICKERING.

In crown 8vo, cloth elegant.

Two Gallant Rebels: A Story of the Great Struggle in La Vendée. By EDGAR PICKERING. With 6 Illustrations by W. H. OVEREND. 3s. 6d.

"There is something very attractive about Mr. Pickering's style. . . . Boys will relish the relation of those dreadful and moving events, which, indeed, will never lose their fascination for readers of all ages."—*The Spectator.*

In Press-Gang Days. By EDGAR PICKERING. With 6 Illustrations by W. S. STACEY. 3s. 6d.

"It is of Marryat we think as we read this delightful story; for it is not only a story of adventure with incidents well conceived and arranged, but the characters are interesting and well-distinguished."—*Academy.*

An Old-Time Yarn: Wherein is set forth divers desperate mischances which befell Anthony Ingram and his shipmates in the West Indies and Mexico with Hawkins and Drake. By EDGAR PICKERING. Illustrated by ALFRED PEARSE. 3s. 6d.

"And a very good yarn it is, with not a dull page from first to last. There is a flavour of *Westward Ho!* in this attractive book."—*Educational Review.*

Silas Verney: A Tale of the Time of Charles II. By EDGAR PICKERING. With 6 page Illustrations by ALFRED PEARSE. 3s. 6d.

"Altogether this is an excellent story for boys."—*Saturday Review.*

A Thane of Wessex: Being the Story of the Great Viking Raid of 845. By CHARLES W. WHISTLER. With 6 Illustrations by W. H. MARGETSON. 3s. 6d.

"This is one of the best books of the season. . . . The story is told with spirit and force, and affords an excellent picture of the life of the period."—*Standard.*

His First Kangaroo: An Australian Story for Boys. By ARTHUR FERRES. Illustrated by PERCY F. S. SPENCE. 3s. 6d.

"A lively story of life on an Australian stock-station, where the monotony of things is agreeably diversified by not only the bounding kangaroo, but also the up-sticking bushranger"—*Scotsman.*

A Champion of the Faith: A Tale of Prince Hal and the Lollards. By J. M. CALLWELL. With 6 page Illustrations by HERBERT J. DRAPER. 4s.

"Will not be less enjoyed than Mr. Henty's books. Sir John Oldcastle's pathetic story, and the history of his brave young squire, will make every boy enjoy this lively story."—*London Quarterly.*

BY ANNIE E. ARMSTRONG.

In crown 8vo, cloth elegant.

Three Bright Girls: A Story of Chance and Mischance. By ANNIE E. ARMSTRONG. Illustrated by W. PARKINSON. 3s. 6d.

"Among many good stories for girls this is undoubtedly one of the very best."—*Teachers' Aid.*

A Very Odd Girl: or, Life at the Gabled Farm. By ANNIE E. ARMSTRONG. Illustrated. 3s. 6d.

"The book is one we can heartily recommend, for it is not only bright and interesting, but also pure and healthy in tone and teaching."—*The Lady.*

The Captured Cruiser: By C. J. HYNE. Illustrated by FRANK BRANGWYN. 3s. 6d.

"The two lads and the two skippers are admirably drawn. Mr. Hyne has now secured a position in the first rank of writers of fiction for boys."—*Spectator.*

Afloat at Last: A Sailor Boy's Log of his Life at Sea. By JOHN C. HUTCHESON. 3s. 6d.

"As healthy and breezy a book as one could wish to put into the hands of a boy."—*Academy.*

Picked up at Sea: or, The Gold Miners of Minturne Creek. By J. C. HUTCHESON. With 6 page Pictures. 3s. 6d.

Brother and Sister: or, The Trials of the Moore Family. By ELIZABETH J. LYSAGHT. 3s. 6d.

The Search for the Talisman: A Story of Labrador. By HENRY FRITH. Illustrated by J. SCHÖNBERG. 3s. 6d.

"Mr. Frith's volume will be among those most read and highest valued. The adventures among seals, whales, and icebergs in Labrador will delight many a young reader."—*Pall Mall Gazette.*

Dora: or, A Girl without a Home. By Mrs. R. H. READ. With 6 page Illustrations. 3s. 6d.

"It is no slight thing, in an age of rubbish, to get a story so pure and healthy as this."—*The Academy.*

Storied Holidays: A Cycle of Red-letter Days. By E. S. BROOKS. With 12 page Illustrations by HOWARD PYLE. 3s. 6d.

"It is a downright good book for a senior boy, and is eminently readable from first to last."—*Schoolmaster.*

In crown 8vo, cloth elegant.

Chivalric Days: Stories of Courtesy and Courage in the Olden Times. By E. S. BROOKS. With 20 Illustrations. 3s. 6d.

"We have seldom come across a prettier collection of tales. These charming stories of boys and girls of olden days are no mere fictitious or imaginary sketches, but are real and actual records of their sayings and doings."—*Literary World.*

Historic Boys: Their Endeavours, their Achievements, and their Times. By E. S. BROOKS. With 12 page Illustrations. 3s. 6d.

"A wholesome book, manly in tone; altogether one that should incite boys to further acquaintance with those rulers of men whose careers are narrated. We advise teachers to put it on their list of prizes."—*Knowledge.*

Dr. Jolliffe's Boys: A Tale of Weston School. By LEWIS HOUGH. With 6 page Pictures. 3s. 6d.

"Young people who appreciate *Tom Brown's School-days* will find this story a worthy companion to that fascinating book."—*Newcastle Journal.*

The Bubbling Teapot. A Wonder Story. By Mrs. L. W. CHAMPNEY. With 12 page Pictures by WALTER SATTERLEE. 3s. 6d.

"Very literally a 'wonder story.' Nevertheless it is made realistic enough, and there is a good deal of information to be gained from it."—*The Times.*

Thorndyke Manor: A Tale of Jacobite Times. By MARY C. ROWSELL. Illustrated by L. LESLIE BROOKE. 3s. 6d.

"Miss Rowsell has never written a more attractive book than *Thorndyke Manor.*"—*Belfast News-Letter.*

Traitor or Patriot? A Tale of the Rye-House Plot. By MARY C. ROWSELL. Illustrated. 3s. 6d.

"Here the Rye-House Plot serves as the groundwork for a romantic love episode, whose true characters are lifelike beings."—*Graphic.*

BLACKIE'S NEW THREE-SHILLING SERIES.

Beautifully illustrated and handsomely bound.

Highways and High Seas: Cyril Harley's Adventures on both. By F. FRANKFORT MOORE. With 6 page Illustrations by ALFRED PEARSE. *New Edition.* 3s.

"This is one of the best stories Mr. Moore has written, perhaps the very best. The exciting adventures are sure to attract boys."—*Spectator.*

Under Hatches: or, Ned Woodthorpe's Adventures. By F. FRANKFORT MOORE. Illustrated by A. FORESTIER. 3s.

"The story as a story is one that will just suit boys all the world over. The characters are well drawn and consistent."—*Schoolmaster.*

THREE-SHILLING SERIES—Continued.

Beautifully illustrated and handsomely bound.

The Missing Merchantman. By HARRY COLLINGWOOD.
With 6 page Illustrations by W. H. OVEREND. 3s.

"One of the author's best sea stories. The hero is as heroic as any boy could desire, and the ending is extremely happy."—*British Weekly.*

Menhardoc: A Story of Cornish Nets and Mines. By G. MANVILLE FENN. Illustrated by C. J. STANILAND, R.I. 3s.

"The Cornish fishermen are drawn from life, and stand out from the pages in their jerseys and sea-boots all sprinkled with silvery pilchard scales."—*Spectator.*

Yussuf the Guide: or, The Mountain Bandits. By G. MANVILLE FENN. With 6 page Illustrations by J. SCHÖNBERG. 3s.

"Told with such real freshness and vigour that the reader feels he is actually one of the party, sharing in the fun and facing the dangers."—*Pall Mall Gazette.*

Patience Wins: or, War in the Works. By GEORGE MANVILLE FENN. With 6 page Illustrations. 3s.

"Mr. Fenn has never hit upon a happier plan than in writing this story of Yorkshire factory life. The whole book is all aglow with life."—*Pall Mall Gazette.*

Mother Carey's Chicken: Her Voyage to the Unknown Isle. By G. MANVILLE FENN. With 6 page Illustrations by A. FORESTIER. 3s.

"Undoubtedly one of the best Mr Fenn has written. The incidents are of thrilling interest, while the characters are drawn with a care and completeness rarely found in a boy's book."—*Literary World.*

Robinson Crusoe. With 100 Illustrations by GORDON BROWNE. 3s.

"One of the best issues, if not absolutely the best, of Defoe's work which has ever appeared."—*The Standard.*

Gulliver's Travels. With 100 Illustrations by GORDON BROWNE. 3s.

"Mr. Gordon Browne is, to my thinking, incomparably the most artistic, spirited, and brilliant of our illustrators of books for boys, and one of the most humorous also, as his illustrations of 'Gulliver' amply testify."—*Truth.*

The Wigwam and the War-path: Stories of the Red Indians. By ASCOTT R. HOPE. With 6 page Illustrations. 3s.

"Is notably good. It gives a very vivid picture of life among the Indians, which will delight the heart of many a schoolboy."—*Spectator.*

THREE-SHILLING SERIES—Continued.

Beautifully illustrated and handsomely bound.

The Loss of John Humble: What Led to It, and What Came of It. By G. NORWAY. With 6 page Illustrations by JOHN SCHÖNBERG. *New Edition.* 3s.

"This story will place the author at once in the front rank. It is full of life and adventure. The interest of the story is sustained without a break from first to last."—*Standard.*

Hussein the Hostage: or, A Boy's Adventures in Persia. By G. NORWAY. With 6 page Illustrations by JOHN SCHÖNBERG. 3s.

"*Hussein the Hostage* is full of originality and vigour. The characters are lifelike, there is plenty of stirring incident, the interest is sustained throughout, and every boy will enjoy following the fortunes of the hero."—*Journal of Education.*

Cousin Geoffrey and I. By CAROLINE AUSTIN. With 6 page Illustrations by W. PARKINSON. 3s.

Reduced Illustration from "Cousin Geoffrey".

"Miss Austin's story is bright, clever, and well developed."—*Saturday Review.*

The Rover's Secret: A Tale of the Pirate Cays and Lagoons of Cuba. By HARRY COLLINGWOOD. With 6 page Illustrations by W. C. SYMONS. 3s.

"*The Rover's Secret* is by far the best sea story we have read for years, and is certain to give unalloyed pleasure to boys."—*Saturday Review.*

The Congo Rovers: A Story of the Slave Squadron. By HARRY COLLINGWOOD. With 6 page Illustrations. 3s.

"No better sea story has lately been written than the *Congo Rovers.* It is as original as any boy could desire."—*Morning Post.*

THREE-SHILLING SERIES—Continued.

Beautifully illustrated and handsomely bound.

Perseverance Island: or, The Robinson Crusoe of the 19th Century. By DOUGLAS FRAZAR. With 6 page Illustrations. 3s.

"This is an interesting story, written with studied simplicity of style, much in Defoe's vein of apparent sincerity and scrupulous veracity; while for practical instruction it is even better than *Robinson Crusoe*."—*Illustrated London News.*

Girl Neighbours: or, The Old Fashion and the New. By SARAH TYTLER. Illustrated by C. T. GARLAND. 3s.

"One of the most effective and quietly humorous of Miss Sarah Tytler's stories. It is very healthy, very agreeable, and very well written."—*The Spectator.*

BLACKIE'S HALF-CROWN SERIES.

Illustrated by eminent Artists. In crown 8vo, cloth elegant.

A Musical Genius. By the Author of the "Two Dorothys".

"It is brightly written, well illustrated, and daintily bound, and can be strongly recommended as a really good prize-book."—*Teachers' Aid.*

For the Sake of a Friend: A Story of School Life. By MARGARET PARKER.

"An excellent school-girl story. . . . Susie Snow and her friend, Trix Beresford, are charming girls."—*Athenæum.*

Under the Black Eagle. By ANDREW HILLIARD.

"The rapid movement of the story, and the strange scenes through which it passes, give it a full interest of surprise and adventure."—*Scotsman.*

The Secret of the Australian Desert. By ERNEST FAVENC.

"We recommend the book most heartily; it is certain to please boys and girls, and even some grown-ups."—*Guardian.*

Reefer and Rifleman: A Tale of the Two Services. By Lieut.-Col. PERCY-GROVES.

"A good, old-fashioned, amphibious story of our fighting with the Frenchmen in the beginning of our century, with a fair sprinkling of fun and frolic."—*Times.*

A Little Handful. By HARRIET J. SCRIPPS.

"He is a real type of a boy."—*The Schoolmaster.*

A Golden Age: A Story of Four Merry Children. By ISMAY THORN. Illustrated by GORDON BROWNE.

"Ought to have a place of honour on the nursery shelf."—*The Athenæum.*

HALF-CROWN SERIES—Continued.

Illustrated by eminent Artists. In crown 8vo, cloth elegant.

BY BEATRICE HARRADEN.

Things Will Take a Turn. By BEATRICE HARRADEN. With 44 Illustrations by JOHN H. BACON.

"Perhaps the most brilliant is *Things Will Take a Turn*. . . . A tale of humble child life in East London. It is a delightful blending of comedy and tragedy, with an excellent plot."—*The Times.*

The Whispering Winds, and the Tales that they Told. By MARY H. DEBENHAM. With 25 Illustrations by PAUL HARDY.

"We wish the winds would tell *us* stories like these. It would be worth while to climb Primrose Hill, or even to the giddy heights of Hampstead Heath in a bitter east wind, if we could only be sure of hearing such a sweet, sad, tender, and stirring story as that of Hilda Brave Heart, or even one that was half so good."—*Academy.*

From "*Things will Take a Turn*". (*Reduced.*)

Hal Hungerford. By J. R. HUTCHINSON, B.A.
"Altogether, Hal Hungerford is a distinct literary success."—*Spectator*

The Secret of the Old House. By E. EVERETT-GREEN.
"Tim, the little Jacobite, is a charming creation."—*Academy.*

White Lilac: or, The Queen of the May. By AMY WALTON.
"Every rural parish ought to add *White Lilac* to its library."—*Academy.*

Miriam's Ambition. By EVELYN EVERETT-GREEN.
"Miss Green's children are real British boys and girls."—*Liverpool Mercury.*

The Brig "Audacious". By ALAN COLE.
"Fresh and wholesome as a breath of sea air."—*Court Journal.*

HALF-CROWN SERIES—Continued.

Illustrated by eminent Artists. In crown 8vo, cloth elegant.

The Saucy May. By HENRY FRITH.
"Mr. Frith gives a new picture of life on the ocean wave."—*Sheffield Independent.*

Jasper's Conquest. By ELIZABETH J. LYSAGHT.
"One of the best boys' books of the season."—*Schoolmaster.*

Little Lady Clare. By EVELYN EVERETT-GREEN.
"Reminds us in its quaintness of Mrs. Ewing's delightful tales."—*Liter. World.*

The Eversley Secrets. By EVELYN EVERETT-GREEN.
"Roy Eversley is a very touching picture of high principle."—*Guardian.*

The Hermit Hunter of the Wilds. By G. STABLES, R.N.
"Will gladden the heart of many a bright boy."—*Methodist Recorder.*

Sturdy and Strong. By G. A. HENTY.
"A hero who stands as a good instance of chivalry in domestic life."—*The Empire.*

Gutta Percha Willie. By GEORGE MACDONALD.
"Get it for your boys and girls to read for themselves."—*Practical Teacher.*

The War of the Axe: or, Adventures in South Africa. By J. PERCY-GROVES.
"The story is well and brilliantly told."—*Literary World.*

The Lads of Little Clayton. By R. STEAD.
"A capital book for boys."—*Schoolmaster.*

Ten Boys who lived on the Road from **Long Ago to Now.** By JANE ANDREWS. With 20 Illustrations.
"The idea is a very happy one, and admirably carried out."—*Practical Teacher.*

A Waif of the Sea: or, The Lost Found. By KATE WOOD.
"Written with tenderness and grace."—*Morning Advertiser.*

Winnie's Secret. By KATE WOOD.
"One of the best story-books we have read."—*Schoolmaster.*

Miss Willowburn's Offer. By SARAH DOUDNEY.
"Patience Willowburn is one of Miss Doudney's best creations."—*Spectator.*

A Garland for Girls. By LOUISA M. ALCOTT.
"These little tales are the beau ideal of girls' stories."—*Christian World.*

Hetty Gray: or, Nobody's Bairn. By ROSA MULHOLLAND.
"Hetty is a delightful creature—piquant, tender, and true."—*World.*

Brothers in Arms: A Story of the Crusades. By F. BAYFORD HARRISON.
"Sure to prove interesting to young people of both sexes."—*Guardian.*

Miss Fenwick's Failures. By ESMÉ STUART.
"A girl true to real life, who will put no nonsense into young heads."—*Graphic.*

Gytha's Message. By EMMA LESLIE.
"This is the sort of book that all girls like."—*Journal of Education.*

HALF-CROWN SERIES—Continued.

Illustrated by eminent Artists. In crown 8vo, cloth elegant.

Hammond's Hard Lines. By SKELTON KUPPORD.

"It is just what a boy would choose if the selection of a story-book is left in his own hand."—*School Guardian.*

Dulcie King: A Story for Girls. By M. CORBET-SEYMOUR.

"An extremely graceful, well-told tale of domestic life. ... The heroine, Dulcie, is a charming person, and worthy of the good fortune which she causes and shares."—*Guardian.*

Hugh Herbert's Inheritance. By CAROLINE AUSTIN.

"Will please by its simplicity, its tenderness, and its healthy interesting motive. It is admirably written."—*Scotsman.*

Nicola: The Career of a Girl Musician. By M. CORBET-SEYMOUR.

Jack o' Lanthorn: A Tale of Adventure. By HENRY FRITH.

Reduced Illustration from "Hammond's Hard Lines"

My Mistress the Queen. By M. A. PAULL.
The Stories of Wasa and Menzikoff.
Stories of the Sea in Former Days.
Tales of Captivity and Exile.
Famous Discoveries by Sea and Land.
Stirring Events of History.
Adventures in Field, Flood, and Forest.

"It would be difficult to place in the hands of young people books which combine interest and instruction in a higher degree."—*Manchester Courier.*

A Rough Road: or, How the Boy Made a Man of Himself. By Mrs. G. LINNÆUS BANKS.

"Mrs. Banks has not written a better book than *A Rough Road.*"—*Spectator.*

HALF-CROWN SERIES—Continued.

Laugh and Learn: The Easiest Book of Nursery Lessons and Nursery Games. By JENNETT HUMPHREYS. Charmingly Illustrated. Square 8vo, cloth extra, 2s. 6d.

"One of the best books of the kind imaginable, full of practical teaching in word and picture, and helping the little ones pleasantly along a right royal road to learning."—*Graphic.*

The Two Dorothys. By Mrs. HERBERT MARTIN.

"A book that will interest and please all girls."—*The Lady.*

Penelope and the Others. By AMY WALTON.

"This is a charming book for children. Miss Walton proves herself a perfect adept in understanding of school-room joys and sorrows."—*Christian Leader.*

A Cruise in Cloudland. By HENRY FRITH.

"A thoroughly interesting story."—*St. James's Gazette.*

Marian and Dorothy. By ANNIE E. ARMSTRONG.

"This is distinctively a book for girls. A bright wholesome story."—*Academy.*

Stimson's Reef: A Tale of Adventure. By C. J. HYNE.

"It may almost vie with Mr. R. L. Stevenson's *Treasure Island.*"—*Guardian.*

Gladys Anstruther. By LOUISA THOMPSON.

"It is a clever book: novel and striking in the highest degree."—*Schoolmistress.*

BLACKIE'S TWO-SHILLING SERIES.

Illustrated by eminent Artists. In crown 8vo, cloth elegant.

In the Days of Drake. Being the Adventures of Humphrey Salkeld. By J. S. FLETCHER.

Wilful Joyce. By W. L. ROOPER.

Proud Miss Sydney. By GERALDINE MOCKLER.

Queen of the Daffodils: A Story of High School Life. By LESLIE LAING.

The Girleen. By EDITH JOHNSTONE.

The Organist's Baby. By KATHLEEN KNOX.

School-Days in France. By AN OLD GIRL.

The Ravensworth Scholarship: A High School Story for Girls. By Mrs. HENRY CLARKE.

Sir Walter's Ward: A Tale of the Crusades. By WILLIAM EVERARD.

Raff's Ranche: A Story of Adventure among Cow-boys and Indians. By F. M. HOLMES.

TWO-SHILLING SERIES—Continued.

Illustrated by eminent Artists. In crown 8vo, cloth elegant.

An Unexpected Hero. By Eliz. J. Lysaght.
The Bushranger's Secret. By Mrs. Henry Clarke, M.A.
The White Squall. By John C. Hutcheson.
The Wreck of the "Nancy Bell". By J. C. Hutcheson.
The Lonely Pyramid. By J. H. Yoxall.
Bab: or, The Triumph of Unselfishness. By Ismay Thorn.
Brave and True, and other Stories. By Gregson Gow.
The Light Princess. By George Mac Donald.
Nutbrown Roger and I. By J. H. Yoxall.
Sam Silvan's Sacrifice. By Jesse Colman.
Insect Ways on Summer Days in Garden, Forest, Field, and Stream. By Jennett Humphreys. With 70 Illustrations.
Susan. By Amy Walton.
A Pair of Clogs. By Amy Walton.
The Hawthorns. By Amy Walton.
Dorothy's Dilemma. By Caroline Austin.
Marie's Home. By Caroline Austin.
A Warrior King. By J. Evelyn.
Aboard the "Atalanta". By Henry Frith.
The Penang Pirate. By John C. Hutcheson.
Teddy: The Story of a "Little Pickle". By John C. Hutcheson.
A Rash Promise. By Cecilia Selby Lowndes.
Linda and the Boys. By Cecilia Selby Lowndes.
Swiss Stories for Children. From the German of Madam Johanna Spyri. By Lucy Wheelock.
The Squire's Grandson. By J. M. Callwell.
Magna Charta Stories. Edited by Arthur Gilman, A.M.
The Wings of Courage; and The Cloud-Spinner. Translated from the French of George Sand, by Mrs. Corkran.
Chirp and Chatter: Or, Lessons from Field and Tree. By Alice Banks. With 54 Illustrations by Gordon Browne.
Four Little Mischiefs. By Rosa Mulholland.

TWO-SHILLING SERIES—Continued.

Illustrated by eminent Artists. In crown 8vo, cloth elegant.

New Light through Old Windows. By GREGSON GOW.
Little Tottie, and Two Other Stories. By THOMAS ARCHER.
Naughty Miss Bunny. By CLARA MULHOLLAND.
Adventures of Mrs. Wishing-to-be. By ALICE CORKRAN.
The Joyous Story of Toto. By LAURA E. RICHARDS.
Our Dolly: Her Words and Ways. By MRS. R. H. READ.
Fairy Fancy: What she Heard and Saw. By MRS. READ.

LIBRARY OF FAMOUS BOOKS FOR BOYS AND GIRLS.

In Crown 8vo. Illustrated. Cloth extra, 1s. 6d. each.

Miss Austen's Northanger Abbey.
Miss Edgeworth's The Good Governess.
Martineau's Feats on the Fiord.
Marryat's Poor Jack.
The Snowstorm. By Mrs. Gore.
Life of Dampier.
The Cruise of the Midge. M. SCOTT.
Lives and Voyages of Drake and Cavendish.
Edgeworth's Moral Tales.
Marryat's The Settlers in Canada.
Michael Scott's Tom Cringle's Log.
White's Natural History of Selborne.
Waterton's Wanderings in S. America.
Anson's Voyage Round the World.
Autobiography of Franklin.
Lamb's Tales from Shakspeare.
Southey's Life of Nelson.
Miss Mitford's Our Village.
Two Years Before the Mast.
Marryat's Children of the New Forest.
Scott's The Talisman.
The Basket of Flowers.
Marryat's Masterman Ready.
Alcott's Little Women.
Cooper's Deerslayer.
The Lamplighter. By Miss CUMMINS.
Cooper's Pathfinder.
The Vicar of Wakefield.
Plutarch's Lives of Greek Heroes.
Poe's Tales of Romance and Fantasy.

BLACKIE'S EIGHTEENPENNY SERIES.

With Illustrations. In crown 8vo, cloth elegant.

The Little Girl from Next Door. By GERALDINE MOCKLER.
Uncle Jem's Stella. By Author of "The Two Dorothys".
The Ball of Fortune. By C. PEARSE.
The Family Failing. By DARLEY DALE.
Warner's Chase: Or, The Gentle Heart. By ANNIE S. SWAN.
Climbing the Hill. By ANNIE S. SWAN.
Into the Haven. By ANNIE S. SWAN.
Down and Up Again. By GREGSON GOW.
Madge's Mistake. By ANNIE E. ARMSTRONG.
The Troubles and Triumphs of Little Tim. By GREGSON GOW.
The Happy Lad: A Story of Peasant Life in Norway. By B. BJÖRNSON.
A Box of Stories. Packed for Young Folk by HORACE HAPPYMAN.
The Patriot Martyr, and other Narratives of Female Heroism.

THE EIGHTEENPENNY SERIES.—Continued.
With Illustrations. In crown 8vo, cloth elegant.

Olive and Robin: or, A Journey to Nowhere. By the author of "The Two Dorothys".

Mona's Trust: A Story for Girls. By PENELOPE LESLIE.

Littlebourne Lock. By F. BAYFORD HARRISON

Wild Meg and Wee Dickie. By MARY E. ROPES.

Grannie. By ELIZABETH J. LYSAGHT.

The Seed She Sowed. By EMMA LESLIE.

Unlucky: A Fragment of a Girl's Life. By CAROLINE AUSTIN.

Everybody's Business; Or, A Friend in Need. By ISMAY THORN.

Tales of Daring and Danger. By G. A. HENTY.

The Seven Golden Keys. By JAMES E. ARNOLD.

The Story of a Queen. By MARY C. ROWSELL.

Edwy: Or, Was he a Coward? By ANNETTE LYSTER.

The Battlefield Treasure. By F. BAYFORD HARRISON.

Joan's Adventures at the North Pole. By ALICE CORKRAN.

Filled with Gold. By J. PERRETT.

Our General: A Story for Girls. By ELIZABETH J. LYSAGHT.

Aunt Hesba's Charge. By ELIZABETH J. LYSAGHT.

By Order of Queen Maude: A Story of Home Life. By LOUISA CROW.

The Late Miss Hollingford. By ROSA MULHOLLAND.

Our Frank. By AMY WALTON.

A Terrible Coward. By G. MANVILLE FENN.

Yarns on the Beach. By G. A. HENTY.

[*Reduced Specimen of the Illustrations.*]
From "*Pleasures and Pranks*".

Little Jimmy: A Story of Adventure. By Rev. D. RICE-JONES, M.A.

Pleasures and Pranks. By ISABELLA PEARSON.

In a Stranger's Garden: A Story for Boys and Girls. By CONSTANCE CUMING.

A Soldier's Son: The Story of a Boy who Succeeded. By ANNETTE LYSTER.

Mischief and Merry-making. By ISABELLA PEARSON.

Tom Finch's Monkey. By J. C. HUTCHESON.

Miss Grantley's Girls, and the Stories she Told Them. By THOS. ARCHER.

The Pedlar and his Dog. By MARY C. ROWSELL.

Town Mice in the Country. By M. E. FRANCIS.

Phil and his Father. By ISMAY THORN.

Prim's Story. By L. E. TIDDEMAN.

** *Also a large selection of Rewards at 1s., 9d., 6d., 3d., 2d., and 1d. A complete list will be sent post free on application to the Publishers.*

BLACKIE'S
SCHOOL AND HOME LIBRARY.

Under the above title the publishers have arranged to issue, for School Libraries and the Home Circle, a selection of the best and most interesting books in the English language. The Library will include lives of heroes, ancient and modern, records of travel and adventure by sea and land, fiction of the highest class, historical romances, books of natural history, and tales of domestic life.

The greatest care will be devoted to the get-up of the Library. The volumes will be clearly printed on good paper, and the binding made specially durable, to withstand the wear and tear to which well-circulated books are necessarily subjected.

In crown 8vo volumes. Strongly bound in imperial cloth. Price 1s. 4d. each.

Dana's Two Years before the Mast.
Southey's Life of Nelson.
Waterton's Wanderings in S. America.
Anson's Voyage Round the World.
Lamb's Tales from Shakspeare.
Autobiography of Benjamin Franklin.
Marryat's Children of the New Forest.
Miss Mitford's Our Village.
Scott's Talisman.
The Basket of Flowers.
Marryat's Masterman Ready.
Alcott's Little Women.
Cooper's Deerslayer.
Parry's Third Voyage.
Dickens' Old Curiosity Shop. 2 vols.
Plutarch's Lives of Greek Heroes.
The Lamplighter.
Cooper's Pathfinder.
The Vicar of Wakefield.
White's Natural History of Selborne.
Scott's Ivanhoe. 2 vols.

Michael Scott's Tom Cringle's Log.
Irving's Conquest of Granada. 2 vols.
Lives of Drake and Cavendish.
Michael Scott's Cruise of the Midge.
Edgeworth's Moral Tales.
Passages in the Life of a Galley-Slave.
The Snowstorm. By Mrs. Gore.
Life of Dampier.
Marryat's The Settlers in Canada.
Martineau's Feats on the Fiord.
Marryat's Poor Jack.
The Good Governess. By Maria Edgeworth.
Northanger Abbey. By Jane Austen.
The Log Book of a Midshipman.
Autobiographies of Boyhood.
Holiday House. By Catherine Sinclair.
Wreck of the "Wager".
What Katy Did. By Miss Coolidge.
What Katy Did at School. By Do.
Scott's Life of Napoleon.

To be followed by a new volume on the first of each month.

"We feel sure that they will form a collection which boys and girls alike, but especially the former, will highly prize; for whilst they contain interesting, and at times very exciting reading, the tone throughout is of that vigorous, stirring kind which is always appreciated by the young."—Sheffield Independent.

Detailed Prospectus and Press Opinions will be sent post free on Application.

LONDON:
BLACKIE & SON, LIMITED, 50 OLD BAILEY, E.C.

www.ingramcontent.com/pod-product-compliance
Lightning Source LLC
Chambersburg PA
CBHW020106010526
44115CB00008B/706